# Balanced Constitutionalism

# Praise for *Balanced Constitutionalism*

How can a court with the power to strike down legislation be less power-ful than one with only the power to declare legislation unconstitutional? Through a careful and detailed analysis of Great Britain and India, Chintan Chandrachud offers a surprising answer. What legislatures do interacts with courts' willingness to say what they really think, and legislative responses are affected by a complex institutional and political environment. By show-ing how complex the institution of constitutional review is in real-world practice, Chandrachud makes an important contribution to constitutional theory.

—*Mark Tushnet, Harvard Law School, USA*

This monograph is a profound work of comparative public law. It describes the different techniques adopted by the courts in India and in the UK to secure rights compliant interpretations of statutes that might be thought to infringe fundamental rights. Out of this emerges an intriguing conundrum. The Indian courts have formally greater powers than the UK courts have in similar circumstances. But in fact, as Dr Chandrachud shows, it is the UK courts that are more successful in securing rights compliant interpreta-tions of statutes. This demonstration requires the mastery of the two legal systems involved but the author is well up to the task. He writes with clarity and great insight into the actual operation of both legal systems. This book will be of great value to any reader seeking a deep understanding of funda-mental rights protection in either of these legal systems.

—*Christopher Forsyth, University of Cambridge, UK*

Dr Chandrachud has explored the working of the two models of judicial control over legislation. In an incisive analysis of the working of Indian power of judicial review and British experience with the model of dec-laration of incompatibility, he finds that the UK courts have, with their model, found it easier to express their interpretation of rights than the Indian courts. The book is a must read not only for students of comparative law and constitutional law, but also for students of political science, for it deconstructs the political dynamics of these two powerful institutions and the comparative effects of two different models on these dynamics.

—*Harish Salve, Senior Advocate, Supreme Court of India*

# Balanced Constitutionalism

*Courts and Legislatures in India and the United Kingdom*

CHINTAN CHANDRACHUD

OXFORD
UNIVERSITY PRESS

# OXFORD
UNIVERSITY PRESS

Oxford University Press is a department of the University of Oxford.
It furthers the University's objective of excellence in research, scholarship,
and education by publishing worldwide. Oxford is a registered trademark of
Oxford University Press in the UK and in certain other countries

Published in India by
Oxford University Press
22 Workspace, 2nd Floor, 1/22 Asaf Ali Road, New Delhi 110 002, India

First Edition published in 2017
Oxford India Paperbacks 2020

ISBN-13: 978-0-19-012767-1
ISBN-10: 0-19-012767-8

Typeset in ITC Giovanni Std 9.5/13
by The Graphics Solution, New Delhi 110092
Printed in India by Rakmo Press, New Delhi 110 020

Affectionately dedicated to Aai and Dad
All that I am and I ever hope to be, I owe to your love

# Contents

# Tables and Figures

## Table

## Figures

# Table of Legislation (Including Constitutions and Constitutional Amendments

## India

## United Kingdom

## Europe

## Miscellaneous

# Table of Cases

## India

## United Kingdom

## European Court of Human Rights

## Miscellaneous

# Acknowledgements

This book germinated as an idea at a conference held at Oxford in 2012. It began to take shape as an MPhil thesis at the University of Oxford and gradually transformed into a PhD thesis at the University of Cambridge. I have incurred many debts along the way. I remain eternally grateful to my supervisors, Aileen Kavanagh and Christopher Forsyth, for their advice and encouragement. Kenneth Armstrong and Harish Salve generously lent their time to examine my thesis and offered detailed suggestions. I have also had the good fortune of receiving comments and feedback from many people over the last few years. They are: Merris Amos, Nick Bamforth, Nick Barber, Mark Elliott, David Feldman, Tom Ginsburg, Tarunabh Khaitan, Jeff King, Dhvani Mehta, Pratap Bhanu Mehta, Cean Murphy, Justine Pila, Thomas Poole, Lavanya Rajamani, Jillaine Seymour, and Mark Tushnet. Anonymous reviewers also offered trenchant commentaries on the manuscript. Thanks are due to all of them. Needless to say, any errors in this book are my own.

Different chapters of this book have been presented as conference papers or lectures between 2012 and 2015. I am grateful to the institutions at which they were organized—Centre for Policy Research (New Delhi), Harvard Law School (Cambridge, Massachusetts), King's College London, London School of Economics, University of Cambridge, University of Chicago, University of Manchester, University of Nottingham, University of Oxford, and Queen Mary University (London)—and all the participants whose questions and suggestions have enriched this book. I am also grateful to the librarians at the Bodleian Law Library (Oxford), British Library (London), Judges' Reference Library (Northern Ireland), Squire Law Library (Cambridge), and the Uttar Pradesh Legislative Assembly Library, for their time and expert assistance.

Pursuing the PhD would not have been possible without funding from Sidney Sussex College (Cambridge) and the Modern Law Review Scholarship. Modified versions of Chapter 2 of this book were published in *Public Law* and the *Georgia Journal of International and Comparative Law*. I am grateful to the editors of those journals for permissions. I would also like to thank the editorial team at Oxford University Press for their patience and attention to detail.

I am indebted to those who played an instrumental role in shaping my thoughts and ideas as a student. They are: Kishu Daswani and Rachita Ratho, my professors at the Government Law College (Mumbai); Parimala Rao, former principal of the Government Law College; Nutan Mitra and Adarsh Wadhwa, my class teachers at the Cathedral & John Connon School (Mumbai); and Meera Isaacs, principal of the Cathedral & John Connon School. I would also like to thank Darius Khambata, Parag Tripathi, and Justice Shiavax Vazifdar, for giving me the opportunity to learn the law under their tutelage. Special thanks are due to Abhijit Joshi, Zia Mody, and Bahram Vakil for their counsel during (and after) my stint at AZB & Partners in Mumbai.

I am grateful to my family and friends for their unwavering support. Although Prabha, Ajju, Nani, and Baba are not here to see the book in its final form, they have all been tremendous sources of inspiration. I wish Aai were here to see this book in print, but her courage and resilience inspires me every day. Dad has always been my role model and mentor—and was my history and biology tutor in the ninth grade! I will never forget their support. I am grateful to Kalpana for her love and support and all the enjoyable teatime conversations. Abhinav has been a source of constant encouragement. I am grateful to Ba, Mom, Papa, and Dimple, for their support and unconditional love. I was sustained by Disha's love through the course of the PhD and the publication of this book.

Margrith and the late Hari Chandrachud, Lata and David Jack, and Wendy, Raman, Alan, and Andrew Chandrachud generously hosted me in Scotland. Sherina Petit made herself available to offer advice on many occasions. Dr Meena and Dr Praful Desai, Madhavi and Jay Desai, Meenakshi and Justice Girish Kulkarni, Sudha and Justice R.M. Lodha, Rajee and Justice S. Radhakrishnan, Anjana and Birendra Saraf, and Meeta and Dr Satyavan Sharma—no words can acknowledge how grateful I am to all of them for what they have done for our family. Many other family members, friends, and colleagues have supported me in different ways. This book could not have been written without all of them.

# Abbreviations and Acronyms

| | |
|---|---|
| ATCSA | Anti-Terrorism, Crime and Security Act, 2001 |
| CoE | Council of Europe |
| Commission | European Commission on Human Rights |
| Convention | European Convention for the Protection of Human Rights and Fundamental Freedoms, 1950 |
| EU | European Union |
| HRA | Human Rights Act, 1998 |
| IPC | Indian Penal Code, 1860 |
| JCHR | Joint Committee on Human Rights |
| LGBT | Lesbian, Gay, Bisexual, and Transgendered |
| NHRC | National Human Rights Commission |
| NGO | Non-governmental Organization |
| PHRA | Protection of Human Rights Act, 1993 |
| RTIA | Right to Information Act, 2005 |
| SOA | Sexual Offences Act, 2003 |
| SSHD | Secretary of State for the Home Department |
| Strasbourg Court | European Court of Human Rights, Strasbourg |
| TADA | Terrorist and Disruptive Activities (Prevention) Act, 1987 |

# Introduction

During the second half of the twentieth century, constitutional designers were presented with a choice between two models for the protection of rights. Parliamentary sovereignty postulated that the legislature, rather than the courts, was the legitimate forum for safeguarding constitutional rights. British orthodoxy demanded that courts be denied the power to strike down legislation enacted by democratically elected representatives. On the other hand, the American model of judicial supremacy entrusted the courts with the power to review and strike down any rights-infringing legislation. Judicial supremacy proliferated swiftly across several nations (including India, France, and Germany) in the aftermath of the Second World War.

It became increasingly clear that each of these models for the protection of rights left something to be desired. Whereas parliamentary sovereignty imperilled the rights of those with inadequate representation in the legislative process, judicial supremacy gave rise to concerns based on democratic legitimacy and counter-majoritarianism. This imperfect binary prompted a novel experiment in constitutional design in parts of the Commonwealth, exemplified by UK's Human Rights Act, 1998 (HRA). For the first time, British courts were empowered to review primary legislation on rights-based parameters. However, courts would not be permitted to invalidate legislation outright; they could only make a declaration of incompatibility, leaving it to the British Parliament to decide whether to amend the law.

The HRA provoked particular interest amongst scholars because, unlike parliamentary sovereignty and judicial supremacy, it offered a 'balanced' model for the protection of rights, which conferred courts with a limited power of review over legislation. Under this model, rights-based decision-making was expected to be balanced amongst courts and the legislature, rather than lopsided in favour of either. The menu of options was no longer restricted to parliamentary sovereignty and judicial supremacy, but included parliamentary sovereignty and *two* distinct models of judicial review.

This book examines the promise of the new model against its performance in practice, by comparing judicial review under the HRA to an exemplar of the old model of judicial review—the Indian Constitution. The book argues that although the HRA fosters a more balanced allocation of powers between the legislature and courts than the Indian Constitution, it does so for a different reason than the one offered by scholars. Political practice suggests that legislatures in the UK and India find it equally difficult to offer their conceptions of rights by rejecting declarations of incompatibility and judgments striking down legislation respectively. In fact, contrary to expectations, the Indian Parliament's responses to strike-downs have been marginally swifter than the Westminster Parliament's responses to declarations of incompatibility. Thus, the HRA fails to achieve more balanced constitutionalism through legislative rejection of judicial decision-making about rights.

The book then proceeds to offer a novel alternative account for the HRA's superiority from the standpoint of balanced constitutionalism. The nature of the remedy itself—the declaration of incompatibility— enables British courts to assert their genuine understanding of rights in situations in which Indian courts find it difficult to do so. The Indian Supreme Court adjudicates in the shadow of the power to strike down legislation, masking its genuine rights reasoning with reasoning that enables it to avoid exercising the power altogether. The new model achieves greater balance not because it enables the legislature to assert its conceptions of rights more easily, but because it encourages courts to do so in circumstances that they would not have been able to under the old model.

———

1997 was a defining year for British constitutionalism. The Labour Party secured victory in the general election, ending 18 years of Conservative Party rule. Prime Minister Tony Blair's 'New Labour' government swiftly pursued many significant constitutional reforms set out in the party's election manifesto, including changing the composition of the House of Lords (the upper house of Parliament), devolving lawmaking authority and some executive powers from Westminster Parliament to Scotland and Wales, and enacting legislation on freedom of information. However, amongst the most profound constitutional changes brought about by the Labour Party was the enactment of the HRA, a domestic statute intended to give effect to the European Convention for the Protection of Human Rights and Fundamental Freedoms, 1950 (or the Convention), which the UK had signed more than four decades earlier.

Historically, the notion of a bill of rights enforced by courts was considered anathema in the UK. As is well known, the UK has no canonical constitutional document. Instead, its Constitution comprises a patchwork of legislation[1] and conventions.[2] Rights were protected as negative liberties—the rights of British citizens consisted not of a set of guarantees embodied in a written instrument, but were the residue of liberties that remained untouched by legislation enacted by Parliament, consisting of the House of Commons and the House of Lords. Rights were safeguarded through parliamentary scrutiny over the exercise of executive power, as well as through protections afforded by courts under the common law. In this context, a bill of rights was viewed with scepticism because of its possible impact on parliamentary democracy and the perceived transfer of power from politicians to judges that such a bill would occasion.[3]

However, towards the latter half of the twentieth century, appeals for the enactment of a bill of rights increased. A realization began to dawn amongst the people that Parliament was no longer an effective check on government.[4] Non-governmental organizations (NGOs) and

[1] This includes the Magna Carta, 1297; Bill of Rights Act, 1689; Representation of the People Acts of 1832, 1867, and 1884; European Communities Act, 1972; and the Constitutional Reform Act, 2005.

[2] These are 'inter-institutional and inter-party social rules' bearing a 'constitutional character'. See Joseph Jaconelli, 'The Nature of Constitutional Convention' (1999) 19 LS 24, pp. 45–6.

[3] David Erdos, 'Ideology, Power Orientation and Policy Drag: Explaining the Elite Politics of Britain's Bill of Rights Debate' (2009) 44 Government and Opposition 20, p. 21.

[4] G.W. Jones, 'The British Bill of Rights' (1990) 43 Parliamentary Affairs 27, p. 31.

pressure groups[5] drafted charters of rights for the UK. The HRA was by no means the first effort to enact a bill of rights—there had been at least three attempts to do so from 1985 onwards.[6] However, in the absence of unequivocal support from either of the two major political parties, these efforts never came to fruition. This changed in 1992, when the Labour Party included the enactment of a bill of rights in its agenda.[7]

The UK was a founder member of the Council of Europe (CoE), a pan-European organization of 47 states, established at the end of the Second World War. The CoE drafted the Convention, a treaty for the protection of human rights and fundamental freedoms in member states. The Convention was an 'international code of civilised conduct'[8] drafted with the aim of preventing sequels to the atrocities perpetrated in Nazi Germany. It contains a catalogue of civil and political rights including the right to life,[9] the right against torture,[10] the right to a fair trial,[11] the right to privacy,[12] and the right to freedom of expression.[13]

The European Court of Human Rights, Strasbourg (or the Strasbourg Court) hears applications concerning allegations that member states have breached rights under the Convention. Judgments of the Strasbourg Court are binding on member states that are parties to the decision.[14] The UK was the very first country to ratify the Convention

---

[5] The best known amongst these are Charter 88 and Liberty (previously called the National Council for Civil Liberties).

[6] These are: a private member's bill introduced in 1987 by Sir Edward Gardner, QC, a Conservative member of Parliament (MP), and two bills introduced in 1994 and 1996 by Lord Lester, a Liberal Democratic MP.

[7] Labour Party, 'It's Time to Get Britain Working Again' (1992 Election Manifesto) <http://www.politicsresources.net/area/uk/man/lab92.htm> accessed 11 August 2016.

[8] Michael D. Goldhaber, *A People's History of the European Court of Human Rights* (Rutgers University Press 2007), p. 4.

[9] Convention, Art. 2.

[10] Convention, Art. 3.

[11] Convention, Art. 6.

[12] Convention, Art. 8.

[13] Convention, Art. 10.

[14] Convention, Art. 46(1). A committee of ministers, comprising the foreign ministers of each member state, monitors compliance with the judgments of the Strasbourg Court.

and accepted the right of individual petition to the Strasbourg Court in 1966. However, until 1998, no domestic statute in the UK incorporated or directly implemented rights under the Convention. This meant that litigants were unable to enforce their Convention rights in the domestic courts and suffered heavy expenses and considerable delays in making claims to the Strasbourg Court.[15]

The buzz phrase during the enactment of the HRA was that it was meant to 'bring rights home' to Britain, by transforming rights that were available to British citizens in an international court into 'British rights' that could be relied upon in domestic courts.[16] The government explicitly set out a threefold rationale for the HRA: First, it would enable citizens to enforce their Convention rights in domestic courts, instead of pursuing the 'long and hard' road to Strasbourg,[17] which at the time took about five years and cost GBP 30,000 on an average.[18] Second, it would ensure that Convention rights would be brought more meaningfully into the jurisprudence of British courts. Until then, courts generally referred to Convention rights indirectly, as an aid in interpreting ambiguous statutory language. Third, it would allow British judges to influence the jurisprudence of Convention rights across Europe.

Incorporated into the Schedule to the HRA were the rights and freedoms embodied in some articles of the Convention and its Protocols.[19] The HRA rendered it unlawful for all public authorities, including courts, to act in a way that was incompatible with one or more Convention rights set out in the Schedule.[20] Decisions of public

---

[15] Until 1998, individuals did not have direct access to the Strasbourg Court. They had to first apply to the European Commission on Human Rights (or the Commission), which would launch a case in the Strasbourg Court on behalf of the individual. The Commission was abolished by Protocol 11 to the Convention, which entered into force on 1 November 1998.

[16] Home Office, *Rights Brought Home: The Human Rights Bill* (Cm 3782, 1997), para 1.14.

[17] Home Office (n. 16), para 1.17.

[18] Home Office (n. 16).

[19] Specifically, Arts 2–12 and 14 of the Convention as well as Arts 1–3 of Protocol 1 and Art. 1 of Protocol 13.

[20] HRA, section 6. On the meaning of 'public authorities', see Stephanie Palmer, 'Public Functions and Private Services: A Gap in Human Rights Protection' (2008) 6 International Journal of Constitutional Law 585, p. 587.

authorities could therefore be set aside or struck down on the basis
that they contravened Convention rights. As is well known, the UK is a
union of England, Wales, Scotland, and Northern Ireland, and the New
Labour government's reforms included the devolution of legislative
powers from the Westminster Parliament to the Scottish Parliament,
the Welsh National Assembly, and the Northern Ireland Assembly.[21]
These three devolved legislatures were also bound by the requirement
to comply with Convention rights, which meant that legislation emanating from Edinburgh, Cardiff, and Belfast could be struck down on
the basis that it violated one or more of the Convention rights that were
incorporated into the Schedule to the HRA.

However, by virtue of being a sovereign legislature, the Westminster
Parliament was specifically exempted from these provisions.[22]
Traditionally, parliamentary sovereignty was the fundamental principle
of the British Constitution. Simply stated, the principle postulated that
anything that the king or queen in Parliament enacted was law. This principle had several implications. First, there could be no legal impediments
on the kind of laws that Parliament could enact—it effectively enjoyed
'unlimited legislative authority'.[23] Second, British courts did not possess
the power to strike down or disapply a statute passed by Parliament. A
third possible implication was that the only thing that Parliament could
not do was to entrench legislation binding its successors, because that
would effectively limit the sovereignty of future Parliaments.

Legal and political developments over the years reshaped this
orthodox notion of parliamentary sovereignty. After the UK's entry
into the EU in 1973, courts began disapplying UK law that conflicted
with EU law.[24] As a member of the CoE, the UK is also under an

---

[21] There is a long history of devolution in Northern Ireland, dating back to
1920; see John Morison, 'Law-making and Devolution: The Northern Ireland
Experience' (2003) 3 Legal Information Management 158. In contrast, the
Scottish Parliament and the Welsh National Assembly were established by statutes of the Westminster Parliament in 1998.

[22] HRA, section 6(3).

[23] A.V. Dicey, *Introduction to the Study of the Law of the Constitution* (6th edn,
Macmillan 1902), p. 39.

[24] Although section 2(4) of the European Communities Act, 1972, an act of
Westminster Parliament, specifically provides for this. See *R v. Secretary of State
for Transport ex p Factortame (No. 2)*, [1991] AC 603.

international obligation to bring its domestic law (including statutes of the Westminster Parliament) into compliance with the judgments of the Strasbourg Court. Based on devolution settlements, the Westminster Parliament, by convention, does not legislate on devolved subjects without the consent of the relevant devolved legislature.[25] Since the turn of the century, senior judges have not only recognized Parliament's ability to protect legislation from implied repeal,[26] but have also threatened to disapply future statutes that clearly attempt to defy the rule of law.[27]

Nevertheless, it is safe to say that the doctrine of parliamentary sovereignty still exerted considerable influence in political circles at the time of the enactment of the HRA. As the home secretary commented in the House of Commons, 'The sovereignty of Parliament must be paramount. By that, I mean that Parliament must be competent to make any law on any matter of its choosing.'[28] Therefore, the challenge was to conceptualize a model that enabled British courts to review Westminster legislation on rights-based grounds, without impinging upon parliamentary sovereignty. Even if there was sufficient agreement on the need to protect further Convention rights domestically, legislative history showed that the devil was in the detail[29]—how would Parliament translate this benevolent objective into the provisions of a statute?

The government mulled over possible options. On the one hand, it considered embracing the approach adopted in the New Zealand Bill of

---

[25] This is called the Sewel Convention (after Lord Sewel, the former parliamentary under-secretary of state for Scotland).

[26] *Thoburn* v. *Sunderland City Council*, [2003] QB 151.

[27] *Jackson* v. *Attorney General*, [2005] UKHL 56: see opinions of Lord Steyn, Baroness Hale, and Lord Hope. See also H.W.R. Wade and C.F. Forsyth, *Administrative Law* (11th edn, Oxford University Press 2014), pp. 22–3.

[28] HC Deb 16 February 1998, vol. 306, col. 770 (Jack Straw).

[29] See, for example, what Lord Archer said in response to the Bill of Rights introduced by Lord Lester in 1996 (HL Deb 5 February 1997, vol. 577, col. 1745):

There is no room for disagreement about the principle underlying the Bill. *The Bill is not about the principle; it is about how best to implement it.* There is no debate as to whether the people of the United Kingdom should have the rights set out in the European Convention.... *What remains is the question of where and how they should enforce them.* (Emphasis added)

Rights Act a few years earlier, in which courts are required to interpret past and future legislation consistently with the rights set out in the act, but cannot do anything further if legislation is inconsistent with those rights.[30] On the other hand, it considered the Canadian model, in which courts can strike down legislation that conflicts with rights, subject to the legislature's ability to re-enact legislation with a 'notwithstanding' clause that would insulate it from judicial review for a defined timespan.[31]

It soon became clear, however, that there was no appetite to give courts the power to strike down legislation, with or without a notwithstanding clause. Many senior judges themselves rejected the idea. As Lord Chief Justice Bingham said at the time, 'That is a power which throughout the recent debates the judges have made clear they do not seek.'[32] Even though the debates about the HRA had a strong comparative flavour,[33] the solution devised was distinctively British. The resulting provisions came in for considerable praise from MPs, having been described as a 'masterly exhibition' of draughtsmanship,[34] an 'adroit scheme' of rights protection,[35] a 'thing of intellectual beauty',[36] and an 'ingenious' solution to the problems that Parliament was confronted with.[37]

The solution was as follows: under section 3 of the HRA, legislation needed to be read, so far as possible, consistently with Convention rights. However, if a rights-compatible interpretation of primary

[30] New Zealand Bill of Rights Act, 1990, section 6.

[31] Canadian Charter of Rights and Freedoms, 1982, section 33.

[32] HL Deb 3 November 1997, vol. 582, col. 1246 (Lord Bingham).

[33] Bills of rights and models of judicial review adopted in other Commonwealth jurisdictions were frequently cited during the debates. See, for example, HL Deb 3 November 1997, vol. 582, col. 1262 (Lord Lester):

> What on earth is wrong with our British judges which disqualifies them from performing the role when the judges of almost every other Commonwealth and European country perform the role of interpreting the broad language of constitutional guarantees of human rights as required by the Bill? Why are our judges uniquely disqualified? What is the threat to them which does not apply to the judges of, for example, India, Canada, New Zealand or the rest of the Commonwealth?

[34] HL Deb 3 November 1997, vol. 582, col. 1234 (Lord Kingsland).

[35] HL Deb 3 November 1997, vol. 582, col. 1282 (Lord Windlesham).

[36] HL Deb 3 November 1997, vol. 582, col. 1286 (Earl Russel).

[37] HL Deb 3 November 1997, vol. 582, col. 1234 (Lord Kingsland).

legislation was not possible, courts could make a declaration of incompatibility under section 4. This declaration would not affect the validity of statutory provisions or render action taken under it unlawful. Instead, it would leave it to Parliament and the government to decide whether and how to address the inconsistency with Convention rights. The declaration would also trigger a ministerial power to amend the incompatible legislation by remedial order if there were compelling reasons to do so.[38] In order to ensure that the declaration of incompatibility did not become a de facto power to strike down legislation, the decision about whether to make a remedial order following a declaration of incompatibility was left to the discretion of the government.[39]

At a conceptual level, the declaration of incompatibility was thus envisioned as an intelligent way of reconciling parliamentary sovereignty and judicial review of primary legislation. However, the remedy excited considerable interest amongst scholars for another reason—by giving courts the power to review legislation without being able to strike it down, it was expected to facilitate a balanced allocation of powers between courts and the legislature in articulating their views about rights. Under this model of rights protection, both institutions were likely to have the opportunity of advancing their views on the compliance of legislation with rights. It was different from parliamentary sovereignty, where the legislature had the upper hand in deciding rights-based questions, and full-scale judicial review or judicial supremacy, where courts enjoyed this privilege.

Which courts were entrusted with the power of making declarations of incompatibility? The structure of the judicial system in the UK is hierarchical but fragmented, since different nations within the UK have different judicial structures. Within each nation, different courts are located at separate levels of the hierarchy based on the subject matter of a dispute. The unifying element between the hierarchy of courts in England & Wales, Scotland, and Northern Ireland is that the Supreme Court, in all cases (barring Scottish criminal cases), stands at the top of the pyramid. The 12-member Supreme Court took over the functions of the Judicial Committee of the House of Lords in 2009.[40] It only

---

[38] HRA, section 10.
[39] HL Deb 27 November 1997, vol. 583, col. 1139 (Lord Chancellor).
[40] See the Constitutional Reform Act, 2005.

determines points of law and hears cases of public or constitutional importance. Panels of five judges typically hear cases in the Supreme Court.[41]

A court of appeal, followed by a high court, constitutes the next two levels of hierarchy in England & Wales and Northern Ireland.[42] In the context of this judicial structure, the power to make declarations of incompatibility was not reserved to the Supreme Court, but was entrusted to all courts at the level of high court and above.[43] The HRA also specified that declarations of incompatibility could be made in any proceeding, subject to the requirement that the government is served notice and given a hearing when a court is considering whether to make such a declaration.[44]

In addition to opening up new avenues of judicial review, the HRA provided for 'pre-enactment political rights review'[45] of legislation. This was done through section 19, which requires the minister in charge of a bill to make a statement that, in his/her view, the provisions of the bill are compatible with Convention rights or that he/she is unable to make a statement of compatibility, but the government 'nevertheless wishes

---

[41] Although three-, seven-, and nine-judge panels are also constituted. Cheryl Thomas, *Decision-making by the United Kingdom Supreme Court and Judicial Committee of the Privy Council: 2009–13: First Consolidated Report of the United Kingdom Supreme Court and Judicial Committee of the Privy Council Project* (UCL Judicial Institute 2013).

[42] The structure is different in Scotland—there is no equivalent of the court of appeal. Instead, the Inner House of the Court of Session is the highest civil court (below the UK Supreme Court) and the High Court of Justiciary is the highest criminal court.

[43] More specifically, the following courts are entitled to make declarations of incompatibility: (a) the Supreme Court; (b) the judicial committee of the Privy Council; (c) the Court Martial Appeal Court; (d) in Scotland, the High Court of Justiciary sitting otherwise than as a trial court or the Court of Session; (e) in England and Wales or Northern Ireland, the high court or the Court of Appeal; and (f) the Court of Protection, in any matter being dealt with by the president of the Family Division, the chancellor of the high court, or a puisne judge of the high court. See HRA, section 4(5).

[44] HRA, section 5.

[45] Stephen Gardbaum, *The New Commonwealth Model of Constitutionalism: Theory and Practice* (Cambridge University Press 2013), p. 79.

the House to proceed' with the bill.[46] The Joint Committee on Human Rights (JCHR), a select committee of both houses of Parliament that scrutinizes draft legislation to determine whether compatibility statements are properly made, gives potency to section 19.[47]

The HRA is an un-entrenched statute, which means that it can be amended or repealed by simple parliamentary majority, without recourse to special majorities or cumbersome amending procedures.[48] This is particularly relevant in the context of the regular threats that have been made by the Conservative Party to repeal the HRA. Nevertheless, it is useful to remember that it is not the HRA which brought the very notion of rights into the UK for the first time. It is for this reason that a hereditary peer in the House of Lords pressed for the word 'additional' or 'enhanced' to be placed before 'Human Rights Act' in the statute's title.[49]

Let us now turn back the clock by almost exactly half a century. In the twilight years of the British Raj, an indirectly elected Constituent Assembly was established to draft a codified constitution for India. Unlike the UK's piecemeal constitutional arrangements, India had its 'big bang' moment of independence in 1947, leading to the adoption of a written Constitution on 26 November 1949. The Indian Constitution—the world's longest[50]—was a comprehensive document that would reflect the values and aspirations of the people. As with many of its post–Second World War counterparts, the Constitution embodied strong individual rights guarantees. Part III contained the chapter on fundamental rights, which included basic civil and political rights such as the right to equality,[51] the freedom of speech and expression,[52] the right to life and personal liberty,[53] and the right to freedom

---

[46]  HRA, section 19(1).

[47]  The JCHR also monitors responses to declarations of incompatibility, a matter that is considered in Chapter 5.

[48]  As a 'constitutional statute'—a written component of the UK's uncodified Constitution—it is immune from implied repeal by subsequent enactments of Parliament. See *Thoburn* (n. 26), para 62.

[49]  HL Deb 27 November 1997, vol. 583, cols 1167–8 (Lord Monson).

[50]  At the time of its enactment, the Indian Constitution consisted of 395 articles and 8 schedules.

[51]  Constitution of India, Art. 14.

[52]  Constitution of India, Art. 19(1)(a).

[53]  Constitution of India, Art. 21.

of religion.[54] Quite remarkably, Art. 32, considered by Dr Ambedkar (Chairman of the Drafting Committee of the Constituent Assembly) as the 'very soul' and 'heart' of the Constitution,[55] guaranteed the right to move the Supreme Court at first instance for the enforcement of these rights.

However, rather more unusually for its time, the Constitution also contained a chapter on social rights. Part IV consisted of the 'Directive Principles of State Policy', modelled on Ireland's 'Directive Principles of Social Policy'. At the time of their adoption, these principles were not considered justiciable, but were 'nevertheless fundamental in the governance of the country'.[56] They imposed several duties on the state, including providing equal pay for equal work,[57] offering free legal aid,[58] and raising the level of nutrition and standard of living amongst the people.[59] India was established as a quasi-federal state, with legislative powers shared between the union and the states. There is a bicameral legislature for the union, comprising the Rajya Sabha (Council of States) and the Lok Sabha (House of People). At the state level, seven of India's 29 states have bicameral legislatures, comprising a Vidhan Parishad (Upper House) and a Vidhan Sabha (Lower House). The remainder have unicameral legislatures.

It was always clear that Indian courts were constitutionally entrusted with the power to strike down primary legislation enacted by the Union and state legislatures. This was a power of not just procedural judicial review, but also substantive judicial review. In other words, courts could not only strike down legislation on the basis that it fell afoul of the federal distribution of powers, but also on the basis that it contravened fundamental rights or other constitutional rights. Some members of the Constituent Assembly persuasively argued that the power of judicial review of legislation was inherent in federal Constitutions with a bill of

[54] Constitution of India, Arts 25–8.

[55] Constituent Assembly of India Debates (Proceedings), 9 December 1948, vol. VII, p. 953.

[56] Constitution of India, Art. 37.

[57] Constitution of India, Art. 39(d).

[58] Constitution of India, Art. 39A.

[59] Constitution of India, Art. 47.

rights.[60] On the face of it, the Indian power to strike down legislation did not engender the benefit that scholars claimed for the HRA. Since the Supreme Court and high courts were the 'ultimate arbiter in all matters involving the interpretation of the Constitution',[61] it was expected that courts would have the final say on questions relating to rights, and that Parliament could not be an equal participant in decision-making about rights.

A few speeches during the Constituent Assembly Debates cast some doubt about whether all members were equally enthusiastic about the courts having the power to strike down legislation on rights-based parameters. No less a person than Dr Ambedkar said (although in the context of whether or not the Indian Constitution should adopt a US-style due process clause):[62]

> In a federal constitution, it is always open to the judiciary to decide whether any particular law passed by the legislature is ultra vires or intra vires in reference to the powers of legislation which are granted by the Constitution to the particular legislature. If the law made by a particular legislature exceeds the authority of the power given to it by the Constitution, such law would be ultra vires and invalid.... The question which arises in considering this matter is this. We have no doubt given the judiciary the power to examine the law made by different legislative bodies on the ground whether that law is in accordance with the powers given to it. The question now raised by the introduction of the phrase 'due process' is whether the judiciary should be given *the additional power to question the laws made by the State on the ground that they violate certain fundamental principles*. (Emphasis added)

Although these observations are remarkably broad, it is likely that they were only meant in the context of whether India should incorporate a US-style due process clause,[63] rather than whether courts, in general,

[60] Constituent Assembly of India Debates (Proceedings) 6 December 1948, vol. VII (Chimanlal Chakkubhai Shah).

[61] Constituent Assembly of India Debates (Proceedings) 23 November 1949, vol. XI (Alladi Krishnaswami Ayyar).

[62] Constituent Assembly of India Debates (Proceedings) 13 December 1948, vol. VII.

[63] US Constitution, 1787, Fifth and Fourteenth Amendments.

possess the power to strike down legislation on the basis that it violates rights. Harder to explain is the statement of Annie Mascarene (a prominent freedom fighter who was later elected as an MP in the first general election in independent India), who, during the final days of the drafting process, observed: 'Our judiciary with its original and appellate jurisdiction and with the right of interpretation of the constitution *differs from that of America, where the judiciary has the right of judicial review of executive and legislative activities*'[64] (emphasis added). One way of reading these observations suggests that Indian courts were not entrusted with the power to strike down legislation that was inconsistent with rights.[65] But any such inferences are powerfully rebutted by the final text of the Constitution itself. Although the power to review and strike down legislation cannot be paired with a single article of the Constitution, it is made manifest by reading several constitutional provisions together.

To begin with, Art. 13(2) proscribes the State from making 'any law which takes away or abridges the rights conferred' by Part III.[66] It then clarifies that 'any law made in contravention of this clause [Art. 13(2)] shall, to the extent of the contravention, be void'. This provision has often been understood to enable courts to strike down primary legislation and executive action.[67] On its own, the provision is under-inclusive and does not encompass the full gamut of judicial review, because it only addresses inconsistencies between legislation and fundamental rights (under Part III), leaving aside the question of

[64] Constituent Assembly of India Debates (Proceedings) 18 November 1949, vol. XI.

[65] The alternative reading is that Mascarene did not intend her observations to mean that Indian courts have no power of judicial review of legislation and executive action; rather, that the jurisdiction of Indian courts was considerably wider than that of their American counterparts.

[66] Art. 13(1) of the Constitution declares that all laws in force in India immediately before the commencement of this Constitution would be void to the extent of their inconsistency with the provisions of Part III.

[67] Maureen Callahan VanderMay, 'The Role of the Judiciary in India's Constitutional Democracy' (1996–7) 20 Hastings International & Comparative Law Review 103, p. 107. See also M.C.J. Kagzi, *The Constitution of India* (2nd edn, Metropolitan Book Company 1967), p. 355. Kagzi says that Art. 13(2) signifies the 'vesting of power of judicial review of legislation'.

inconsistencies between legislation and other justiciable provisions of the Constitution.

Interestingly, Art. 13 did not provoke much debate in the Constituent Assembly.[68] The most likely inference is that a consensus prevailed about the necessity of including this provision in the Constitution. Granville Austin records that members of an ad hoc committee of the Constituent Assembly had urged the Assembly to include this explicit provision for judicial review, in the knowledge that in the US, the power of judicial review had to be inferred by the Supreme Court.[69] It should also be noted that one of the possible reasons for which Art. 13 was not debated at length was because the nature of the remedy available to courts was a sideshow at the time of the Constitution's enactment (although, as this book demonstrates, it became increasingly significant after the Constitution entered into force). The Indian Constitution was meant to be a transformative one, seeking to address complex social problems such as untouchability, illiteracy, and the unequal distribution of wealth. It is only natural then that the framers focused their energies on these seemingly more pressing matters. This is in contrast to the UK, where on account of the tradition of parliamentary sovereignty, the remedy formed a central plank of the parliamentary debates at the time of enactment of the HRA.

Next, there are Arts 372(1) and 245(1) of the Constitution—the former applies to pre-constitutional laws,[70] and the latter to post-constitutional laws.[71] Art. 372(1) provides that 'subject to the provisions of the Constitution, all laws in force in the territory of India immediately before the commencement of the Constitution shall continue in force therein until altered or repealed or amended by a competent Legislature or other competent authority' (emphasis added). In the context of judicial review of legislation, this provision bears two implications:

---

[68] The only real point of debate concerned the definition of 'law' in this article. See Constituent Assembly of India Debates (Proceedings) 29 November 1948, vol. VII (Art. 13 was draft Art. 8).

[69] Granville Austin, *The Indian Constitution: Cornerstone of a Nation* (Oxford University Press 1972), p. 171. See *Marbury v. Madison*, (1803) 5 US 137.

[70] This refers to all laws in force immediately before the commencement of the Constitution (that is, before 26 January 1950).

[71] This refers to all laws that come into force after the commencement of the Constitution (that is, after 26 January 1950).

First, it signals that all laws in force prior to the commencement of the Constitution can be tested for compliance with the provisions of the Constitution by courts. Second, since the term 'laws', as per Art. 372, includes common law,[72] the power of judicial review of legislation (which was part of common law applicable in India before the Constitution entered into force[73]) would continue to vest in the Indian courts.

Article 245(1) reads as follows: *'Subject to the provisions of this Constitution,* Parliament may make laws for the whole or any part of the territory of India, and the Legislature of a State may make laws for the whole or any part of the State' (emphasis added). This provision, on the other hand, seems to suggest that post-constitutional legislation that violates provisions of the Constitution can be reviewed (and struck down as invalid) by Indian courts.[74] Overall, this network of constitutional provisions clearly shows that judicial review of primary legislation, coupled with the power to strike it down, formed part of the scheme of the Indian Constitution at the time of its founding.

The Indian Constitution established a unitary judicial structure with the Supreme Court at the top. The Supreme Court is the final court of appeal in civil and criminal cases and is the authoritative interpreter of the Constitution. Comprising maximum 31 judges including the Chief Justice, the Supreme Court sits in panels of two or more judges.[75] The Constitution declares that judgments of the Supreme Court are binding on all other courts in the country.[76] Twenty-four high courts,

---

[72] *Union of India* v. *SICOM,* (2009) 2 SCC 121, para 11.

[73] *R* v. *Burah,* (1878) 3 AC 889. Although this seemed to be limited to review on procedural grounds.

[74] Some authors have attempted to read Arts 13, 372(1), and 245(1) together by arguing that they perform separate functions in the context of judicial review. Thus, whereas Arts 372(1) and 245(1) constitute the textual basis of judicial review, confirming that Indian courts do have this power, Art. 13 regulates the extent to which legislation that is repugnant with Part III alone is void (and not the other provisions of the Constitution). See V.S. Deshpande, *Judicial Review of Legislation* (Eastern Book Company 1975), p. 59.

[75] Substantial questions of law as to the interpretation of the Constitution are decided by benches of at least five judges. See Constitution of India, Art. 145(3).

[76] Constitution of India, Art. 141.

representing the states and union territories in India,[77] are at the second tier of this hierarchy. High courts exercise appellate and original jurisdiction. As is the case with declarations of incompatibility in the UK, only the higher courts in India (the Supreme Court and the state high courts) have the power to strike down any legislation on the basis that it violates constitutional rights.[78]

It is important to note some of the differences between the Supreme Court of the UK and the Supreme Court of India—these differences often reflect the manner in which judgments are drafted and reasoned in both courts. The Indian Supreme Court is more in the nature of an ordinary appellate court rather than what one might associate with being the foremost court for a jurisdiction. The UK Supreme Court, although not an exclusively constitutional court in the continental European sense, is like a conventional Supreme Court that decides a select group of cases. The UK Supreme Court hears about 65 cases a year,[79] while the overburdened Indian Supreme Court hears close to 50,000 cases a year,[80] with over 60,000 cases awaiting hearing.[81] Decisions of the UK Supreme Court are usually made by panels of five judges, whereas two-judge panels are the norm in the Indian Supreme Court.[82] Unlike in the UK, the staggering volume of cases in

[77] Some High Courts have jurisdiction over two or more states and union territories.

[78] See Civil Procedure Code, 1908, section 113; Code of Criminal Procedure, 1973, section 395; *Shreeshyla Crowns* v. *Union of India*, AIR 1983 Kar 130, para 22. However, some administrative tribunals can adjudicate upon challenges to the constitutional validity of statutes; see *L. Chandra Kumar* v. *Union of India*, AIR 1997 SC 1125. That the Supreme Court would not have the exclusive power to decide issues of rights was clear from the early days of the Constitution's drafting—see Austin (n. 69), p. 170.

[79] This figure is based on an average of the total number of cases heard between 2009 and 2013. See Thomas (n. 41).

[80] Nick Robinson, 'A Court Adrift' *Frontline* (New Delhi, 3 May 2013). These are the figures for 'admissions' matters alone.

[81] This is based on the Supreme Court's official figures. See <http://supremecourtofindia.nic.in/p_stat/pm01022014.pdf> accessed 18 February 2014.

[82] For a critical discussion of the panel composition on the Supreme Court of India, see Chintan Chandrachud, 'The Supreme Court's Practice of Referring Cases to Larger Benches: A Need for Review' (2010) 1 SCC 37.

India makes it difficult for the academics to analyse the jurisprudence of the Supreme Court critically and comprehensively over any given period of time.[83] Judicial review is no exception to this phenomenon: every UK Supreme Court judgment under sections 3 and 4 of the HRA is the subject of widespread academic commentary, while many Indian Supreme Court judgments on judicial review of primary legislation tend to fall under the radar.[84]

Pre-enactment political rights review in India is not as broad-based as it is under the HRA. At the level of the Union Parliament, the government department in charge of a bill refers legislative proposals to the Union Ministry of Law and Justice for advice as to 'its feasibility from legal and constitutional points of view'.[85] This review is expected to be of a top-level nature, since (unlike in the UK) it takes place before the legislative proposals are formally translated into a bill.[86] Before the bill is finalized and introduced in Parliament, the department in charge of the bill is expected to submit a pro forma document indicating compliance with constitutional and procedural requirements for the bill to the relevant minister.[87] Although the pro forma requires the department to specify if the bill contains any provisions 'placing restrictions on or regulation of [sic] fundamental rights',[88] it does not require the

---

[83] Tarunabh Khaitan, 'Koushal v Naz: The Legislative Court' (*UK Constitutional Law Association*, 22 December 2013) <https://ukconstitutional-law.org/2013/12/22/tarunabh-khaitan-koushal-v-naz-the-legislative-court/> accessed 11 August 2016.

[84] *Noor Aga* v. *State of Punjab*, (2008) 16 SCC 417 is a good example. In this case, the Supreme Court reinterpreted provisions of the Narcotic Drugs and Psychotropic Substances Act, 1985 in a manner that contradicted the express terms of the statute. This judgment seems to have received little or no serious academic comment.

[85] Ministry of Parliamentary Affairs, 'Manual on Parliamentary Procedures in the Government of India' (Ministry of Parliamentary Affairs, Government of India, June 2004) <http://mpa.nic.in/mpa/manual_EV.aspx> accessed 19 February 2014, para 9.2(b).

[86] The manual itself recognizes that the Ministry of Law and Justice will not go 'into details' about the constitutional validity of the legislative proposals. See Ministry of Parliamentary Affairs (n. 85), para 9.2(b).

[87] Ministry of Parliamentary Affairs (n. 85), para 9.7.4 and annex 8.

[88] Ministry of Parliamentary Affairs (n. 85), para 9.7.4 and annex 8.

question of the legislation's compatibility with rights to be considered during parliamentary proceedings.

The Indian Constitution, as a canonical constitutional document, is entrenched to a far greater extent than the HRA. Amendments to the Constitution can only be made by a two-thirds' majority in the Union Parliament.[89] Amendments of certain matters, such as the distribution of legislative power between the union and the states, also require ratification of at least half of the states.[90] In its seminal judgment in *Kesavananda Bharati* v. *State of Kerala*,[91] the Supreme Court established a jurisdiction to review and strike down constitutional amendments that alter or destroy the 'basic structure' of the Constitution.[92] It developed what is effectively a judicially imposed absolute entrenchment of the Constitution's basic features.

Comparative constitutional law is a relatively nascent field in the social sciences, and is still in its formative years. It is unsurprising that it is often asked whether there is any value in comparing constitutional systems. Is it at all useful to compare systems with different cultures, political histories, and linguistic identities? Reference to foreign judgments in constitutional decision-making has also generated significant controversy. As Justice Scalia from the US Supreme Court famously said, 'We must never forget that it is a Constitution for the United States of America we are expounding ... where there is first not a settled consensus among our own people, the views of other nations, however enlightened the Justices of this Court may think them to be, cannot be imposed upon Americans through the Constitution.'[93] These are

---

[89]  Constitution of India, Art. 368.

[90]  These requirements notwithstanding, the Indian Constitution is frequently amended—there have been 100 amendments since it came into force in 1950.

[91]  AIR 1973 SC 1461 (Basic Structure case).

[92]  This judgment marked the culmination of a hard-fought battle, spanning several years, between the judiciary and the executive. For a detailed analysis, see S.P. Sathe, 'Judicial Activism: The Indian Experience' (2001) 6 Washington University Journal of Law & Policy 29.

[93]  *Thompson* v. *Oklahoma*, (1988) 487 US 815, p. 868. For a similar statement from the Bench in India, see *Mahadeb Jiew* v. *B.B. Sen*, AIR 1951 Cal 563, para 37: 'The craze for American precedents can soon become a snare. A blind and uncritical adherence to American precedents must be avoided or else there

hard issues that have received compelling treatment elsewhere.[94] But the case for the constitutional scholar, rather than the court, is easier— comparing experiences from different constitutional systems enables us to learn from them, and better understand the system with which we are most familiar. As Robert Leckey says: 'If knowledge is power, favorable foreign judicial texts, and the periodical articles that disseminate them to new audiences, are part of the relevant knowledge.'[95]

Nevertheless, comparative constitutional law also carries its share of challenges for scholars. As with all comparative law, it involves an opportunity cost—looking at multiple systems often demands compromising the depth in which each system is examined. Resources from all jurisdictions may not be equally accessible.[96] Language barriers may require scholars to learn foreign tongues or rely on translations (an issue which this piece of work did not face, since English is the official language for the UK [de jure] and India [de facto]). These challenges need to be accommodated bearing in mind the nature and purpose of the research undertaken.

This book seeks to measure the promise of the new model against its performance—by comparing judicial review in one of the world's oldest existing democracies, the UK, to that under the Constitution of the world's largest democracy, India. As was explained in the preceding discussion, in terms of constitutional design, India and the UK lie along different parts of the spectrum of judicial review. The Indian Supreme

---

will soon be a perverted American Constitution operating in this land under the delusive garb of the Indian Constitution. We are interpreting and expounding our own Constitution.' It bears mentioning that this extract does not represent Indian courts' general or current position on citing foreign precedent.

[94] See, for example, Sarah K. Harding, 'Comparative Reasoning and Judicial Review' (2003) 28 Yale Journal of International Law 409; Robert J. Delahunty and John Yoo, 'Against Foreign Law' (2005) 29 Harvard Journal of Law & Public Policy 291; Cheryl Saunders, 'The Use and Misuse of Comparative Constitutional Law' (2006) 13 Indiana Journal of Global Legal Studies 37.

[95] Robert Leckey, 'Thick Instrumentalism and Comparative Constitutionalism: The Case of Gay Rights' (2009) 40 Columbia Human Rights Law Review 425, p. 433.

[96] Vicki C. Jackson, 'Methodological Challenges in Comparative Constitutional Law' (2010) 28 Pennsylvania State International Law Review 319, p. 323.

Court and high courts have the power to review primary legislation on both substantive and procedural grounds. The remedy available to them is more familiar to the constitutional scholar than the declaration of incompatibility—legislation that violates constitutional rights can be struck down. In contrast with the HRA, this court-centric model of review is believed to supply the judiciary with an advantage in deciding rights-based questions. Constitutional review is based not on an un-entrenched statute of Parliament, but on an entrenched, 'codified' Constitution. Ever since its enactment in 1949, the Indian Constitution has remained safe from existential threats posed by changing political majorities, barring a brief period of national emergency during Prime Minister Indira Gandhi's tenure in the 1970s.

Many scholars have argued that judicial review in the UK (and in other jurisdictions with similar versions of judicial review) is superior to models of judicial supremacy, where courts have the power to strike down legislation, because it enables the legislature to assert its own—more democratically grounded—conceptions of rights. This is by virtue of the fact that the legislature can reject judicial understandings of rights through ordinary majorities, without needing to take recourse to cumbersome amendment procedures or court-packing plans. The primary issue that this book seeks to focus on is: which model of judicial review, between that of India and the UK, enables both the legislature and courts to assert their understanding of rights more freely? This will be broken down into two questions: the first, addressed to the legislature, and the second, addressed to courts. Examining these questions will entail thorough investigation into many facets of the declaration of incompatibility (in the UK) and the power to strike down legislation (in India), including legislatures' perceptions of them, courts' willingness to issue them, and the role of institutions that strengthen or weaken their normative force.

An obvious issue that then arises is why India has been selected as the comparator jurisdiction for this task. Most studies thus far have focused on the US as the exemplar of judicial supremacy.[97] From that

---

[97] See, for example, Mark Tushnet, *Weak Courts, Strong Rights: Judicial Review and Social Welfare Rights in Comparative Constitutional Law* (Princeton University Press 2009); Rosalind Dixon, 'Weak-Form Judicial Review and American Exceptionalism' (2012) 32 OJLS 487. This is attributable, at least partly, to the large number of comparative law scholars and journals based in the US.

perspective, this book breaks away from the existing scholarship on models of judicial review. The reason for this is that unlike the US, India exhibits the combination of a system that is characterized by judicial supremacy within a tradition of parliamentary democracy. In parliamentary systems of government, since there is no formal separation between the legislature and the executive,[98] it is crucial to enable the two key prongs of authority—the legislature and courts—to assert their competing conceptions of rights.[99]

Parliamentary systems do not possess 'dual democratic legitimacy' shared between the executive and the legislature.[100] In parliamentary systems, the legislature alone represents the popular will in the rights discourse. The UK and India share this characteristic. To compare the UK's HRA with the US or other jurisdictions with an elected executive suffers the drawback that in presidential systems, there is an alternative source of democratic legitimacy: ignoring the executive's contribution to the rights discourse misses an important part of the landscape.

Although India and the UK have been compared in other areas of the law,[101] it is somewhat surprising that no detailed work comparing the UK's experience under the HRA with judicial review in India has

[98] Anthony W. Bradley and Cesare Pinelli, 'Parliamentarism' in Michael Rosenfeld and Andras Sajo (eds), *Oxford Handbook of Comparative Constitutional Law* (Oxford University Press 2012), p. 652.

[99] In contrast, in presidential systems, models that encourage each of the three branches of government to express their understanding of constitutional rights are often advocated. See, for example, the discussion of 'departmentalism' in the US in Mark Tushnet, 'Alternative Forms of Judicial Review' (2003) 101 Michigan Law Review 2781, p. 2782.

[100] Juan J. Linz, 'The Perils of Presidentialism' (1990) 1 Journal of Democracy 51, p. 63.

[101] See, for example, Simon Deakin, Priya Lele, and Mathias Siems, 'The Evolution of Labour Law: Calibrating and Comparing Regulatory Regimes' (2007) 146 International Labour Review 133; Manoranjan Ayilyath, 'Character Merchandising and Personality Merchandising—The Need for Protection: An Analysis in the Light of UK and Indian Laws' (2012) Entertainment Law Review 43; Tarunabh Khaitan, *A Theory of Discrimination Law* (Oxford University Press 2015). See also, Charles R. Epp, *The Rights Revolution: Lawyers, Activists, and Supreme Courts in Comparative Perspective* (University of Chicago 1998), published before the HRA was enacted.

surfaced, particularly since the two nations share a common history, and the two legal systems continue to influence one another. Scholars have also demanded a greater focus on South Asia in constitutional research.[102] This book may be considered as an attempt to fulfil such demands by focusing attention on a jurisdiction whose constitutional complexities remain under-theorized and are still not fully understood.

The book adopts what can be situated in the scholarship as a 'small-n'[103] approach—focusing on two jurisdictions in considerable detail and depth. Recent scholarship has emphasized upon the value of developing causality in comparative constitutional law;[104] for instance, that the way in which a Constitution is drafted establishes an 'incentive structure that affects behaviour' in one way or another.[105] Given the complex number of variables at play, this book is sceptical about drawing any distinct generalizations,[106] although it speculates about some towards the end. The focus, rather, is on concept thickening[107]—understanding and explaining the way in which judicial review operates in

---

[102] See Edward J. Eberle, 'The Method and Role of Comparative Law' (2009) 8 Washington University Global Studies Law Review 451, p. 454, where the author explains: 'Comparative law should also focus more intently on non-Western legal orders. Especially crucial for consideration are the legal cultures of Asia, most notably, those of China and India—two rising superpowers—and of Japan, which is already an important player on the world stage.'

[103] 'Small-n' approaches focus on a small number of case studies in depth.

[104] Ran Hirschl, 'The Question of Case Selection in Comparative Constitutional Law' (2005) 53 American Journal of Comparative Law 125; Christopher A. Whytock, 'Taking Causality Seriously in Comparative Constitutional Law: Insights from Comparative Politics and Comparative Political Economy' (2008) 41 Loyola of Los Angeles Law Review 629; Ran Hirschl, *Comparative Matters: The Renaissance of Comparative Constitutional Law* (Oxford University Press 2014), chapter 6.

[105] Robert D. Cooter, *The Strategic Constitution* (Princeton University Press 2000), p. 360.

[106] Vicki C. Jackson, 'Comparative Constitutional Law: Methodologies' in Rosenfeld and Sajo (n. 98), p. 65.

[107] Leckey (n. 95), p. 437. As the author says: 'The thin understanding [of Constitutions] regards them as utilitarian, rule-based, and represented satisfactorily by their texts…. By contrast, the thick understanding apprehends constitutions as symbolic, cultural, discursively embedded, and operative in multiple sites.'

both jurisdictions. This work will compare not only the formal legal rules and texts in both jurisdictions, but also the manner in which they operate in practice.

The book, therefore, relies on the functionalist methodology. Functionalism has four characteristics:[108] First, it is factual, and 'focuses not on rules but on their effects' and not on doctrinal form, but on function. Second, social context plays an important role in functionalism: the objects of study are considered in the light of the socio-political context in which they operate. Third, an excessive focus on nomenclature is cast aside, and institutions are treated as comparable if they are functionally equivalent. Fourth, functionality serves as an 'evaluative criterion' to determine which institutions fulfil certain functions better than others.

Functionalism is amongst the most widely applied, yet heavily contested, methodologies in comparative law. As one scholar observes, it has become 'both the mantra and the bête noire of comparative law'.[109] Functionalist approaches also lie at the fulcrum of two opposing tensions—on the one hand, they must avoid specifying functions too generally, and on the other, must also avoid specifying functions so precisely that the benefits of comparison are all but lost.[110] This book attempts to avoid these tensions by defining the 'function'—maintaining a balance between the legislature and courts on the interpretation of rights—at an appropriate level of abstraction.

Functionalism is also condemned for assuming that societies confront similar social problems.[111] Then there is the organicist critique, which posits that only a constitutional regime that emanates organically from within a society will be accepted by it.[112] An effective way

---

[108] Ralf Michaels, 'The Functional Method of Comparative Law' in Mathias Reimann and Reinhard Zimmermann (eds), *The Oxford Handbook of Comparative Law* (Oxford University Press 2006), p. 342.

[109] Michaels (n. 108), p. 340.

[110] Mark Tushnet, 'The Possibilities of Comparative Constitutional Law' (1999) 108 Yale Law Journal 1225, p. 1238.

[111] James Q. Whitman, 'The Neo-romantic Turn' in Pierre Legrand and Roderick Munday (eds), *Comparative Legal Studies: Traditions and Transitions* (Cambridge University Press 2003), p. 313.

[112] Mark Tushnet, 'Returning with Interest: Observations on Some Putative Benefits of Studying Comparative Constitutional Law' (1998) 1 Journal of Constitutional Law 325, p. 333.

of dealing with these critiques is by deploying a moderate form of functionalism,[113] which is sensitive to differences in social and political context and cautious about making direct causal inferences. This moderate form of functionalism recognizes that rules and institutions form part of a larger social context. Mindful of this, this chapter has attempted to supply some context to the discussion that follows in the book.

The book pursues the following trajectory: Chapter 1 establishes the theoretical framework, and more fully develops the questions that the book engages with. Chapters 2 and 3 consider political responses to declarations of incompatibility in the UK and striking down of legislation in India, with the objective of determining whether the Westminster Parliament has greater room for manoeuvre than the Indian legislature, as many scholars would have expected soon after the HRA was enacted. Chapter 4 moves to the judicial dimension—whether, in the context of the constitutional remedies available to them, courts in both jurisdictions are able to assert their understanding of rights unreservedly. Chapter 5 then examines the institutional structure surrounding the remedies, with reference to the work of the JCHR in the UK, the Strasbourg Court under the Convention, and the National Human Rights Commission (NHRC) in India. Chapter 6 concludes and considers broader inferences that may be drawn from this book.

[113] Jaakko Husa, 'Farewell to Functionalism or Methodological Tolerance?' (2003) 67 Rabel Journal of Comparative and International Private Law 419.

# 1 Balancing Decision-making amongst Courts and Legislatures

This chapter sets out the theoretical framework within which the constitutional practice of the two jurisdictions, India and the UK, will be examined. At the outset, it is worth clarifying what the chapter does and does not seek to achieve. The chapter develops a theoretical framework, or a skeleton, upon which later chapters add the practice, or the proverbial flesh. On the other hand, what this chapter does not do is engage in depth with democratic theory or theories of rights, subjects on which many volumes have been written and which deserve consideration spanning beyond a few pages.[1]

This chapter has three aims: (a) to situate the arguments made in this book in the broader comparative constitutional law scholarship on models of judicial review;[2] (b) to develop a normative theoretical framework within which the models of rights protection in India and

---

[1] Some of the most prominent examples are: Ronald Dworkin, *Taking Rights Seriously* (Harvard University Press 1978); John Hart Ely, *Democracy and Distrust: A Theory of Judicial Review* (Harvard University Press 1980); Ronald Dworkin, *A Matter of Principle* (Harvard University Press 1986); and Jeremy Waldron, *Law and Disagreement* (Oxford University Press 1999).

[2] The author refers to judicial review in the sense of constitutional judicial review (or judicial review of primary legislation) rather than judicial review of executive action. This is discussed later in the chapter, in the section titled 'Issues of Scope and Typology'.

the UK are later evaluated; and (c) to introduce the two primary claims made by this book based on the normative framework identified.

## Three Models of Rights Protection

Over the last two centuries, constitutional experience from around the world has shown that there are two divergent models of rights protection. They represent differing constitutional arrangements in the way in which they balance decision-making power between the legislature and the judiciary. On the one hand, parliamentary sovereignty acknowledges that the legislature is the supreme lawmaking authority, and that courts are not permitted to ignore or reject legislation that has been properly enacted by the body that is representative of the people's interests. The absence of judicial review over legislation does not mean that rights remain unprotected. Rather, the primary forum for rights protection is the legislature, not the courts.

Political parties that represent contrasting interests and offer differing perspectives safeguard rights through the democratic process. Governments that impinge upon the rights of citizens through primary legislation are not directly sanctioned by courts, but are confronted with paying the political price to the electorate. Parliamentary sovereignty, a concept most famously expounded by A.V. Dicey,[3] the Vinerian Professor of English Law at the University of Oxford, emerged in Britain and travelled to former British colonies, including Australia[4] and New Zealand.

On the other hand, the model of judicial supremacy (or 'strong-form judicial review'[5]) prevails in jurisdictions that have a codified, canonical constitution. In systems of judicial supremacy, legislative power is subjected to constitutional limitations that are enforced by courts by

---

[3] A.V. Dicey, *Introduction to the Study of the Law of the Constitution* (6th edn, Macmillan 1902).

[4] On the influence of parliamentary sovereignty in Australia, see Cheryl Saunders and Anna Dziedzic, 'Parliamentary Sovereignty and Written Constitutions in Comparative Perspective' in A. Welikala (ed.), *The Sri Lankan Republic at 40: Reflections on Constitutional History, Theory and Practice* (vol. 1, Centre for Policy Alternatives 2012), p. 477.

[5] Mark Tushnet, 'New Forms of Judicial Review and the Persistence of Rights- and Democracy-Based Worries' (2003) 38 Wake Forest Law Review 813, p. 814.

the exercise of a power to strike down, invalidate, or disapply primary legislation. Courts enjoy the last word on the resolution of issues relating to rights, at least within the existing constitution or bill of rights.[6] In other words, judges, who have more modest representative credentials than legislators, are entrusted with policing the boundaries of rights. This model of judicial review, which is most common amongst constitutional democracies of today,[7] proliferated after, and quite significantly as a result of, the Second World War.[8] The typical post-War constitution, if there is such a thing, is a written document giving the courts the power to review primary legislation on substantive and procedural grounds. This model of constitutionalism was put into place in Italy (1947), Germany (1949), India (1949), France (1958), Greece (1975), Spain (1978), and many other jurisdictions.

These models reflected a binary choice that lay before newly independent nations or those undergoing constitutional transition. Based on the logic of the US Supreme Court's judgment in *Marbury* v. *Madison*,[9] they would need to decide between a higher-law written Constitution or bill of rights policed by independent courts, and a constitution that is 'on par with regular law', which left questions of rights resolution to elected representatives.[10] It should be noted, however, that these traditional models did not represent monoliths, and there remained scope for variation *within* them. So, for example, within parliamentary sovereignty, a sovereign legislature may or may not have been empowered to enact legislation prescribing the 'manner and form'

[6] Stephen Gardbaum, *The New Commonwealth Model of Constitutionalism: Theory and Practice* (Cambridge University Press 2013).

[7] Bruce Ackerman, 'The Rise of World Constitutionalism' (1997) 83 Virginia Law Review 771.

[8] Tom Ginsburg, 'The Global Spread of Constitutional Review' in Keith E. Whittington, R. Daniel Keleman, and Gregory A. Caldeira (eds), *The Oxford Handbook of Law and Politics* (Oxford University Press 2008), p. 81.

[9] (1803) 5 US 137, p. 177. Chief Justice John Marshall famously held that '[t]he Constitution is either a superior paramount law, unchangeable by ordinary means, or it is on a level with ordinary legislative acts, and, like other acts, is alterable when the legislature shall please to alter it'.

[10] Rivka Weill, 'The New Commonwealth Model of Constitutionalism Notwithstanding: On Judicial Review and Constitution-Making' (2014) 62 American Journal of Comparative Law 127, pp. 128–9.

of future legislation, thereby effectively imposing limits upon itself.[11] Within models of judicial supremacy, the authority to determine the rights-compatibility of legislation could be centralized in a constitutional court or superior courts, or dispersed among courts at all levels.[12] Further, courts could be empowered simply to disapply legislation or to strike it down, removing it from the statute book altogether as though it had been repealed.[13] These variations represented options *within* each of the traditional models, but left little room for any significant convergence *between* them.

Each of these traditional models is, in some sense, considered imperfect. Parliamentary sovereignty, although democratically legitimate, bears the risk of leaving behind minorities that suffer inadequate representation in the democratic process. Judicial supremacy, which leaves the process of adjudication of rights to independent courts, gives rise to apprehensions of democratic legitimacy that are well captured by the notion of the 'countermajoritarian difficulty'.[14] The principal concern is whether it is legitimate, in systems of judicial supremacy, to allow unaccountable judges to thwart decisions that are reflective of the public will.

Over the last three decades, a third alternative to these traditional models has emerged. This model seeks to capture the best aspects of the two traditional models, while leaving aside their weaknesses. The highlight of the new model is that it enables both courts and the legislature to assert their competing understanding of rights. Courts have a limited power of review over primary legislation, which can be assailed by the legislature, acting in its ordinary capacity, in different ways. In Canada,

---

[11] Ivor Jennings, *The Law and the Constitution* (3rd edn, London University Press 1943), p. 146; R.F.V. Heuston, *Essays in Constitutional Law* (2nd edn, Stevens 1964), pp. 1–31.

[12] Paul Craig, 'Constitutional and Non-Constitutional Review' (2001) 54 Current Legal Problems 147, pp. 148–50.

[13] Jeremy Waldron, 'The Core of the Case against Judicial Review' (2006) 115 Yale Law Journal 1346, p. 1354.

[14] Barry Friedman, 'The History of the Countermajoritarian Difficulty, Part One: The Road to Judicial Supremacy' (1998) 73 New York University Law Review 333. The classic exposition is Alexander M. Bickel, *The Least Dangerous Branch: The Supreme Court at the Bar of Politics* (2nd edn, Vail-Ballou 1986), p. 16.

section 33 of the Charter of Rights and Freedoms, 1982 empowers the legislature to declare, by ordinary majority, that a statute (or one of its provisions) will operate 'notwithstanding' certain provisions of the Charter. In New Zealand (under the New Zealand Bill of Rights Act, 1990), the UK (under the HRA), the Australian Capital Territory (under the Human Rights Act, 2004), and the Australian state of Victoria (under the Victorian Charter of Human Rights and Responsibilities Act, 2006), courts can make a declaration of inconsistency or incompatibility when they consider primary legislation to be inconsistent with rights.[15] However, it remains the task of the legislature to decide whether to take heed of such a declaration by amending the legislation in any way. In this manner, the model seeks to tactfully reconcile democratic legitimacy with rights-based judicial review.

Constitutional scholars ascribe many labels to this third alternative. These include 'the new commonwealth model of constitutionalism',[16] 'weak-form judicial review',[17] the 'parliamentary bill of rights' model,[18] the 'hybrid model' of judicial review,[19] the 'third way' or 'third wave' bill of rights,[20] the 'democratic dialogue' model,[21] and 'weak-form bills of rights'[22] (for the sake of convenience, these will collectively be referred to as the 'new model labels'). While recognizing subtle differences between them, Stephen Gardbaum, amongst the most well-known

---

[15] However, the power in New Zealand is implied rather than expressed. See *Moonen* v. *Film and Literature Board of Review*, [2000] 2 NZLR 9. A declaration of inconsistency was issued by the High Court in *Taylor* v. *Attorney General*, [2015] NZHC 1706.

[16] Gardbaum (n. 6).

[17] Mark Tushnet, 'Alternative Forms of Judicial Review' (2003) 101 Michigan Law Review 2781, p. 2782.

[18] Janet L. Hiebert, 'Parliamentary Bills of Rights: An Alternative Model?' (2006) 69 MLR 7.

[19] Jeffrey Goldsworthy, 'Homogenizing Constitutions' (2003) 23(3) OJLS 483, p. 483.

[20] Francesca Klug, 'The Human Rights Act: A "Third Way" or "Third Wave" Bill of Rights' (2001) 4 EHRLR 361.

[21] Alison Young, *Parliamentary Sovereignty and the Human Rights Act* (Hart 2009), chapters 4 and 5.

[22] Christine Bateup, 'Reassessing the Dialogic Possibilities of Weak-form Bills of Rights' (2009) 32 Hastings International & Comparative Law Review 529.

proponents of this new model, acknowledges that all these descriptions are alternative terms for the same phenomenon.[23] This is probably an overstatement—the more accurate way of understanding these labels is that all their proponents agree about the centrality of one aspect of the model: the fact that courts have the power to review primary legislation without being ascribed a definitive role in the process.[24]

However, apart from this central aspect of the third model, the different labels used by scholars reflect underlying differences in focus. So, for example, Tushnet's use of the label 'weak-form judicial review' is suitable to his heavy focus on decisions of courts in his vast scholarship on the subject.[25] Although he defends the model as a general one,[26] Gardbaum's use of the 'commonwealth' tag suggests that the new model will be better suited to commonwealth jurisdictions.[27] Klug's

[23]  Gardbuam (n. 6), p. 14.

[24]  Aileen Kavanagh, 'What's So Weak about "Weak-form" Review? The Case of the UK Human Rights Act 1998' (2015) 13 International Journal of Constitutional Law 1008.

[25]  Tushnet (n. 17); Mark Tushnet, 'Forms of Judicial Review as Expressions of Constitutional Patriotism' (2003) 22 Law and Philosophy 353; Mark Tushnet, 'Weak-form Judicial Review: Its Implications for Legislatures' (2004) 2 NZJPIL 7; Mark Tushnet, 'Social Welfare Rights and the Forms of Judicial Review' (2004) 82 Texas Law Review 1895; Mark Tushnet, 'Weak-form Judicial Review and "Core" Civil Liberties' (2006) 41 Harvard Civil Rights-Civil Liberties Law Review 1; Mark Tushnet, *Weak Courts, Strong Rights: Judicial Review and Social Welfare Rights in Comparative Constitutional Law* (Princeton University Press 2008); Mark Tushnet, 'The Rise of Weak-form Judicial Review' in Tom Ginsburg and Rosalind Dixon (eds), *Comparative Constitutional Law* (Edward Elgar 2011), p. 321; Mark Tushnet and Rosalind Dixon, 'Weak-form Review and Its Constitutional Relatives: An Asian Perspective' in Rosalind Dixon and Tom Ginsburg (eds), *Comparative Constitutional Law in Asia* (Edward Elgar 2014), p. 102.

[26]  Stephen Gardbaum, 'The Single and General New Commonwealth Model: A Response to Ran Hirschl and Sujit Choudhry' (2013) 11 International Journal of Constitutional Law 1100.

[27]  See Ran Hirschl, 'How Consequential Is the Commonwealth Constitutional Model?' (2013) 11 International Journal of Constitutional Law 1086, p. 1088, suggesting, in response to Gardbaum's work, that there could be something 'in the combination of characteristics shared by the countries under study—all relatively prosperous, stable democracies, and all current or former British colonies sharing a roughly similar legal tradition—that makes them conducive to this particular model of judicial review'.

use of the 'third wave' bill of rights idea clearly reflects her attention to the changing understanding of human rights across different periods of history. Alison Young's chosen label—the 'dialogue model'—reflects her emphasis on the importance of dialogic interactions between the courts and the legislature under this new model of judicial review, an issue which is addressed later in the chapter.

Scholars also hold different views about what the new model includes—more specifically, whether 'pre-enactment political rights review'[28] or executive/legislative review of statutory provisions before they are enacted as law, forms an essential element of the new model of constitutionalism. In his early work on the subject, Gardbaum did not include political rights review in expounding upon the new model of constitutionalism.[29] However, in his book that was published more than a decade later, he described the new model as a 'combination' of mandatory pre-enactment political rights review and weak-form judicial review.[30]

What becomes clear from these discussions is that the ability of courts to review primary legislation for compliance with rights without enjoying primacy over the legislative will is the sine qua non of the new model of rights protection, however one chooses to package it overall. It is inconceivable to consider a constitution or bill of rights as embodying the new model unless it contains a judicial power to review legislation (without being able to disapply it or strike it down) for compliance with rights, or alternatively, something resembling the Canadian 'notwithstanding' clause, enabling the legislature to override, by simple majority, a judgment which strikes down legislation. It is this central feature of the new model of constitutionalism—which can properly be described as its core—that this book will focus on. Adding pre-enactment political rights review would possibly advance, but certainly not detract from, the primary objective of the model—that both

---

[28] Stephen Gardbaum, *The New Commonwealth Model of Constitutionalism: Theory and Practice* (Cambridge University Press 2013), p. 79.

[29] Stephen Gardbaum, 'The New Commonwealth Model of Constitutionalism' (2001) 49 American Journal of Comparative Law 707.

[30] Gardbaum (n. 6), p. 25. Similarly, Hiebert (n. 18) argues that the new model consists of political rights review as well as judicial review with an opportunity for legislative disagreement.

courts and the legislature be given an opportunity to put forward their conception of rights.[31]

At this stage, it is useful to consider whether this framework ascribes undue importance to section 4 of the HRA, ignoring the equally important directive under section 3 for British courts, 'so far as it is possible to do so', to read legislation in compliance with rights under the European Convention for the Protection of Human Rights and Fundamental Freedoms, 1950 (Convention). Two things should be made quite clear. First, section 3 (rather than section 4) is the principal remedy under the HRA. This was evident from the Lord Chancellor's observation in Parliament during the debates on the HRA that in 99 per cent of cases, there would be no need for declarations of incompatibility.[32] Over the last few years, the case law has reflected this bias in favour of section 3.[33] As Appendix B shows, between the years 2000 and 2015, there have been only 20 declarations of incompatibility under the HRA that have survived appeal. Second, section 3 enables courts to depart from the intention of the legislature enacting the statute that needs to be read in compliance with Convention rights.

Both these matters are unexceptionable. In most constitutional systems, courts do their best to interpret legislation consistently with rights before exploring alternatives. Indeed, such interpretation sometimes departs from legislative intent, and there are well-known examples of this in Indian case law,[34] as well as UK case law predating the HRA.[35] But rights-compliant interpretation tends to convey the message that the government and Parliament have a 'clean bill of health' in human rights terms.[36] Declarations of incompatibility are different—they involve open recognition of the fact that Parliament has legislated

---

[31] Gardbaum (n. 26). Cf. Sujit Choudhury, 'The Commonwealth Constitutional Model or Models?' (2013) 11 International Journal of Constitutional Law 1094.

[32] HL Deb 5 February 1998, vol. 585, col. 840. This observation was cited by Lord Steyn in *Ghaidan* v. *Mendoza*, [2004] UKHL 30, p. 46.

[33] Christopher Crawford, 'Dialogue and Rights-compatible Interpretations under Section 3 of the Human Rights Act 1998' (2014) 25 KLJ 34.

[34] *Githa Hariharan* v. *RBI*, AIR 1999 SC 228.

[35] *R* v. *Cheltenham Commissioners*, (1841) 1 QB 467; *Anisminic Ltd* v. *Foreign Compensation Commission*, [1969] 2 AC 467.

[36] Kavanagh (n. 24).

contrary to Convention rights, and that such legislation can neither be quashed nor be saved from the shadow of inconsistency through a rights-compliant interpretation. Therefore, even though section 3 is the HRA's primary remedy, section 4 is, in common with its equivalents in other jurisdictions embodying the new model, its distinctive feature.

Continuing the discussion on the meaning and scope of the new model, some scholars have used one or more of the new model labels to refer to more than just the ability of courts to review, without presumptive finality, statutes enacted by democratically elected representatives. Aileen Kavanagh points out, for instance, that Tushnet has, across his different writings, used the 'weak-form' terminology to refer to 'institutions, courts, issues, rights, statutes, cultures, or remedies'.[37] On the other hand, Dixon has used the 'weak-form' label to refer to approaches to rights adjudication, rights themselves, as well as remedies,[38] while Khosla uses it in the context of the intensity of judicial review.[39] This book will avoid these expansive uses of the new model labels, and focus on the new model as a choice of formal constitutional design. It will consider the new model as a way of seeking to design institutional arrangements on the basis of 'speculative predictions' (made at the time of enactment of the constitution, bill of rights, or constitutional document), of how institutions will 'actually function'.[40]

Treating the new model as a function of constitutional design enables us to effectively judge the promise of the new model against its performance in particular jurisdictions (in this case, the UK). For example, the formal design of the HRA makes it clear that it set up the new model, a compromise between parliamentary sovereignty and judicial supremacy. This is done principally (though not exclusively) through section 4, which empowers courts to make a declaration of incompatibility when primary legislation is inconsistent with Convention rights.

---

[37] Kavanagh (n. 24), p. 1033.

[38] Rosalind Dixon, 'Creating Dialogue about Socioeconomic Rights: Strong-form versus Weak-form Judicial Review Revisited' (2007) 5 International Journal of Constitutional Law 391.

[39] Madhav Khosla, 'Making Social Rights Conditional: Lessons from India' (2010) 8 International Journal of Constitutional Law 739.

[40] Tom Ginsburg, 'Introduction' in Tom Ginsburg (ed.), *Comparative Constitutional Design* (Cambridge University Press 2012) 1, p. 1.

The expectation was that it would offer a more balanced allocation of the power of rights resolution between the Westminster Parliament and the courts. After examining the functioning of the HRA, it may turn out that this balanced allocation has not been achieved, and that either Parliament or the courts enjoy the upper hand in asserting their understanding of rights. It is precisely this exercise of setting out the promise of the HRA against its performance in practice (compared with the performance of the model of judicial supremacy in India), that this book engages in.

Similarly, judicial supremacy (in India) will also be defined from the standpoint of constitutional design. As explained in the Introduction, from the institutional arrangements established by the Indian Constitution, it was clear that courts were entrusted with the power to strike down primary legislation that violates rights. The expectation in jurisdictions that establish judicial supremacy is that courts will have the definitive word on the meaning of rights. Practice may meet this expectation—for example, the legislature may indeed have little option but to go along with courts' understanding of rights with which it disagrees. On the other hand, constitutional practice may defy expectations—by giving the legislature a greater role in rights resolution than expected.

It is worth pointing out that constitutional design, which assists us in deciding which of the three options (parliamentary sovereignty, judicial supremacy, or the new model) has been put into place in a new constitutional settlement, does not simply boil down to the constitutional text.[41] This would be an under-inclusive understanding of constitutional design. A better approach would be to consider constitutional design as relating to the institutional arrangements put in place by a constitutional document or bill of rights—the text being an important part of, but not the only, evidence of such arrangements. The most obvious example of this understanding comes from the US. Although the power of judicial review did not flow directly from the constitutional

---

[41] Rivka Weill makes this (in my view, mistaken) argument: 'Leading scholars of this Commonwealth model ... have described "weak-form" or intermediate constitutionalism as dependent upon the specific constitutional text found in the various countries sharing the Commonwealth model.' See Weill (n. 10), p. 129.

text, scholars have argued that *Marbury* was not simply an act of 'self-articulation' by judges, but reflected institutional arrangements that were put in place at the time of the Constitution's founding.[42]

The Indian Constitution offers us another good example. There is no single provision of the constitutional text that categorically states that courts have the power to review legislation on substantive, rights-based grounds. Some scholars have pointed to Art. 13(2), which provides 'The State shall not make any law which takes away or abridges the rights conferred by this Part and any law made in contravention of this clause shall, to the extent of the contravention, be void.'[43] But this provision seems under-inclusive, because it only applies to one part of the Constitution (the chapter on fundamental rights), whereas Indian courts have the power to strike down legislation that impinges upon any mandatory provision of the Constitution. Others have pointed to Arts 372(1)[44] and 245(1)[45] of the Indian Constitution.[46] Once again, the former is under-inclusive, because it applies only to laws that were enacted before the Constitution entered into force, whereas the latter only seems to mark the division of legislative competence between the Union and the states. Nevertheless, it has always been clear that the

---

[42] Robert Lowry Clinton, 'Game Theory, Legal History, and the Origins of Judicial Review: A Revisionist Analysis of Marbury v. Madison' (1994) 38 American Journal of Political Science 285; Tom Ginsburg, *Judicial Review in New Democracies: Constitutional Courts in Asian Cases* (Cambridge University Press 2003), p. 58.

[43] M.C.J. Kagzi, *The Constitution of India* (2nd edn, Metropolitan Book Co. 1967), p. 355, arguing that Art. 13(2) signifies the 'vesting of power of judicial review of legislation'; Maureen Callahan VanderMay, 'The Role of the Judiciary in India's Constitutional Democracy' (1996–7) 20 Hastings International & Comparative Law Review 103, p. 107.

[44] Article 372(1) provides that '*subject to the other provisions of this Constitution*, all the laws in force in the territory of India immediately before the commencement of this Constitution, shall continue in force' (emphasis added).

[45] Article 245(1) reads as follows: '*Subject to the provisions of this Constitution*, Parliament may make laws for the whole or any part of the territory of India, and the Legislature of a State may make laws for the whole or any part of the State' (emphasis added).

[46] V.S. Deshpande, *Judicial Review of Legislation* (Eastern Book Company 1975), pp. 5, 59.

institutional arrangements established by the Constitution empowered courts with reviewing (and striking down) primary legislation that violates constitutional rights.[47]

Understanding these models of constitutionalism as choices in constitutional design also leads us towards a useful starting point for the comparative analysis of two systems which have, in design terms, adopted quite different models of rights protection. Failing to do so gives rise to classificatory challenges that have prompted scholars to arrive at widely differing categorizations of the two constitutional systems being studied. The UK and India have each, on different occasions, been labelled as 'weak-form' (or new model) and 'strong-form' (or judicial supremacy) systems.[48] This book avoids such classificatory knots by safely categorizing the HRA as embodying the new model of judicial review (since it empowers courts to review primary legislation without presumptive finality) and the Indian Constitution as representing the traditional model of judicial supremacy (since it enables courts to strike down legislation without the possibility of being overridden by ordinary legislative procedures). As mentioned earlier, whether these models actually achieve the outcomes that they were expected to achieve is an issue that this book explores.

Subject to what has been said about conceiving of models of rights protection as functions of formal constitutional design, this book will not insist upon the use of any one of the new model labels to describe this third model of judicial review. Throughout the book, the 'new commonwealth model', 'new model', or 'weak-form review' labels will be used interchangeably. The only label that will be consciously avoided is the phrase 'dialogic review'. This is because the metaphor of dialogue is over-inclusive. It is difficult to conceive of any system of

---

[47] Ivor Jennings, *Some Characteristics of the Indian Constitution* (Oxford University Press 1953), p. 38; Durga Das Basu, *Commentary on the Constitution of India* (8th edn, LexisNexis Butterworths Wadhwa 2007), p. 725.

[48] For example, the HRA has been categorized as a model of weak-form judicial review by Tushnet (n. 17), p. 2785, and a model approaching strong-form judicial review by Kavanagh (n. 24), although she is highly sceptical of the strong-form versus weak-form distinction. India, on the other hand, has been categorized as a system of 'quasi-weak-form review' by Tushnet and Dixon (n. 25), p. 108 and 'strong-form' review by Weill (n. 10), p. 169.

judicial review which does not facilitate inter-branch dialogue, or some kind of interaction between courts and the legislature.[49]

An example from India sheds light on the inter-branch dialogue that takes place in systems of judicial supremacy, just as it does in systems of weak-form judicial review. In 2005, the legislature of Maharashtra enacted primary legislation[50] imposing a ban on dance performances in bars, except in certain establishments (such as hotels rated three stars and above). The Indian Supreme Court struck down this ban as being unconstitutional on two grounds: that it was discriminatory and that it deprived the dancers of their right to livelihood.[51] The state government sidestepped compliance with the judgment and soon thereafter, the legislature passed a bill banning dance performances in all bars in the state.[52] Even though it is unlikely that the newer legislation will survive judicial review, this clearly instantiates the dialogic interactions that can, and often do, take place between courts and the legislature in systems of judicial supremacy.

## The Benefits and Drawbacks of the New Model

The previous section alluded to some benefits of the new model of constitutionalism. The two general benefits of the model are that first, it secures a more balanced distribution of power between the legislature and courts on questions of rights, and second, it enables both institutions to assert freely their competing understanding of rights. Courts and legislators are treated as 'joint or supplementary rather than alternative exclusive protectors and promoters of rights'.[53] The new model seeks to avoid the underlying tension between democratic

[49] Aileen Kavanagh, *Constitutional Review under the UK Human Rights Act* (Cambridge University Press 2009), p. 129; Gardbaum (n. 6), pp. 15–16.

[50] Bombay Police Act, 1951, sections 33A, 33B.

[51] *State of Maharashtra* v. *Indian Hotel and Restaurants Association*, AIR 2013 SC 2582. This decision affirmed the judgment of the Bombay High Court in *Indian Hotel and Restaurants Association* v. *State of Maharashtra*, (2006) 3 Bom CR 705.

[52] Priyanka Kakodkar, 'Maharashtra Legislature Passes Bill Banning Dance Bars' *The Hindu* (Chennai, 13 June 2014).

[53] Gardbaum (n. 6), p. 7.

self-governance and judicial policing of constitutional limitations.[54] It also provides an unparalleled 'opportunity for judicial oversight of legislation without displacing the ultimate power of legislatures to determine public policy'.[55] Courts can impose a high burden of justification on the legislature, and in considering how to respond to the issue of rights, the legislature has the benefit of a careful judicial analysis of the rights issues at stake.[56]

How is the new model superior to the two traditional alternatives? Scholars argue that it is preferable to parliamentary sovereignty because it grants greater responsibility to the courts for the protection of rights, and by implication, grants a greater role for legal argument in political decision-making.[57] On the other hand, it is preferable to judicial supremacy because it leaves room for the legislature to reject judicial understanding of rights by ordinary legislative majority—either by invoking the power to override or by refusing to comply with a declaration of incompatibility or inconsistency. Tushnet argues that under the new model, the legislature can revise judicial understanding of rights in the short run.[58]

In models of judicial supremacy, the legislature can only do so in the 'longish run'.[59] The reason for this seems intuitive and obvious: it is much harder to override a judgment through extraordinary procedures such as constitutional amendments (requiring greater-than simple majorities) or court-packing plans than it is to do the same through ordinary, everyday legislative procedures. The former would be expected to require much greater political traction, which would be harder, and more time-consuming, to mobilize. Thus, it is clear that the element of time plays a major role in scholars' explanations of the superiority of the new model over models of judicial supremacy. The new model is said to be superior, then, not merely because it enables the legislature

---

[54]  Tushnet, *Weak Courts, Strong Rights* (n. 25), p. 22.

[55]  Mark Tushnet, 'New Forms of Judicial Review and the Persistence of Rights- and Democracy-based Worries' (2003) 38 Wake Forest Law Review 813, p. 831.

[56]  Choudhury (n. 31), p. 1095.

[57]  Gardbaum (n. 6), p. 44.

[58]  Tushnet, *Weak Courts, Strong Rights* (n. 25), p. 34.

[59]  Tushnet, *Weak Courts, Strong Rights* (n. 25), p. 34.

to assert its competing conception of rights, but because it allows it to do so relatively swiftly and easily.

Proponents of the new model recognize that it suffers from some drawbacks—that in spite of seeking to achieve the golden mean between two extremes, it may, in practice, slide back into parliamentary sovereignty or judicial supremacy.[60] Hence, for example, if declarations of incompatibility under the HRA variety of the new model are invariably acted upon by the legislature, the model could, in practice, become indistinguishable from judicial supremacy. If, on the other hand, the legislature always ignores judicial declarations of incompatibility, treating them as merely exhortative instructions, the new model would begin resembling parliamentary sovereignty. Weak-form review thus risks becoming parliamentary sovereignty or strong-form review 'in disguise'.[61] This will be referred to as the problem of 'internal stability'.

The new model also faces an 'external stability' problem. Unlike systems of judicial supremacy, in which the written Constitution is relatively immune (at least in the strictly legal sense) from changing political tides, un-entrenched bills of rights under the new model are subject to the shifting preferences of ruling political coalitions. This external stability problem is brought out best by political developments in the UK. After increasing dissatisfaction with the functioning of the HRA and the influence of the Strasbourg Court on domestic adjudication, the Conservative Party included the repeal of the HRA in its manifesto for the 2015 general elections.[62] Commentators in the UK agree that with the Conservative Party's win in the general elections of 2015, the future of the HRA is uncertain. The arguments made in this book touch upon the problems of both internal stability and external stability associated with the new model, as it is manifested in the UK.

---

[60] Gardbaum acknowledges upfront that the new model may prove to be 'a comet that shone brightly and beguilingly in the constitutional firmament for a brief moment but quickly burned up'. See Gardbaum (n. 6), p. 1.

[61] Tushnet, *Weak Courts, Strong Rights* (n. 25), p. 47.

[62] David Barrett, 'Tory Manifesto Will Promise to Scrap Labour's Human Rights Act, Says Theresa May' *The Telegraph* (London, 30 September 2013); Brice Dickson, 'If the Human Rights Act Were Repealed, Could the Common Law Fill the Void?' *Oxford Human Rights Hub* (27 November 2013) <http://ohrh.law. ox.ac.uk/if-the-human-rights-act-were-repealed-could-the-common-law-fill-the-void/> accessed 23 August 2016.

## Criteria for Evaluating Models of Rights Protection

The new model of judicial review is based on the premise that people may reasonably disagree about the correct answers to questions concerning rights. Very often, in disputed questions about rights, people will agree about the specific rights that are at play in a particular case. But, as Jeremy Waldron, the most well-known proponent of the notion of reasonable disagreements on rights points out, bills of rights often consist of 'bland rhetoric',[63] offering little guidance in deciding genuine disagreements. Courts, legislatures, and citizens are likely to agree, for example, that a general right to equality exists. But, when it is framed at a high level of abstraction (in India, for example: 'The State shall not deny to any person equality before the law or the equal protection of the laws within the territory of India'[64]), they are also likely to disagree about what its implications are in particular cases.[65] In such situations, whose reasonable answer to the rights question should prevail? Democratic theory requires us to favour a reasonable legislative judgment over a reasonable judicial one.[66] The legitimacy of the decision-making process is crucial: unlike courts, the legislature is representative of the people whose rights are at stake in these disagreements.[67] Legislative judgments allow those who are required to comply with a decision about the implications of rights to secure a voice in the decision-making process.[68]

Let us consider a few examples from the two jurisdictions that this book focuses on. When the constitution guarantees a general right

[63] Waldron (n. 13), p. 1369. It should be noted, however, that he does not subscribe to the view that there are no right answers to questions about rights; it may just be difficult to know what they are. See Waldron (n. 1), p. 164.

[64] Constitution of India, Art. 14.

[65] Wojciech Sadurski, 'Judicial Review and the Protection of Constitutional Rights' (2002) 22 OJLS 275, p. 283.

[66] Gardbuam (n. 6), p. 65, explaining Waldron's argument. It should be noted that there are many critiques of, and alternatives to, Waldron's thesis on democracy. The most well-known of critics is Ronald Dworkin, who argues that the meaning of rights themselves, as opposed to who decides them, is crucial. See, for example, Dworkin, *Taking Rights Seriously* (n. 1).

[67] Waldron (n. 13), p. 1369.

[68] Jeremy Waldron, 'A Right-based Critique of Constitutional Rights' (1993) 13 OJLS 18, p. 38.

to life and personal liberty, does that include patients' right to die through the withdrawal of life support when they are in a permanent vegetative state?[69] There are many reasonable answers to this question—for example, that withdrawal of life support should only be permitted if there is a 'living will', or that it should also be permitted when responsible medical opinion considers it as being in the best interests of the patient. Or, does a statute enabling state prohibition on the publication of journals to secure 'public safety' or the 'maintenance of public order' violate the constitutionally protected freedom of expression?[70] Or, to take one of the most controversial issues under the HRA, does a general prohibition on prisoners' right to vote violate the free expression of opinion in citizens' 'choice of the legislature'?[71] Again, there are many reasonable positions on this question—that a general prohibition is consistent with the right, that a prohibition should only be applicable to prisoners facing a stated minimum term of imprisonment, or indeed, that the right mandates no prohibition whatsoever on prisoners' voting.

The new model brings to bear different perspectives of the courts and legislature on such questions.[72] If courts arrive at a reasonable answer with which the legislature disagrees, then the legislature should be able to assert its alternative reasonable interpretation of the rights question in place of that of the courts. Different possibilities under the new model—for example, rejection or ignorance of a declaration of incompatibility in the UK or the invocation of the 'notwithstanding' power in Canada—are intended to function as a legislative safety valve against judicial interpretation of rights.[73]

[69] This question arose before the Indian Supreme Court in *Aruna Shanbaug* v. *Union of India*, AIR 2011 SC 1290.

[70] See *Romesh Thapar* v. *State of Madras*, AIR 1950 SC 124.

[71] See *Hirst* v. *United Kingdom (No 2)*, [2005] ECHR 681; *Smith* v. *Scott*, [2007] CSIH 9; *Scoppola* v. *Italy (No 3)*, (2013) 56 EHRR 19.

[72] Gardbaum (n. 6), p. 63.

[73] See Richard Fallon, 'The Core of an Uneasy Case for Judicial Review' (2008) 121 Harvard Law Review 1693, p. 1734, where the author argues that 'Under conditions of reasonable disagreement, democratic institutions should not be too disabled from making periodic reassessments of where and how to strike the balance in weighing the comparative risks and moral costs of the over- and underenforcement of fundamental rights.'

The normative framework that is developed hereafter, and the arguments made in this book more generally, rests on two premises (which are also set up as assumptions in Waldron's classic article on judicial review),[74] both of which are required if the new model's claim (manifested through the UK) to a more balanced allocation of power between the legislature and courts is to be meaningfully tested against the Indian system of judicial supremacy. The first premise is that democratic institutions are in 'reasonably good working order', and include a representative legislature elected on the basis of universal adult suffrage.[75] The second premise is that the courts, established on a non-representative basis, are also in reasonably good working order.[76] For, if the legislatures or the courts of either jurisdiction are not in working order, then it may be necessary for the views of one institution to predominate over those of the other on rights-based questions.

Both these premises prevail in the jurisdictions under discussion—India and the UK. But it may be worth considering possible challenges to these premises before moving to the normative framework set up by this chapter. In the context of the UK, it is difficult to dispute that the Westminster Parliament and the courts are, despite their imperfections, in reasonably good working order. Perhaps the argument worth addressing is that the House of Lords is not a genuinely representative institution, since a majority of its members are appointed.[77] This argument however fails to carry through, because the House of Commons is an elected body whose representatives are chosen based on universal adult suffrage. Moreover, there is a heavy imbalance of power in favour of the House of Commons over the House of Lords. This imbalance stems from the Commons' veto power over legislation, its ability to rely on the Parliament Acts of 1911 and 1949 to enact legislation without

---

[74]  Waldron (n. 13).

[75]  Waldron (n. 13), p. 1360.

[76]  Waldron (n. 13), p. 1360.

[77]  See Hugh Bochel and Andrew Defty, 'Representation and the House of Lords' (2012) 18 Journal of Legislative Studies 82, noting that 'there remain significant grounds for questioning the representative nature of the House of Lords'. For details on reform of the House of Lords since the early twentieth century, see Vernon Bogdanor, *The New British Constitution* (Hart 2009), pp. 145–72.

the approval of the House of Lords, and the procedure for enacting money bills.

In the case of India, the challenge is slightly more compelling. Commentators have often argued that India's Parliament, and many of its state legislatures, are in a state of disarray.[78] Obstructionism in the Parliament has led to significant plenary bottlenecks and legislative paralysis.[79] Reports on the functioning of the 2009–14 Lok Sabha indicate that frequent disruptions resulted in its working for only 61 per cent of the scheduled time (its worst performance in over 50 years).[80] The corresponding figure for the Rajya Sabha for the same period was only marginally better, at 66 per cent.[81] 'Criminalization of politics', a phrase which is commonly used in India, reflects, amongst other things, the fact that a fair proportion of parliamentarians face criminal charges (some of them as serious as murder and rape).[82]

Serious as these matters are, they do not reflect the existence of a pathological condition that has denied the legislature from performing its essential representative function. Several important pieces of legislation, including the Right to Education Act, 2009,[83] the Lokpal and Lokayuktas Act, 2013, and the National Food Security Act, 2013, were enacted after debate during the previous Lok Sabha. Scholars have also

---

[78] See Devesh Kapur and Pratap Bhanu Mehta, 'The Indian Parliament as an Institution of Accountability' (2006) UNRISD Democracy, Governance and Human Rights Programme Paper No. 23.

[79] Tarunabh Khaitan, 'The Real Price of Parliamentary Obstruction' (2013) 642 Seminar 37. See also Hari Narayan, 'Opposing to Govern, Not to Obstruct' *The Hindu* (Chennai, 1 May 2014).

[80] Kusum Malik and Mandira Kala, 'Vital Stats: Performance of Parliament during the 15th Lok Sabha' (*PRS Legislative Research*, 21 February 2014) <http://www.prsindia.org/parliamenttrack/vital-stats/performance-of-parliament-during-the-15th-lok-sabha-3146/> accessed 3 August 2014.

[81] Malik and Kala (n. 80).

[82] Nithya Nagarathinam, 'Criminalisation of Politics' (*The Hindu*, 30 April 2014) <http://www.thehinducentre.com/verdict/get-the-fact/article5962667.ece> accessed 4 August 2014. See also Matthieu Chemin, 'Welfare Effects of Criminal Politicians: A Discontinuity-based Approach' (2012) 55 Journal of Law and Economics 667, p. 670.

[83] Officially, the Right of Children to Free and Compulsory Education Act, 2009.

relied upon legislative inertia as a justification for judicial activism by the Supreme Court and high courts of India.[84] However, the reality is that the courts are themselves plagued by serious institutional problems, including a mammoth backlog of cases,[85] a large proportion of unfilled judicial vacancies,[86] and a process of appointments that is seen to be increasingly opaque and problematic.[87] However, all things considered, it would be difficult to disagree with the fact that the legislature and courts in India are, albeit imperfect, in reasonable working order, and are performing their primary institutional roles—cases are decided, and legislation is passed. Even if one were to consider that the Indian legislature is to some extent dysfunctional, the relative performance of courts has only been marginally better.

As explained earlier, the hallmark of the new model of constitutionalism is that it provides for a more balanced allocation of powers between the legislature and courts on questions of rights. This balanced allocation of powers is considered a virtue, given that disagreements about the implications of rights often entail disagreements between two or more reasonable positions (or reasonable articulations of the effect of the right in question). In order to answer the question about which model (between the new model in the UK and judicial supremacy in India) provides for a more balanced allocation of powers, two sub-questions need to be asked. These are: (a) which legislatures, post–judicial review, are able to assert their genuine understanding of

[84] Abhishek Manu Singhvi, 'Judicial Activism is Like an Unruly Horse' *The Indian Express* (New Delhi, 3 May 2007); Nick Robinson, 'Expanding Judiciaries: India and the Rise of the Good Governance Court' (2009) 8 Washington University Global Studies Law Review 1.

[85] Abhishek Singhvi, 'Beating the Backlog: Less Talk, More Work' (2007) 2 SCC (Jour) 9; Nick Robinson, 'A Quantitative Analysis of the Indian Supreme Court's Workload' (2013) 10 Journal of Empirical Legal Studies 570.

[86] J. Venkatesan, 'In 2014, Supreme Court Will Witness Three CJIs' *The Hindu* (Chennai, 1 January 2014).

[87] Abhinav Chandrachud, 'The Insulation of India's Constitutional Judiciary' (2010) 45 Economic and Political Weekly 38. The Parliament attempted to replace the existing appointment process through a constitutional amendment—the Constitution (Ninety-ninth Amendment) Act, 2014. This amendment was struck down by the Supreme Court in *Supreme Court Advocates on Record Association* v. *Union of India*, 2016 5 SCC 1.

rights more freely? (b) which courts, through judicial review, are able to assert their genuine understanding of rights more freely? The first sub-question involves legislatures asserting their understanding of rights at the stage following judicial review of the statute (after the court has expressed its own view on the issue). This will be the normative framework used to compare the new model of constitutionalism in the UK with judicial supremacy in India.

Thus, the principal question and the two sub-questions that form the framework within which arguments are made in this book are as follows:

(General) question: Which model of rights protection provides for a more balanced allocation of powers between the legislature and courts?
Sub-question 1: Which legislature(s)[88] can assert their genuine understanding of rights more freely?
Sub-question 2: Which courts can assert their genuine understanding of rights more freely?

It should be noted that if either of the two sub-questions is answered in favour of the UK and India does not 'win' on the other sub-question, then it will be considered proven that the HRA provides for a more balanced allocation of powers than the Indian Constitution. So, for example, if the Westminster Parliament can freely assert its genuine understanding of rights more than the Indian legislature, and if British courts and Indian courts can assert their genuine understanding of rights equally freely, then the British system provides for a more balanced allocation of powers. If, on the other hand, India trumps the UK on either sub-question and there is no 'winner' for the other sub-question, then the Indian system provides for a more balanced allocation of powers. If India and the UK both 'win' on one sub-question each, then there is no clear overall answer for which system provides for the more balanced allocation of powers—the answer would depend upon margins of victory and defeat.

The following hypothetical tables make the analysis clearer. In each table, '✓' indicates that a particular jurisdiction has 'won' on a particular

88 In the UK, the new model operates only vis-à-vis one legislative body—the Westminster Parliament.

sub-question, '×' indicates that a jurisdiction has 'lost' on a particular sub-question, and '–' indicates that neither jurisdiction has won or lost on a particular sub-question.[89]

In each of the following three tables below, the new model in the UK would be proven to facilitate a greater balanced allocation of powers between the legislature and courts. In the first table, the UK wins on both sub-questions, and therefore also wins on the general question.

|  | UK | India |
| --- | --- | --- |
| Sub-question 1 | ✓ | × |
| Sub-question 2 | ✓ | × |

In the next table, the UK wins on sub-question 1, and there is no winner on sub-question 2. Therefore, the UK wins on the general question.

|  | UK | India |
| --- | --- | --- |
| Sub-question 1 | ✓ | × |
| Sub-question 2 | – | – |

In the next table, the UK wins on sub-question 2, and there is no winner on sub-question 1. Therefore, the UK wins on the general question.

|  | UK | India |
| --- | --- | --- |
| Sub-question 1 | – | – |
| Sub-question 2 | ✓ | × |

On the other hand, in the next three tables, judicial supremacy in India would be proven to facilitate a greater balanced allocation of powers between legislatures and courts. In the following table, India wins on both sub-questions, and therefore also wins on the general question.

|  | UK | India |
| --- | --- | --- |
| Sub-question 1 | × | ✓ |
| Sub-question 2 | × | ✓ |

[89] The author is conscious that these tables suggest a mathematical precision that is unachievable in an analysis that examines a complex body of case law and political practice. The tables are only intended to demonstrate the nature of the argument made in this book in an uncluttered (albeit simplistic) way.

The next table shows that India wins on sub-question 1, and there is no winner on sub-question 2. Therefore, India wins on the general question.

|                | UK | India |
| -------------- | -- | ----- |
| Sub-question 1 | ✗ | ✓ |
| Sub-question 2 | – | – |

In the next table, India wins on sub-question 2, and there is no winner on sub-question 1. Therefore, the India wins on the general question.

|                | UK | India |
| -------------- | -- | ----- |
| Sub-question 1 | – | – |
| Sub-question 2 | ✗ | ✓ |

Finally, in next two tables, there is no clear answer about which model provides for a greater balanced allocation of powers. The answer in these cases would depend on margins of victory and defeat. In the following table, the UK wins on sub-question 1, and India wins on sub-question 2. Therefore, there is no clear winner on the general question. In the final table, India wins on sub-question 1, and the UK wins on sub-question 2. Therefore, there is no clear winner on the general question.

|                | UK | India |
| -------------- | -- | ----- |
| Sub-question 1 | ✓ | ✗ |
| Sub-question 2 | ✗ | ✓ |

|                | UK | India |
| -------------- | -- | ----- |
| Sub-question 1 | ✗ | ✓ |
| Sub-question 2 | ✓ | ✗ |

Two clarifications are necessary at this stage. First, when the question of whether the legislature or courts are able to assert freely their genuine understanding of rights is asked, the focus is on whether both sets of institutions are able, in practice, to express their opinions on questions of rights unreservedly. Therefore, this is not merely a matter of whether courts and the legislature possess the institutional apparatus to assert their understanding of rights. The inquiry is a richer, practice-based one, which will examine whether they are in a position to engage that apparatus meaningfully. This inquiry goes to the heart of the new model, because its proponents claim that it is preferable to judicial supremacy by giving the *legislature* a greater role in rights resolution, and greater than parliamentary sovereignty because it gives *courts* a greater role in rights resolution.

Second, the sub-questions have been deliberately phrased in relative terminology. The focus of both sub-questions is on which institutions can assert their understanding of rights '*more* freely' than the corresponding institutions in the other jurisdiction. Hence, the effort remains explicitly comparative, and concentrates solely on how courts and legislatures in both jurisdictions compare with one another. No objective assessment of how the institution performs generally (or perhaps, in comparison with corresponding institutions from other countries) is answered by these sub-questions. This also explains why the tables do not contemplate the possibility of both jurisdictions 'losing' on any particular sub-question. This is simply impossible under the analysis that is undertaken, even though it may only, hypothetically speaking, reflect that one institution may be doing a 'less bad' job (or more specifically, playing a less 'non-rights-assertive' role) than the other.

The existing scholarship seems to suggest that the new model is superior to judicial supremacy from the perspective of ensuring a more balanced allocation of powers based on the second table. In other words, whereas courts in jurisdictions with the new model and judicial supremacy are able to assert their understanding of rights equally freely, legislatures in jurisdictions with the new model are able to assert their understanding of rights more freely than legislatures in jurisdictions with judicial supremacy. This is on account of the ability of the legislature to exercise its override power (in Canada), or its power to reject (or simply ignore) declarations of incompatibility (in the UK). As stated earlier, scholars such as Tushnet do not overlook the possibility that decisions taken during judicial review in systems of judicial supremacy may be overridden. But this, they argue, is an arduous and time-consuming process involving extraordinary procedures such as constitutional amendments.

The claim that this book makes, using India and the UK as comparator jurisdictions, is that when it comes to questions of rights, the new model in the UK does provide for a more balanced allocation of powers than judicial supremacy in India. But the explanation offered in the existing scholarship does not bear out in these two jurisdictions. Chapters 2 and 3 establish that in both jurisdictions, the legislature can respond to decisions in judicial review equally swiftly, notwithstanding differences in the constitutional procedures available for such responses. However, there is an alternative explanation for the superiority of the HRA's model of rights protection over that in the Indian Constitution. That explanation comes from the third table, not the second.

While the legislature in both jurisdictions can express their understanding of rights equally easily, courts in the UK are able to express their understanding of rights more easily than courts in India. This stems from the nature of the remedy—the power to strike down legislation—available to Indian courts in proceedings for judicial review. As Chapter 4 explains, Indian courts sometimes hesitate to assert their true understanding of rights because it would entail exercising the power to strike down legislation. Instead, they allow the 'remedial tail to wag the adjudicative dog'[90]—by rethinking their original view that a statute is unconstitutional. In similar situations, British courts may choose to make declarations of incompatibility, leaving it to Parliament and the government to rectify the inconsistency with Convention rights.[91] The analysis also bears implications for the stability concerns associated with systems that have incorporated the new model. Whereas the concern of internal stability is not borne out in the UK, the HRA has faced serious threats to its external stability. The Conclusion notes that this danger to external stability is the price that jurisdictions adopting the new model pay for the more balanced allocation of powers between the legislature and courts than models of judicial supremacy.

---

[90] The author is grateful to David Feldman and Mark Elliott, professors at University of Cambridge, for this colourful phrase.

[91] This explanation for the superiority of the new model of rights protection may not hold true for jurisdictions such as Canada, in which courts do possess the power to strike down legislation, albeit in the shadow of a legislative power to override.

## Issues of Scope and Typology

Before closing, a few matters concerning the scope of this book and typology should be noted. This book deals with judicial review of primary legislation or legislation emanating from the highest lawmaking authorities in both jurisdictions that are examined. In India, since there is a division of legislative competence between the Union and the states, this includes legislation enacted by the Parliament as well as the state legislatures. On the other hand, in UK, primary legislation has a very specific meaning under the HRA.[92] It includes legislation emanating from Westminster Parliament, but does not include legislation enacted by the devolved legislature of each of Scotland, Wales, and Northern Ireland.[93] It is this definition of primary legislation that will be adopted vis-à-vis the UK.

To be clear, the kind of law that courts grapple with most frequently is not primary legislation.[94] Most often, the courts deal with government policy, ministerial decisions, departmental guidelines, and the like during judicial review, all of which would be excluded from the scope of this book. Interesting judicial decisions that cancelled the arbitrary grant of telecom licences,[95] annulled the appointment of unfit candidates to statutory vigilance bodies,[96] or quashed an executive

---

[92] Under section 21(1) of the HRA:

'[P]rimary legislation' means any (a) public general Act; (b) local and personal Act; (c) private Act; (d) Measure of the Church Assembly; (e) Measure of the General Synod of the Church of England; (f) Order in Council—(i) made in exercise of Her Majesty's Royal Prerogative; (ii) made under section 38(1)(a) of the Northern Ireland Constitution Act 1973 or the corresponding provision of the Northern Ireland Act 1998; or (iii) amending an Act of a kind mentioned in paragraph (a), (b) or (c).

[93] As explained in the Introduction, legislation enacted by the devolved legislatures can be struck down on the basis that they violate Convention rights.

[94] Kreimer has argued, in the context of the US Supreme Court, that most cases of judicial review involve the enforcement of constitutional norms against low-level bureaucrats. See Seth F. Kreimer, 'Exploring the Dark Matter of Judicial Review: A Constitutional Census of the 1990s' (1997) 5 William and Mary Bill of Rights Journal 427.

[95] *Centre for Public Interest Litigation* v. *Union of India*, (2012) 3 SCC 1.

[96] *Centre for Public Interest Litigation* v. *Union of India*, AIR 2011 SC 1267.

decision to delay consideration of asylum applications[97] fall out of scope. Yet, from the perspective of constitutional law, judicial review of primary legislation by courts is most significant and controversial. It is this kind of judicial review (often described as 'constitutional judicial review'[98]) that has preoccupied strong democrats such as Jeremy Waldron[99] and James Allan.[100] This is because primary legislation emanates directly from the people's elected representatives and gives rise to the strongest concerns of counter-majoritarianism. Unlike delegated legislation, it goes through a formal process of enactment, including readings, parliamentary committee reports, and amendments.[101] This open and transparent process gives primary legislation a different sanctity from delegated legislation,[102] even when delegated legislation requires a formal parliamentary vote of approval, as is often the case.

Another point to note is that the UK's model of rights protection, based on the Convention, enforces principally civil and political rights.[103] On the other hand, as explained in the Introduction, the Indian

[97] *R (S)* v. *SSHD*, [2007] EWCA Civ 546.

[98] Jeffrey Jowell, 'Beyond the Rule of Law: Towards Constitutional Judicial Review' [2000] PL 671.

[99] Waldron (n. 13), p. 1353.

[100] James Allan, 'Oh That I Were Made Judge in the Land' (2002) 30 Federal Law Review 561.

[101] Although, under the HRA, there is a peculiarity of legislation emanating from (elected) devolved legislatures being treated as subordinate legislation. See N.W. Barber and Alison L. Young, 'The Rise of Prospective Henry VIII Clauses and Their Implications for Sovereignty' [2003] PL 112, p. 118. Put differently, being a sovereign lawmaking body, the Westminster Parliament may be considered as the 'odd one out' [*Whaley* v. *Lord Watson*, (2000) SCLR 279]. The new model does not operate vis-à-vis such legislation, since courts have the power to strike it down if it breaches Convention rights.

[102] See Aileen McHarg, 'What is Delegated Legislation?' [2006] PL 539, pp. 555–6.

[103] Robin C.A. White and Clare Ovey, *Jacobs, White and Ovey: The European Convention on Human Rights* (5th edn, Oxford University Press 2010), p. 8. A notable exception is the right to education under Art. 2 of Protocol 1 to the Convention. The European Social Charter, 1961 is the Council of Europe's primary instrument governing socio-economic rights. The HRA does not give effect to this Charter. See K.D. Ewing, 'The Unbalanced Constitution' in Tom Campbell, K.D. Ewing, and Adam Tomkins (eds), *Sceptical Essays on Human*

Constitution guarantees many socio-economic rights in addition to civil and political rights. This book makes a general comparison of the UK's model of judicial review with the Indian model of judicial supremacy and draws inferences that are not restricted to particular categories of rights. A conscious effort has been made to cite cases involving a diverse range of rights in both jurisdictions to provide evidence of the generality of the conclusions that can be drawn from the book. The only exception is Chapter 4, which adopts a methodology that directly compares specific cases of judicial review in India and the UK. That chapter only relies upon civil and political rights cases from India in order to rebut the claim that the approach of the Indian courts in the selected cases, in contrast to that of British courts, was heavily influenced by the nature of rights they were adjudicating upon.

Finally, a point on typology—debates surrounding constitutional adjudication in India, in particular, have often tended to adopt the language of judicial activism and restraint.[104] These terms are entirely inappropriate for the analysis that is conducted in this book. As the book unfolds, it will become clear that courts in both jurisdictions are highly strategic, political actors that keep a close eye on the goings-on in in the other branches of government, and whose decisions are heavily influenced by predictions of what their consequences are likely to be. In this context, the phrases judicial 'activism' and 'restraint', which are often flung around as epithets,[105] risk masking the highly sophisticated

---

*Rights* (Oxford University Press 2001), p. 104, arguing that the failure to incorporate social rights in the British Constitution risks 'undermining and diminishing' the overall regime of human rights protection.

[104] Jamie Cassels, 'Judicial Activism and Public Interest Litigation in India: Attempting the Impossible?' (1989) 37 American Journal of Comparative Law 495; Arvind Verma, 'Taking Justice Outside the Courts: Judicial Activism in India' (2001) 40 Howard Journal of Criminal Justice 148; S.P. Sathe, *Judicial Activism in India: Transgressing Borders and Enforcing Limits* (Oxford University Press 2003); T.R. Andhyarujina, 'Disturbing Trends in Judicial Activism' *The Hindu* (Chennai, 6 August 2012); T.R. Andhyarujina, 'The Unique Judicial Activism of the Supreme Court of India' (2014) 130 LQR 53.

[105] Kent Roach, *The Supreme Court on Trial: Judicial Activism or Democratic Dialogue* (Irwin Law 2001), p. 9.

nature of the relationship between courts and the legislature in these jurisdictions.

\*\*\*

This chapter has sought to provide the theoretical grounding for the subsequent, practice-heavy, chapters in the book. It has set up a normative framework, and offered eight possibilities that may ensue from the comparison between India and the UK on the question of which jurisdiction provides for a more balanced allocation of powers between legislatures and courts. The chapter provided a quick glimpse into the answer—that the new model in the UK engenders a more balanced allocation of powers between these institutions than judicial supremacy in India, not because of the Westminster Parliament's putative liberty to ignore declarations of incompatibility, but on account of the greater ability of British courts to assert freely their understanding of rights compared to their Indian counterparts. These claims will be thoroughly investigated in the chapters that follow.

# 2 Judicial Review and Political Responses

This chapter begins developing the negative claim made by the book—that the HRA does not enable the legislature to assert its understanding of rights more freely than judicial supremacy under the Indian Constitution. In fact, political practice shows that it is similarly burdensome to respond to declarations of incompatibility in the UK as it is to respond to the striking down of legislation in India. In the Indian context, constitutional amendments of two kinds (which I refer to as 'fundamental rights amendments' and 'Ninth Schedule amendments') have been invoked by Parliament to respond to judgments striking down primary legislation. In the UK, Parliament has some room for manoeuvre when responding to declarations of incompatibility, and even though no such declaration has yet been rejected outright, such a rejection cannot be ruled out. The following section examines political responses[1] to judicial strike-downs in India, while the subsequent one will focus on declarations of incompatibility and political responses under the HRA.

## Political Responses to Striking Down of Legislation in India

It is useful to begin with the default position—when the Supreme Court and high courts strike down legislation, political compliance with the

---

[1] Throughout this chapter, 'political responses' will refer to responses by the relevant legislatures and governments—not responses across the spectrum of political parties.

courts' judgments is often automatic. However, even when the Indian Parliament wishes to reject such judgments, it is difficult for it to do so through ordinary legislation, as striking down of legislation is based on constitutional grounds and has immediate effect. However, as with legislatures from other parts of the world, it has sought to reject such judgments indirectly, by amending the provisions of the Constitution itself—thereby dismantling the foundation of the court's judgments.

Parliament has relied on two mechanisms to respond to strike-downs—fundamental rights amendments and Ninth Schedule amendments. Both these response mechanisms were actually conceptualized by the Constituent Assembly of India, but while acting in different capacities. The power to amend the Constitution (including the chapter on fundamental rights) formed part of the original constitutional text enacted in 1949, and was a product of the debates of the Constituent Assembly. Ninth Schedule amendments are a special species of constitutional amendments that were developed by the Constituent Assembly, in its capacity as Provisional Parliament of India,[2] shortly after the Constitution entered into force. The invocation of these response mechanisms make it clear that strike-downs have not necessarily constituted a 'final word' on the validity of primary legislation violating fundamental rights,[3] but have instead left room for political response. This enables us to begin questioning whether proponents of the new model are justified in claiming that responses are easier in jurisdictions where judgments can be overridden through ordinary legislative procedures.

## Fundamental Rights Amendments

This amendment is an attempt to undo the justice that the courts of law have given. When the highest tribunal in our land has declared that it is immoral and unconstitutional, now we are trying to change the rules of the game. We have lost the game; so now we go and cheat. We change

---

[2] See Arudra Burra, 'The Cobwebs of Imperial Rule' (2010) 615 Seminar 79, p. 81.

[3] Many scholars argue that in systems of judicial supremacy, courts enjoy the 'final word' on questions of rights. See Robert Justin Lipkin, 'We Are All Judicial Activists Now' (2008) 77 University of Cincinnati Law Review 181, p. 191; Stephen Gardbaum, 'A Democratic Defense of Constitutional Balancing' (2010) 4 Law & Ethics of Human Rights 78.

the rules so that what was unlawful and unconstitutional now becomes constitutional.[4]

The general power to amend the Constitution is set out in Art. 368.[5] The relevant portion of this provision reads as follows:

(1) Notwithstanding anything in this Constitution, Parliament may in exercise of its constituent power amend by way of addition, variation or repeal any provision of this Constitution in accordance with the procedure laid down in this article.

(2) An amendment of this Constitution may be initiated only by the introduction of a Bill for the purpose in either House of Parliament, and when the Bill is passed in each House by a majority of the total membership of that House and by a majority of not less than two-thirds of the members of that House present and voting, it shall be presented to the President who shall give his assent to the Bill and thereupon the Constitution shall stand amended in accordance with the terms of the Bill:

Provided that if such amendment seeks to make any change in—

(a) Article 54, Article 55, Article 73, Article 162 or Article 241, or
(b) Chapter IV of Part V, Chapter V of Part VI, or Chapter I of Part XI, or
(c) any of the Lists in the Seventh Schedule, or
(d) the representation of States in Parliament, or
(e) the provisions of this article,[6]

the amendment shall also require to be ratified by the Legislatures of not less than one-half of the States by resolutions to that effect passed by those Legislatures before the Bill making provision for such amendment is presented to the President for assent.

---

[4] This statement was made by M.R. Masani, an opposition member of Parliament (MP), during the debates on the Constitution (Seventeenth Amendment) Act, 1964. Lok Sabha Debates, 1964, vol. XXXII, col. 365 (M.R. Masani).

[5] Some provisions of the Indian Constitution (for example, Arts 4, 169, 239A, 239AA(7), 243M(4), 243ZC(3), 244A, 312, Fifth Schedule, and Sixth Schedule) are un-entrenched, and can be amended by a simple parliamentary majority. However, these provisions expressly state that they are not to be considered as 'amendments to the Constitution' for the purposes of Art. 368.

[6] These are matters affecting federal–state relations.

Article 368 thus provides for a 'dual majority'[7] procedure for constitutional amendments. An amendment needs to be passed by a simple majority of the *total membership* in the Lok Sabha and Rajya Sabha. It also needs to be passed by a majority of not less than two-thirds of the members of each House, *present and voting*. No explicit limitation on Parliament's amending power was originally included in the Constitution.[8] As the terms of Art. 368 bear out, the amendment of some constitutional provisions concerning federal matters requires ratification by the legislatures of at least half the states in India. All existing fundamental rights, however, can be amended without the ratification of state legislatures.

In nearly seven decades since it entered into force, the Constitution has been amended on numerous occasions. One hundred constitutional amendments were passed up to May 2015, while several others were on the anvil. Some of these involved minor changes to the Constitution[9] while others, such as the Constitution (Forty-second Amendment) Act, 1976, sought to radically transform parts of the Constitution.[10] While certain portions of the Constitution have remained unamended,[11] others, including the chapter on fundamental rights, have been amended quite frequently. Although some people argue that these amendments have been motivated by 'narrow political ends' and to pander to 'vote-bank politics',[12] it is unfair to paint all constitutional amendments with the same motivational brush.[13]

[7] Arvind Datar, *Commentary on the Constitution of India* (2nd edn, LexisNexis Butterworths Wadhwa 2007), p. 2017.

[8] The Supreme Court imposed doctrinal limits on the power to amend the Constitution in *Kesavananda Bharati* v. *State of Kerala*, AIR 1973 SC 1461 (Basic Structure case), which is discussed later.

[9] See, for example, the Constitution (Ninety-sixth Amendment) Act, 2011, which altered the name of one of the languages recognized in the Eighth Schedule of the Constitution.

[10] Nani A. Palkhivala, *We the People* (UBS Publishers' Distributors 2007), p. 201.

[11] See, for example, Part XVII, Chapters I and II.

[12] Madhav Godbole, *The Judiciary and Governance in India* (Rupa 2009), p. 32.

[13] See Setalvad's defence of the amendments made during the first 15 years of constitutional experience in India: M.C. Setalvad, *The Indian Constitution, 1950–1965* (University of Bombay 1967), p. 40.

Some of these constitutional amendments share a common feature: they have been enacted with the objective of indirectly nullifying Supreme Court and high court decisions striking down legislation. In other words, the substratum of judgments invalidating legislation held to breach fundamental rights has been removed through amendment of the higher law from which they derived their authority. These are referred to as 'fundamental rights amendments'. At least four[14] constitutional amendments can be identified as fundamental rights amendments meeting this description.

In order to analyse the manner in which fundamental rights amendments can be employed as a political response mechanism, it is useful briefly to introduce the 'doctrine of eclipse' in Indian constitutional law. This is a judicially crafted doctrine that postulates that when a statute or parts of it are struck down for violating a fundamental right, it is not treated as having been wiped off the statute book altogether.[15] A shadow descends over the statute or its invalid provisions, which is lifted when the constitutional bar ceases to operate. It also continues to remain in force with respect to persons who do not enjoy the fundamental right in question.[16]

---

[14] Constitution (First Amendment) Act, 1951; Constitution (Fourth Amendment) Act, 1955; Constitution (Seventeenth Amendment) Act, 1964; Constitution (Twenty-fifth Amendment) Act, 1971. Some of these amendments repudiated more than one judgment of the Supreme Court/high courts.

[15] Mahendra Pal Singh, *V.N. Shukla's Constitution of India* (10th edn, Eastern Book Company 2003), p. 31. This reflects the difference between Parliament's power to repeal a statute and courts' powers to strike down a statute. Deshpande J. describes the former as 'express repeal' and the latter as 'implied repeal' (*P.L. Mehra v. D.R. Khanna*, AIR 1971 Del 1, para 28). This terminology is however linguistically jarring, since courts do not repeal legislation in any sense of the term: they simply disapply legislation that violates fundamental rights. Further, implied repeal is an expression that is often used in the context of Parliament enacting legislation that is inconsistent with (but does not expressly supersede) existing legislation. See also 'What Is the Effect of a Court's Declaring a Legislative Act Unconstitutional?' (1926) 39 Harvard Law Review 373; Earl Crawford, 'The Legislative Status of an Unconstitutional Statute' (1951) 49 Michigan Law Review 645.

[16] For instance, in *State of Gujarat v. Shri Ambica Mills*, AIR 1974 SC 1300, a law was struck down for contravening a fundamental right enjoyed by citizens. The Supreme Court held that the law would continue to apply to non-citizens.

The statute thus remains in a 'state of suspension'[17] or, as Prime Minister Nehru described it, 'half-dead',[18] and can be brought back into operation when the constitutional provision based on which the legislation was struck down is itself amended.[19] The constitutional barrier having been removed, the eclipse over the legislation would stand lifted.[20] To take an example, in *Bhikaji* v. *State of Madhya Pradesh*,[21] the Supreme Court held that the eclipse cast over a 1947 statute,[22] which contravened fundamental rights, lifted when the relevant fundamental rights were later amended to remove the conflict. Thus, the statute was once again enforceable.

That the doctrine of eclipse can operate to resuscitate pre-constitutional legislation[23] is a matter of judicial consensus.[24] What remains contested is whether the doctrine applies to post-constitutional legislation.[25] In some cases, the Supreme Court[26] and high courts[27] have

[17] *Mehra* (n. 15), para 29 (dissenting opinion of Deshpande J.).

[18] Lok Sabha Debates, vol. XII, no. II, col. 9080 (Jawaharlal Nehru).

[19] Field describes amending the Constitution as a 'difficult but perfectly feasible method of removing constitutional obstacles from the path of statutes or of enlarging legislative powers'. See Oliver Field, *The Effect of an Unconstitutional Statute* (University of Minnesota Press 1935), p. 288.

[20] Crawford (n. 15).

[21] AIR 1955 SC 781.

[22] CP & Berar Motor Vehicles (Amendment) Act, 1947.

[23] This refers to all laws in force immediately before the commencement of the Constitution (that is, before 26 January 1950).

[24] *Keshavan Madhava Menon* v. *State of Bombay*, AIR 1951 SC 128; *Bhikaji Dhakras* v. *State of Madhya Pradesh*, AIR 1955 SC 781; *Behram Pesikaka* v. *State of Bombay*, AIR 1955 SC 123.

[25] This refers to all laws that come into force after the commencement of the Constitution (that is, after 26 January 1950). This is both peculiar and counter-intuitive, as it effectively places colonial legislation on a higher plane compared to legislation passed after the Indian Constitution was enacted.

[26] *Sundararamier* v. *State of Andhra Pradesh*, AIR 1958 SC 468; *Shri Ambica Mills* (n. 16); *K.K. Poonacha* v. *State of Karnataka*, (2010) 9 SCC 671. In the last-mentioned case, however, the Court observed that the doctrine of eclipse operates vis-à-vis post-constitutional laws that fail to comply with procedural requirements laid down in Part III of the Constitution, not post-constitutional laws that take away substantive rights provided for in Part III.

[27] The dissenting opinion of Deshpande J. in *Mehra* (n. 15) is the most elaborate defence of the doctrine of eclipse from the Bench. See also *Minoo*

held that the doctrine would apply equally to post-constitutional laws, saving Parliament from the costs of re-enactment of a statute which is struck down. Other decisions by the Supreme Court[28] and high court[29] suggest that the doctrine only applies to laws that came into being before the Constitution, and that post-constitutional legislation that contravenes fundamental rights is 'stillborn' and would be considered a nullity.[30] Academic opinion on the issue is also deeply divided.[31]

The operation of the doctrine of eclipse vis-à-vis post-constitutional laws violating the fundamental rights has some important practical implications. The legislature that enacted the law which is resuscitated through the doctrine of eclipse does not have to take recourse to fresh parliamentary procedure and majorities. Constitutional amendments, on the other hand, need to be passed by a special majority in Parliament. Even so, the political relevance of the doctrine would be substantial in situations where the fresh enactment of a statute invalidated by a court may not secure a simple majority vote in Parliament, whereas a constitutional amendment *having the effect of* resuscitating the invalidated statute may find sufficient support to secure a two-thirds majority in Parliament.

---

*Framroze Balsara* v. *Union of India*, AIR 1992 Bom 375; *Nataraj* v. *State of UP*, AIR 1996 All 375, paras 62–8, 158–62.

[28] The judgments of the Supreme Court that arrived at this conclusion are as follows: *Deep Chand* v. *State of UP*, AIR 1959 SC 648; *Mahendra Lal Jaini* v. *State of UP*, AIR 1963 SC 1019; *Rakesh Vij* v. *Raminder Sethi*, AIR 2005 SC 3593.

[29] *Bawa Singh* v. *Union of India*, (1970) 6 DLT 409; *Ram Chand* v. *State of Haryana*, (1971) 73 PLR 958; *Mehra* (n. 15) (Hardayal Hardy J.); *Dharam Pal* v. *Kaushalya Devi*, AIR 1990 Raj 135, paras 16–17.

[30] In still other cases, the Court left the question open. See *State of Maharashtra* v. *Kamal Durgule*, (1985) 1 SCC 234.

[31] The following commentators subscribe to the view that the doctrine of eclipse should apply to post-constitutional laws: S. Venkataraman, 'The Status of an Unconstitutional Statute' (1960) 2 JILI 401, p. 418; H.M. Seervai, *Constitutional Law of India* (4th edn, N.M. Tripathi 1996), pp. 420–1; Singh (n. 15), pp. 38–40. However, many others are in the opposite camp: Durga Das Basu, *Limited Government and Judicial Review* (S.C. Sarkar 1972), pp. 423–88; Sushila Rao, 'The Doctrine of Eclipse in Constitutional Law: A Critical Reappraisal of Its Contemporary Scope and Relevance' (2006) 18 Student Bar Review 45; Datar (n. 7), p. 53; Chakradhar Jha, *Judicial Review of Legislative Acts* (2nd edn, LexisNexis Butterworths Wadhwa 2009), p. 321.

It is not difficult to imagine situations where consensus prevails over broad constitutional principles, but not over the manner in which those principles should be given effect—the devil is often in the detail. However, the specific terms in which a constitutional amendment is enacted may obviate the need to invoke the doctrine of eclipse. Hence, where a constitutional amendment contains a specific savings clause reviving legislation that has been previously declared invalid by the courts,[32] it performs the same task as the doctrine of eclipse would in the circumstances.

Precisely how can the power to amend fundamental rights under the Constitution be employed by Parliament as a response mechanism to overcome judicial decisions striking down primary legislation? The possibilities depend crucially upon two factors: whether the doctrine of eclipse is applicable in the circumstances (alternatively, whether the amendment contains a specific savings clause of the kind just described) and whether the constitutional amendment applies prospectively or retrospectively. A hypothetical example (as follows) brings out the alternatives.

The Indian Constitution entered into force in 1950. In 1965, a statute, 'UnconStat', is enacted by Parliament. In 1966, the Supreme Court strikes down UnconStat on the basis that it violates a fundamental right. Parliament would have the following options before it in, say, 1970. If the doctrine of eclipse applies in the circumstances or if the amendment contains a specific savings clause, a *retrospective* constitutional amendment would resuscitate UnconStat, which would once again become operative without needing fresh enactment.[33] In this scenario, a *prospective* constitutional amendment would not lift UnconStat out of the shadow of invalidity, since the amendment would apply to statutes enacted after 1970.

---

[32] See, for example, Constitution (First Amendment) Act, 1951, section 3(2):

No law in force in the territory of India immediately before the commencement of the Constitution which is consistent with the provisions of article 19 of the Constitution as amended by sub-section (1) of this section shall be deemed to be void, *or ever to have become void*, on the ground only that, being a law which takes away or abridges the right conferred by sub-clause (a) of clause (1) of the said article, its operation was not saved by clause (2) of that article as originally enacted. (Emphasis added)

[33] *Mehra* (n. 15) (dissenting opinion of Deshpande J.).

If the doctrine of eclipse does not apply and if the amendment does not contain a specific savings clause, even a *retrospective* constitutional amendment would not resuscitate UnconStat, since it cannot be revived from its state of unconstitutionality. However, in this case, if a law identical to UnconStat is passed after 1965 (say, in 1968) and remains to be struck down as unconstitutional until 1970 (after the constitutional amendment is passed), the law would be protected by the amendment. Finally, if the doctrine of eclipse applies or if the amendment contains a specific savings clause and the constitutional amendment is *prospective*, the cause of unconstitutionality is treated as having been removed only in 1970.[34] Thus, the 1968 statute which is still to be struck down will, for all times to come, remain unprotected by the amendment. Only fresh statutes enacted after 1970 would be protected by it. All these possibilities are set out in Table 2.1 below.

**Table 2.1**    Effect of Doctrine of Eclipse or Specific Savings Clause on the Validity of Legislation Struck Down

| Does the doctrine of eclipse apply or is there a specific savings clause? | Is the constitutional amendment enacted in 1970 prospective or retrospective? | Is UnconStat (enacted in 1965, struck down in 1966) revived without re-enactment? |
| --- | --- | --- |
| Yes | Retrospective | Yes |
| Yes | Prospective | No |
| No | Retrospective | No (But an identical law enacted between 1965 and 1970, which has not been struck down, is protected by the amendment) |
| No | Prospective | No |

Of course, in all cases where UnconStat is not resuscitated automatically by the constitutional amendment, it can be re-enacted by Parliament in the same terms with the expectation that, the Constitution having been amended, it cannot be struck down based on the same

---

[34] Durga Das Basu, *Commentary on the Constitution of India* (8th edn, LexisNexis Butterworths Wadhwa 2007), p. 939.

infirmity. What the doctrine of eclipse (or a specific savings clause) does is to render constitutional amendments more potent as response mechanisms than they would have been in its absence, since retrospective constitutional amendments coupled with the doctrine of eclipse or a specific savings clause automatically validate legislation that is struck down as unconstitutional.

To establish the broader argument in this chapter, few judgments of the Supreme Court and high courts, nullified through constitutional amendments (set out in Appendix A), have been selected on the basis of two characteristics. First, only cases that involved a challenge to primary legislation have been considered, since the book compares responses to judicial review of primary legislation in India and the UK. Delegated legislation, emanating from the executive rather than the legislature, is an entirely different animal,[35] and British courts also have the power to strike down delegated legislation that contravenes rights under the Convention. Second, only those cases where legislation was struck down for violating fundamental rights under Part III have been selected, although this need not have been the court's only reason for doing so. This naturally means that no judgments striking down primary legislation for breaching constitutional rights outside of Part III have been considered. The underlying rationale for this is to ensure a comparison between equals, since judicial review of primary legislation for breaching Convention rights in the UK cannot be meaningfully compared with judicial review in India based, for instance, on the federal distribution of powers or the freedom of interstate trade.

The judgments selected are worth examining in order to expound upon the manner in which fundamental rights amendments have been employed as a response mechanism by Parliament. Particularly in the early years of constitutional experience, a frequent governmental response to judicial decisions whose reasoning on rights Parliament or government disagreed with was to veer towards a change in the Constitution.[36] As one member of parliament (MP) put it while

---

[35] As Lord Kerr said in *R (Nicklinson)* v. *Ministry of Justice*, [2014] UKSC 38, para 365, the HRA treats '[primary] legislation and executive action entirely separately'.

[36] Pratap Bhanu Mehta, 'The Rise of Judicial Sovereignty' in Sumit Ganguly, Larry Diamond, and Mark F. Plattner (eds), *The State of India's Democracy* (Johns

debating one of these constitutional amendments, albeit somewhat histrionically: 'I [personifying Parliament] bow my head to the Supreme Court or any other court to interpret the law [the Constitution]. If the law does not express what I want, what I wish, then I am at full liberty to amend it any number of times. It may even be 50 times.'[37] In some cases, MPs urged litigants not to approach the courts seeking the invalidation of a specific piece of legislation, on the ground that if necessary, Parliament would be ready to amend the Constitution to nullify the basis of the judgment.[38]

Let us consider some examples: in *Shaila Bala Devi* v. *Chief Secretary*,[39] the petitioner sought a judgment from the Patna High Court that section 4(1)(a) of the Indian Press (Emergency Powers) Act, 1931, that penalized the publication of any document which incited or encouraged the commission of murder or any cognizable offences involving violence, breached the right to freedom of speech and expression under Art. 19(1)(a) of the Constitution. The majority on the Bench struck down the provision on the basis that it violated the right to freedom of speech and expression and did not fall under the permissible exceptions under Art. 19(2). At the time, the only exception was law relating to libel, slander, defamation, contempt of court, or 'any matter which offends against decency or morality or which undermines the security of, or tends to overthrow the State'. Similarly, in *Romesh Thapar* v. *State of Madras*,[40] the Supreme Court found section 9(1A) of the Madras Maintenance of Public Order Act, 1949 (which authorized a ban on the circulation of documents to secure 'public safety' and 'public order') overbroad as it violated Art. 19(1)(a) without falling within the scope of the exceptions laid down in Art. 19(2).

---

Hopkins University Press 2007). As Irani said, it was 'common' for parliamentarians to demand constitutional amendments to nullify important judicial pronouncements that they disagreed with—see Phiroze K. Irani, 'The Courts and the Legislature in India' (1965) 14 International and Comparative Law Quarterly 950, p. 952.

[37] Lok Sabha Debates, 1971, vol. IX, no. XIII, cols 276–7 (Era Sezhiyan).

[38] Lok Sabha Debates, 1951, vol. XII, no. II, col. 10052 (Seth Govind Das).

[39] AIR 1951 Pat 12.

[40] AIR 1950 SC 124.

Parliament was quick to respond. By the first amendment to the Constitution,[41] the exceptions provided for in Art. 19(2) were expanded to encompass clearly cases such as *Shaila Bala* and *Romesh Thapar*.[42] The amendment was retrospective in operation and contained a specific savings clause protecting legislation that was declared void under the original unamended version of Art. 19.[43] Parliament thus effectively nullified the two judgments and revived the statutes by altering the constitutionally permissible restrictions on the right to freedom of expression. In fact, when *Shaila Bala* went in appeal to the Supreme Court after the amendment was enacted, the Patna High Court's judgment was reversed on the basis that the constitutional amendment had decisively concluded the matter.[44] Parliament was thus able to replace courts' conception of the right to freedom of expression with its own.

In *State of West Bengal* v. *Bella Banerjee*,[45] the constitutionality of a provision of the West Bengal Land Development and Planning Act, 1948 was at issue before the Supreme Court. The statute was enacted primarily for the settlement of immigrants who had migrated into the province of West Bengal and provided for the acquisition and development of land. Those whose land was acquired under the statute contended that section 8, which restricted the amount of compensation payable on acquisition so as not to exceed the market value of the land on a fixed date, violated the right to compensation under the

[41] Constitution (First Amendment) Act, 1951.

[42] The constitutional amendment also nullified four other judgments which struck down statutes for violating the right to freedom of speech and expression: *Brij Bhushan* v. *State of Delhi*, AIR 1950 SC 129; *Amar Nath Bali* v. *State*, AIR 1951 Punj 18; *Srinivasa* v. *State of Madras*, AIR 1951 Mad 70; *Tara Singh* v. *State*, AIR 1951 Punj 27. See Arudra Burra, 'Arguments from Colonial Continuity: The Constitution (First Amendment) Act, 1951' (*SSRN*, 7 December 2008) <http://papers.ssrn.com/sol3/papers.cfm?abstract_id=2052659> accessed 28 June 2013.

[43] This savings clause in section 3(2) of Constitution (First Amendment) Act, 1951 obviated the need to invoke the doctrine of eclipse in order to revive the statutory provision declared invalid. See n. 32 for text of section 3(2).

[44] *State of Bihar* v. *Shaila Bala*, AIR 1952 SC 329.

[45] AIR 1954 SC 170.

(erstwhile)[46] fundamental right to property laid down in Art. 31(2) of the Constitution. The Court accepted the argument and struck down the relevant section for failing to comply with the 'letter and spirit' of the article.[47] Parliament promptly altered the Supreme Court's reasoning of rights through a constitutional amendment which excluded the inquiry into the adequacy of compensation paid for acquisition of land from judicial consideration.[48] The judgment of the Supreme Court was therefore neutralized by amending the constitutional provision upon which it rested.

Along similar lines, the Constitution (Seventeenth Amendment) Act, 1964 was enacted by Parliament to nullify two judgments. In the first,[49] the Supreme Court struck down the Kerala Agrarian Relations Act, 1961 in relation to its application to certain kinds of land, as it violated the right to equality under Art. 14. The Court rejected the government's argument that the statute fell within the protective umbrella of Art. 31A, which protected laws providing for the acquisition of estates from scrutiny under Arts 14,[50] 19,[51] and 31[52] of the Constitution. In the second case,[53] the same statute was found by the Kerala High Court to violate Arts 14, 19, and 31 of the Constitution. The constitutional amendment passed by Parliament expanded the scope of Art. 31A to include within its protective cloak the kind of legislation that was at

---

[46] The fundamental right to property under Arts 19(1)(f) and 31 of the Constitution were deleted by the Constitution (Forty-fourth Amendment) Act, 1978. However, the amendment inserted Art. 300A into the Constitution, which reads: 'Persons not to be deprived of property save by authority of law. No person shall be deprived of his property save by authority of law.' Thus, the right to property remains a (non-fundamental) constitutional right.

[47] *Bella Banerjee* (n. 45), para 11.

[48] Constitution (Fourth Amendment) Act, 1955. Parliament also inserted the West Bengal Land Development and Planning Act, 1948 into the Ninth Schedule of the Constitution, the significance of which are discussed in the following section in this chapter.

[49] *Kunhikoman* v. *State of Kerala*, AIR 1962 SC 273.

[50] The right to equality before the law and the equal protection of the laws.

[51] The right to certain freedoms, including the freedom of speech and the freedom of trade.

[52] The right to property, see n. 46.

[53] *Sukapuram* v. *State of Kerala*, AIR 1963 Ker 101.

issue in the two cases. The Supreme Court upheld the validity of the constitutional amendment in two subsequent decisions.[54] Since the amendment did not contain a specific savings clause (and the doctrine of eclipse was not invoked), the state legislature enacted fresh legislation[55] with similar objectives in place of the invalidated statute.

*R.C. Cooper* v. *Union of India*,[56] better known as the Bank Nationalization case, provides yet another example of parliamentary rejection of a judgment striking down legislation. The petitioner, a shareholder and director of a bank, challenged primary legislation[57] that sought to nationalize 14 Indian banks. An 11-judge bench of the Supreme Court struck down the statute on the basis that it breached the right to equality under Art. 14, the right to freedom of trade under Art. 19(1)(g), and the rights to property protected by Arts 19(1)(f) and 31(2). Looked upon by many within government as a judgment that impeded the 'building of a socialist economy',[58] Parliament passed a constitutional amendment[59] to roll back the effects of the decision. Subsequently, the Supreme Court upheld the amendment (barring one portion of it).[60] Once again, since the amendment did not contain a specific savings clause, Parliament enacted another statute[61] with the

---

[54] *Sajjan Singh* v. *State of Rajasthan*, AIR 1965 SC 845; *Golak Nath* v. *State of Punjab*, AIR 1967 SC 1643. In *Golak Nath*, the constitutional amendment was upheld subject to the qualification that Parliament could no longer amend Part III of the Constitution after the date of the Court's decision; this view was later overruled in the Basic Structure case (n. 8). Both *Golak Nath* and the Basic Structure case are discussed later in the chapter.

[55] Kerala Land Reforms Act, 1963. This statute was also inserted into the Ninth Schedule, the relevance of which will be discussed below. See Constitution (Seventeenth Amendment) Act, 1964 and Constitution of India, Ninth Schedule (Entry 39).

[56] AIR 1970 SC 564.

[57] Banking Companies (Acquisition and Transfer of Undertakings) Act, 1969.

[58] S. Mohan Kumaramangalam, 'Slide-back on Compensation: Bank Nationalisation Judgment' (1970) 5 Economic and Political Weekly 356.

[59] Constitution (Twenty-fifth Amendment) Act, 1971.

[60] Basic Structure case (n. 8).

[61] Banking Companies (Acquisition and Transfer of Undertakings) Act, 1970. This statute applied retrospectively and predated the constitutional amendment.

same objectives, which, in the light of the constitutional amendment, was not open to constitutional challenge on the same basis.

What is interesting to note from these cases is that for the large part, courts upheld fundamental rights amendments passed by successive Parliaments.[62] In the words of Patanjali Sastri J.: '[T]o make a law which contravenes the constitution constitutionally valid is a matter ... [which courts considered to be] within the exclusive power of Parliament.'[63] This statement provides a useful lead into questions concerning the scope of the amending power.

Frequent constitutional amendments over the years gave rise to one of the most politically loaded questions of Indian constitutional law. Are there any limitations on the amending power of Parliament? Art. 13(2) of the Constitution proscribes the state from making 'any law which takes away or abridges the rights conferred' by Part III of the Constitution.[64] A difficult issue that arose in litigation was whether the term 'law' in Art. 13 included constitutional amendments. If it did, then that would mean that Parliament lacked the constitutional authority to amend fundamental rights, as it had been doing soon after the Constitution was enacted.

When the Supreme Court was first confronted with this question, a unanimous five-judge bench[65] decided that 'law' did not include constitutional amendments, paving the way for Parliament to amend any part of the Constitution, including Part III.[66] Thirteen years later, the majority on a five-judge bench of the Supreme Court agreed.[67] However, two judges expressed scepticism about the correctness of this

---

[62] See *Shankari Prasad* v. *Union of India*, [1952] 1 SCR 89; *Sajjan Singh* (n. 54); *Golak Nath* (n. 54) ; Basic Structure case (n. 8).

[63] *Shankari Prasad* (n. 62), para 30.

[64] Art. 13(2) of the Indian Constitution reads as follows: 'The State shall not make any law which takes away or abridges the rights conferred by this Part [the chapter on fundamental rights] and any law made in contravention of this clause shall, to the extent of the contravention, be void.'

[65] In the Supreme Court of India, only Benches comprising the same or larger number of judges can overrule precedent. See Chintan Chandrachud, 'The Supreme Court's Practice of Referring Cases to Larger Benches: A Need for Review' (2010) 1 SCC (Jour) 37.

[66] *Shankari Prasad* (n. 62).

[67] *Sajjan Singh* (n. 54) (Gajendragadkar C.J.).

conclusion. Hidayatullah J. said that 'stronger reasons' were required in order to arrive at this decision.[68] Mudholkar J., on the other hand, articulated that the Constituent Assembly might have intended to give permanency to the 'basic features of the Constitution'.[69] But he chose not to develop what the 'basic features' of the Constitution were in any detail.

A few years later, the question was referred to a bench of 11 judges of the Supreme Court in *Golak Nath*.[70] Aggrieved by the impact of land reform legislation, several litigants filed writ petitions in the Supreme Court.[71] They claimed that such legislation, along with certain constitutional amendments that protected the legislation, should be struck down for breaching their fundamental rights. On this occasion, by a thin majority of 6:5, the Supreme Court held that constitutional amendments were 'law' within the purview of Art. 13(2), rendering Part III of the Constitution inviolate.[72] However, the majority applied the doctrine of 'prospective overruling' to avoid the chaos and confusion that they expected would follow the invalidation of existing constitutional amendments and the statutes on which they were based.[73]

In 1973, *Golak Nath* was reconsidered by an unprecedented 13-judge bench of the Supreme Court in the Basic Structure case.[74] This case arose out of six writ petitions challenging land redistribution legislation and the constitutional amendments that protected it. The reported name of the case, *Kesavananda Bharati v. State of Kerala*, comes from the title of one of the petitioners, His Holiness Swami Kesavananda

---

[68] *Sajjan Singh* (n. 54), para 49 (Hidayatullah J.).

[69] *Sajjan Singh* (n. 54), para 61 (Mudholkar J.).

[70] See n. 54.

[71] Art. 32 of the Constitution guarantees the right to move the Supreme Court of India at first instance for the enforcement of fundamental rights under Part III.

[72] Since Art. 13(2) only prevents Parliament from making any law which 'takes away or abridges' the rights conferred by Part III, *Golak Nath* did not imply that the fundamental rights could not be enlarged or advanced through constitutional amendment. See R.S. Gae, *The Bank Nationalisation Case and the Constitution* (N.M. Tripathi 1971), p. 139.

[73] The doctrine of prospective overruling is discussed more fully in Chapter 4.

[74] See n. 8.

Bharati, the head of a religious establishment. Eleven separate opinions were delivered in what was one of the longest appellate decisions,[75] comprising over 400,000 words, of the last century.

What complicates the judgments in the Basic Structure case is the discord between what the judges *said* and what they were *understood to mean* by subsequent benches, which relied on a questionable 'summary' of the majority's decision signed by 9 of the 13 judges.[76] It is difficult to find common ground between the seven judges that form the 'majority' in the case;[77] however, subsequent judgments of the Supreme Court consider the ratio decidendi of the Basic Structure case to be that although the term 'law' in Art. 13(2) does not include constitutional amendments and that Parliament could amend any part of the Constitution (including Part III), the power of amendment under Art. 368 of the Constitution does not include the power to alter, abrogate, or destroy the basic structure of the Constitution.[78]

Thus, the 'basic structure' doctrine (also referred to as the 'basic features' doctrine and the 'essential features' doctrine) postulates that although Parliament may amend any part of the Constitution, a constitutional amendment that destroys, alters, or abrogates its basic structure can be struck down as an 'unconstitutional constitutional amendment'. What comprised the basic structure of the Constitution was left open, allowing judges to develop the concept incrementally. The following are amongst the principles that have been included within the purview of the basic structure doctrine, in the Basic Structure case and subsequent

[75] Vivek Krishnamurthy, 'Colonial Cousins: Explaining India and Canada's Unwritten Constitutional Principles' (2009) 34 Yale Journal of International Law 207.

[76] Seervai (n. 31), p. 3114; T.R. Andhyarujina, *The Kesavananda Bharati Case: The Untold Story of Struggle for Supremacy by Supreme Court and Parliament* (Universal Law Publishing 2011), pp. 63–7.

[77] Granville Austin, *Working a Democratic Constitution: A History of the Indian Experience* (Oxford University Press 2003), p. 265; Sudhir Krishnaswamy, *Democracy and Constitutionalism in India: A Study of the Basic Structure Doctrine* (Oxford University Press 2010), p. 27; Andhiyarujina (n. 76), p. 49.

[78] *Indira Gandhi* v. *Raj Narain*, AIR 1975 SC 2299; *Minerva Mills* v. *Union of India*, AIR 1980 SC 1789 (Chandrachud C.J.); *Waman Rao* v. *Union of India*, AIR 1981 SC 271.

decisions: the supremacy of the Constitution,[79] secularism,[80] the sovereignty of India,[81] federalism,[82] judicial review,[83] the limited power to amend the Constitution,[84] and free and fair elections.[85] For the purposes of this chapter, the key difference between *Golak Nath* and the Basic Structure case is that where the former embodied a rigid restriction on the amendability of Part III, the latter incorporated functional flexibility, allowing Parliament to amend any part of the Constitution subject to the 'basic structure' qualification.[86]

Thus, the Indian Parliament's formally unlimited power to amend the Constitution has been attenuated by the Basic Structure case and subsequent decisions. The existing position of law on Parliament's ability to nullify judgments that strike down legislation for violating of fundamental rights through constitutional amendments is as follows. Not all fundamental rights form part of the basic structure of the Constitution—if they did, the relative flexibility in the Basic Structure case, in comparison with *Golak Nath*, would have been meaningless.[87] However, Parliament cannot amend a fundamental right to the extent that the basic structure of the Constitution would be abrogated.

---

[79] Basic Structure case (n. 8), paras 1171 (Ray J.), 302 (Sikri J.), 599 (Shelat J. and Grover J.). However, it seems a tautology to say that Parliament's power to amend the Constitution is restricted by the supremacy of the very Constitution that it seeks to amend.

[80] Basic Structure case (n. 8), paras 1171 (Ray J.), 302 (Sikri J.), 599 (Shelat J. and Grover J.).

[81] Basic Structure case (n. 8), paras 1171 (Ray J.), 599 (Shelat J. and Grover J.), 682 (Hegde J. and Mukherjea J.).

[82] Basic Structure case (n. 8), paras 302 (Sikri J.), 599 (Shelat J. and Grover J.).

[83] *L. Chandra Kumar* v. *Union of India*, AIR 1997 SC 1125.

[84] *Minerva Mills* (n. 78).

[85] *Special Reference No 1 of 2002*, AIR 2003 SC 87.

[86] M.P. Jain, 'The Supreme Court and Fundamental Rights' in Indian Law Institute, *Fifty Years of the Supreme Court of India: Its Grasp and Reach* (Oxford University Press 2003), pp. 11–12.

[87] Initially, Khanna J.'s judgment in the Basic Structure case was understood by some to mean that no fundamental rights formed part of the basic structure of the Constitution. But Khanna J. later issued a clarification stating that his opinion was not intended to suggest this—see *Indira Gandhi* (n. 78), paras 251–2.

However, it is still open to Parliament to nullify a judgment striking down legislation by amending a fundamental right without altering the basic structure of the Constitution. The possibility of Parliament responding to strike-downs in this way through fundamental rights amendments, without having an impact on the basic structure of the Constitution, is discussed later in greater detail.

## Ninth Schedule Amendments

[T]he Indian is the only constitution ... providing for protection against itself.[88]

The Ninth Schedule resembles an appendix to the Constitution and is associated with a special species of constitutional amendments. It is linked to Art. 31B, which reads as follows:

> Validation of certain Acts and Regulations: Without prejudice to the generality of the provisions contained in Article 31A, none of the Acts and Regulations specified in the Ninth Schedule nor any of the provisions thereof shall be deemed to be void, or ever to have become void, on the ground that such Act, Regulation or provision is inconsistent with, or takes away or abridges any of the rights conferred by, any provisions of this Part [Part III of the Constitution], and notwithstanding any judgment, decree or order of any court or tribunal to the contrary, each of the said Acts and Regulations shall, subject to the power of any competent Legislature to repeal or amend it, continue in force.

Although it is tempting to draw associations between the Ninth Schedule and the Canadian 'notwithstanding clause',[89] there

---

[88] Granville Austin, citing what Gajendragadkar C.J. had, according to 'judicial lore', said about the Ninth Schedule—see Austin (n. 77), p. 85. This statement was putatively made well before the 'notwithstanding clause' under section 33 of the Canadian Charter of Rights and Freedoms, 1982 (Canadian Charter) and similar mechanisms (such as under section 8 of the Israeli Basic Law: Freedom of Occupation) came into existence.

[89] Section 33 of the Canadian Charter, better known as the 'notwithstanding clause', reads as follows:

(1) Parliament or the legislature of a province may expressly declare in an Act of Parliament or of the legislature, as the case may be, that the Act or a provision thereof shall operate notwithstanding a provision included in section 2 or sections 7 to 15.

are some crucial differences between the two. Unlike in Canada (where the notwithstanding clause can be invoked by ordinary legislative majorities), the Ninth Schedule is treated as a part of the Constitution and statutes can only be added to it through the supermajority procedure prescribed for constitutional amendments in Art. 368. This is important, because if the Ninth Schedule could be invoked through the ordinary legislative process, then the Indian system could not have been formally classified as one characterized by judicial supremacy.

Although federal or state legislation may be placed in the Ninth Schedule, only the Union Parliament, which is entrusted with the power of amending the Constitution, can do so.[90] There is no limit on the number of statutes that can be added to the Ninth Schedule through a single constitutional amendment.[91] In fact, in only one case has a constitutional amendment inserted just a single statute into the Ninth Schedule.[92] Finally, being more difficult to invoke, the Ninth Schedule is also in a sense more potent than the notwithstanding clause: there is no time limit specified for the insulation of statutes inserted into the

---

(2) An Act or a provision of an Act in respect of which a declaration made under this section is in effect shall have such operation as it would have but for the provision of this Charter referred to in the declaration.

(3) A declaration made under subsection (1) shall cease to have effect five years after it comes into force or on such earlier date as may be specified in the declaration.

(4) Parliament or the legislature of a province may re-enact a declaration made under subsection (1).

(5) Subsection (3) applies in respect of a re-enactment made under subsection (4).

For commentary, see Tsvi Kahana, 'Understanding the Notwithstanding Mechanism' (2002) 52 University of Toronto Law Journal 221.

[90] In Canada, the notwithstanding clause may be invoked by Parliament or provincial legislatures.

[91] This reduces the per-legislation cost of adding each statute to the Ninth Schedule. See Shruti Rajagopalan, 'Independent Judiciary and Rent Seeking: Evidence from the Indian Constitution' (SSRN, October 2012) <http://ssrn.com/abstract=2172070> accessed 11 November 2014.

[92] See the Constitution (Seventy-Sixth Amendment) Act, 1994.

Ninth Schedule from judicial review.[93] Statutes in the Ninth Schedule, in other words, were meant to remain protected in perpetuity.

Since Art. 31B itself contains a specific savings clause protecting legislation notwithstanding any judgment, by automatically reviving laws that are struck down and later inserted into the Ninth Schedule without fresh enactment, it performs the same task that the doctrine of eclipse would have in the circumstances. This explains why the doctrine of eclipse does not need to be invoked in cases where Parliament responds to a judgment by inserting legislation into Ninth Schedule.[94]

Legislative override through Art. 31B and the Ninth Schedule was not originally part of the Constitution. It was included through a constitutional amendment in 1951 in order to immunize agrarian reform legislation from judicial scrutiny for contravening one or more fundamental rights under Part III.[95] More than 280 statutes currently lie within the confines of the Ninth Schedule,[96] some of which have little to do with land reform.[97] State legislation comprises more than 85 per cent of the statutes in the Ninth Schedule.[98]

There are three stages at which Parliament may decide to insert legislation into the Ninth Schedule. First, it could choose to insert legislation into the Schedule as a precaution against an adverse judicial decision in the future.[99] Second, it could pre-empt a final decision

[93] The Canadian notwithstanding clause protects statutes for renewable five-year periods.

[94] *Jagannath* v. *Authorised Officer*, AIR 1972 SC 425, paras 33–4.

[95] Constitution (First Amendment) Act, 1951, 'Statement of Objects and Reasons'. Austin describes the Ninth Schedule as a 'constitutional vault' to which the judges were denied the key—see Austin (n. 77), p. 98.

[96] There are currently 282 statutes in the Ninth Schedule. Although the schedule lists 284 items, some of them have been deleted.

[97] See, for example, the Essential Commodities Act, 1955 (Entry 126), Smugglers and Foreign Exchange Manipulators (Forfeiture of Property) Act, 1976 (Entry 127), and Levy Sugar Price Equalisation Fund Act, 1976 (Entry 131). Baldev Singh categorized the legislation inserted into the Ninth Schedule up to 1990; see Baldev Singh, 'Ninth Schedule to Constitution of India: A Study' (1995) 37 JILI 457, p. 467. His analysis shows that a little over 87 per cent of statutes inserted into the schedule dealt with agrarian/land reform.

[98] To be precise, 247 of the 282 statutes in the Ninth Schedule.

[99] See, for example, Constitution (Forty-seventh Amendment) Act, 1984, 'Statement of Objects and Reasons'; Constitution (Sixty-sixth Amendment) Act, 1990, 'Statement of Objects and Reasons'.

by a court by inserting legislation into the Schedule in cases where a court has granted interim relief suspending its operation during the pendency of a case.[100] Third, it could insert legislation that has already been struck down into the Ninth Schedule to lift it from the shadow of unconstitutionality, since the legislation would be treated as never having become void.[101] This section will focus on the third use of the Ninth Schedule—as a response mechanism that takes the form of an attempt to immunize statutes (or specific statutory provisions) that were finally adjudicated upon and struck down by the Supreme Court and high courts. These uses of the Ninth Schedule will be referred to as 'Ninth Schedule amendments'. At least five[102] of the 100 constitutional amendments enacted up to May 2015 represent Ninth Schedule amendments.[103]

A few examples shed light on how Parliament has responded to judgments striking down legislation for violating fundamental rights through Ninth Schedule amendments. In *Balmadies Plantations* v. *State of Tamil Nadu*,[104] a group of petitions challenged the constitutional validity of legislation[105] that sought to transfer private forest lands to the state government. The Madras High Court dismissed the petitions.[106] In appeal, the Supreme Court upheld the validity of the statute except in so far as it related to the transfer of forests in certain private estates to the government, which in its view violated Arts 14,[107] 19,[108] and 31[109] of the Constitution. In a little over two years, Parliament passed a constitutional amendment inserting the

---

[100] See, for example, Constitution (Fortieth Amendment) Act, 1976, 'Statement of Objects and Reasons'.

[101] Constitution of India, Art. 31B.

[102] Constitution (First Amendment) Act, 1951; Constitution (Fourth Amendment) Act, 1955; Constitution (Twenty-ninth Amendment) Act, 1972; Constitution (Thirty-fourth Amendment) Act, 1974; Constitution (Sixty-sixth Amendment) Act, 1990.

[103] See Appendix A.

[104] AIR 1972 SC 2240.

[105] Gudalur Janmam Estates (Abolition and Conversion into Ryotwari) Act, 1969.

[106] *Nilambur Kovilagam* v. *State of Tamil Nadu*, (1971) 1 MLJ 255.

[107] The right to equality before the law and the equal protection of the laws.

[108] The right to freedom.

[109] The erstwhile fundamental right to property (see n. 46).

statute into the Ninth Schedule.[110] This *ipso facto* revived the portion of legislation that was struck down.

In another case, Kerala enacted the Kerala Land Reforms Act, 1963 as the primary land reform law for the state. The statute was inserted into the Ninth Schedule to protect it from constitutional challenge on the touchstone of violating fundamental rights.[111] In 1969, extensive amendments were made to the law by an amending statute,[112] which was not itself inserted into the Ninth Schedule. The amended provisions of the Kerala Land Reforms Act were challenged before the Kerala High Court on the basis that they were unconstitutional. The court held that since the amending statute was not inserted into the Ninth Schedule, the provisions of the original legislation, as amended by the subsequent statute, could not receive the protection of Art. 31B.[113] It struck down some statutory provisions for violating the right to equality under Art. 14 and the right to property under Art. 19(1)(f) of the Constitution.[114]

In appeal, the Supreme Court substantially confirmed the conclusions of the high court.[115] In a separate group of petitions, the Supreme Court also struck down another discrete aspect of the statute, as amended in 1969.[116] Within two months of the Supreme Court's judgments, Parliament inserted the amending act of 1969 into the Ninth Schedule with the avowed objective of nullifying the effects of this group of decisions.[117] The statement of objects and reasons accompanying the amendment made it clear that Parliament was consciously revising the judgments:[118]

---

[110] Constitution (Thirty-fourth Amendment) Act 1974 and Constitution of India, Ninth Schedule (Entry 80). The insertion of the statute into the Ninth Schedule was later upheld by the Supreme Court in *Glanrock Estate* v. *State of Tamil Nadu*, (2010) 10 SCC 96.

[111] Constitution (Seventeenth Amendment) Act, 1964 and Constitution of India, Ninth Schedule (Entry 39).

[112] Kerala Land Reforms (Amendment) Act, 1969.

[113] *Narayanan Nair* v. *State of Kerala* AIR 1971 Ker 98.

[114] *Narayanan Nair* (n. 113).

[115] *Kunjukutty Sahib* v. *State of Kerala*, AIR 1972 SC 2097.

[116] *Malankara Rubber* v. *State of Kerala*, AIR 1972 SC 2027.

[117] Constitution (Twenty-ninth Amendment) Act, 1972 and Constitution of India, Ninth Schedule (Entry 65).

[118] Constitution (Twenty-ninth Amendment) Act 1972, 'Statement of Objects and Reasons'.

Although the High Court of Kerala has generally upheld the scheme of land reforms envisaged [in the statute] ... a few vital provisions have been struck down.... The Supreme Court ... [has also] generally upheld the scheme of land reforms as envisaged in the principal Act as amended but agreed with the High Court invalidating certain crucial provisions. It is feared that this will have far-reaching adverse [e]ffects on the implementation of the programme of land reforms in the State and thousands of tenants will be adversely affected by some of the provisions which have been either struck down or rendered ineffective.

The invalidated legislation was thus automatically revived without requiring re-enactment.

In *Paschimbanga* v. *State of West Bengal*,[119] the Calcutta High Court considered the validity of the West Bengal Land Holding Revenue Act, 1979, a statute that provided for the levy of revenue on landholdings in the state. Section 2(c) was struck down for granting excessive powers to the authority prescribed under the statute.[120] Since the court considered that this provision was not severable from the rest of the statute, the entire statute was rendered unenforceable. About four years later, Parliament passed a constitutional amendment validating the act by inserting it into the Ninth Schedule.[121] Yet again, the Ninth Schedule was engaged as a constitutional device to roll back the effects of a judicial decision that had struck down primary legislation for breaching fundamental rights.

Following the judgment in the Basic Structure case, there appeared to be a zone of conflict between the accepted effect of the case and the Ninth Schedule. While Art. 31B, along with the Ninth Schedule, sought to confer unlimited powers of constitutional amendment on Parliament to protect legislation from judicial review, the Basic Structure case was an attempt to limit Parliament's amending power and subject it to judicial scrutiny.[122]

---

[119] MANU/WB/0564/1986.

[120] Invalidity on the basis of excessive delegation is inextricably linked to a breach of the right to equality under Art. 14 of the Constitution—see *Trustees for the Improvement of Calcutta* v. *Chandra Sekhar*, AIR 1977 SC 2034, para 7.

[121] Constitution (Sixty-sixth Amendment) Act, 1990 and Constitution of India, Ninth Schedule (Entry 250).

[122] Madhav Khosla, 'Addressing Judicial Activism in the Indian Supreme Court: Towards an Evolved Debate' (2009) 32 Hastings International & Comparative Law Review 55. See also Harish Salve, 'Citizen Supreme' *India Today* (New Delhi, 29 January 2007).

The conflict reflected contrasting political narratives—the first, in which the founding fathers of the nation, many of whom became MPs, believed that they had a special claim to expounding the Constitution's meaning—one that was superior to that of the judges,[123] and the second, in which the judges assumed responsibility for curbing governmental excesses through an unprecedented jurisdiction to review constitutional amendments.

This conflict was ultimately reconciled by the Supreme Court in *I.R. Coelho* v. *State of Tamil Nadu*.[124] A unanimous nine-judge bench held that primary legislation which was inserted into the Ninth Schedule after the decision in the Basic Structure case would be subjected to the 'basic structure' test laid down in that decision. In other words, the insertion of legislation into the Ninth Schedule would be struck down if it altered, abrogated, or destroyed the basic structure of the Constitution. The Court also held that some fundamental rights[125] pertained to the basic structure of the Constitution. The insertion of legislation into the Ninth Schedule would also be struck down if the statute abrogated these fundamental rights. The test that would be employed to determine whether a fundamental right pertaining to the basic structure was abrogated was the 'rights test', according to which the impact and effect of the constitutional amendment on the fundamental rights would be relevant. Thus, the status and level of protection accorded to statutes inserted into the Ninth Schedule has been circumscribed. However, even after the decision in *Coelho*, the possibility of Parliament repudiating judicial reasoning of rights by validly inserting legislation that has been struck down for violating fundamental rights into the Ninth Schedule remains open.[126]

---

[123] This matter that will be touched upon in Chapter 3.

[124] AIR 2007 SC 861. This case reconsidered the Supreme Court's judgment in *Waman Rao* (n. 78), which adjudged the same question.

[125] These rights include Art. 14 (the right to equality), Art. 19 (which protects the freedom of speech and other rights), and Art. 21 (the right to life and personal liberty). The jury is out on precisely which fundamental rights pertain or do not pertain to the basic structure of the Constitution, since judicial decisions on this issue have been nebulous. See Kamala Sankaran, 'From Brooding Omnipresence to Concrete Textual Provisions: IR Coelho Judgment and Basic Structure Doctrine' (2007) 49 JILI 240.

[126] Virendra Kumar, 'Basic Structure of the Indian Constitution: Doctrine of Constitutionally Controlled Governance' (2007) 49 JILI 365.

Thus, the important point to be made is that some operational space for legislative response remains available after *Coelho*, albeit in restricted form. Some scholars disagree with this analysis. Soli Sorabjee, for instance, argues that the decision in *Coelho* 'in effect' renders fundamental rights under the Indian Constitution unamendable.[127] This argument thus questions the status of constitutional amendments to fundamental rights as a political response mechanism to judicial review. Randhawa reads *Coelho* as indicating that the inclusion of a statute that violated fundamental rights in the Ninth Schedule would invariably be invalidated through the basic structure doctrine.[128] Jaising makes a similar argument, stating that *Coelho* 'virtually repeals' Art. 31B of the Constitution and renders any violation of fundamental rights as an interference with the basic structure of the Constitution.[129] If one were to accept their arguments, the Ninth Schedule would be effectively eliminated as a response mechanism and Parliament could no longer invoke it in order to respond to judgments striking down legislation. These arguments are now worth considering.

Sorabjee's contention fails to consider that *Coelho* and subsequent judgments emphasize that different tests must be applied in determining the validity of constitutional amendments altering the substantive content of fundamental rights and those merely inserting legislation into the Ninth Schedule, seeking to protect it from judicial scrutiny. In the case of the former, the 'essence of rights test' (as opposed to the

---

[127] Soli Sorabjee, 'Evolution of the Basic Structure Doctrine: Its Implications and Impact on Constitutional Amendments' (Lecture at Oslo University, Oslo, 6 October 2008).

[128] Jasdeep Randhawa, 'Understanding Judicialization of Mega-Politics: The Basic Structure Doctrine and Minimum Core' (*Jus Politicum*, 2011) <http://juspoliticum.com/article/Understanding-Judicialization-Of-Mega-Politics-The-Basic-Structure-Doctrine-And-Minimum-Core-401.html> accessed 25 August 2016. She posits that the Supreme Court has exercised restraint in subsequent cases. The more satisfactory position is that *Coelho* itself exhibits elements of restraint, leaving a fair amount of space to the legislature.

[129] Indira Jaising, 'Ninth Schedule: What the Supreme Court Judgment Means' (*Rediff*, 11 January 2007) <http://www.rediff.com/news/2007/jan/11indira.htm> accessed 28 June 2014.

'rights test') is applied,[130] according to which the court focuses on the impact of the amendment on the overarching principles espoused by the Constitution rather than on the specific rights amended.[131] This means that fundamental rights could, quite plausibly, be amended to protect certain kinds of legislation that would otherwise be invalidated, without breaching the overarching principles forming part of the basic structure, for instance, secularism and federalism.

The Supreme Court's judgment in *Indian Medical Association* v. *Union of India*[132] confirms this claim. In 2005, Parliament inserted Art. 15(5) into Part III of the Constitution through a constitutional amendment.[133] The amendment was directed at nullifying earlier decisions[134] of the Supreme Court holding that state-sanctioned imposition of reservation policy on non-minority unaided educational institutions breached the freedom to carry on any occupation, trade, or business under Art. 19(1)(g). Delhi enacted primary legislation,[135] which, in the absence of Art.15(5), would have been struck down as invalid. The constitutionality of the insertion of Art. 15(5) into the Constitution was challenged on the touchstone of the basic structure doctrine. Rejecting the challenge, the Court observed that the question was not whether a fundamental right itself was amended, but whether, applying the 'essence of rights' test, the overarching constitutional principles connecting fundamental rights were abrogated.[136] Thus, an amendment

---

[130] The 'essence of rights' test and the 'rights' test have elsewhere been described by the Supreme Court as the 'identity' test and the 'width' test respectively. See M. *Nagaraj* v. *Union of India*, AIR 2007 SC 71, para 77; *Pramati Educational and Cultural Trust* v. *Union of India*, AIR 2014 SC 2114, para 23.

[131] The Court has held that the basic structure doctrine consists of foundational principles drawn from the provisions of the Constitution itself: *Supreme Court Advocates on Record Association* v. *Union of India*, (2016) 5 SCC 1, para 220 (Khehar J.).

[132] AIR 2011 SC 2365.

[133] Constitution (Ninety-third Amendment) Act, 2005.

[134] *T.M.A. Pai Foundation* v. *State of Karnataka*, (2002) 8 SCC 481; *P.A. Inamdar* v. *State of Maharashtra*, (2005) 6 SCC 37.

[135] The Delhi Professional Colleges or Institutions (Prohibition of Capitation Fee, Regulation of Admission, Fixation of Non-exploitative Fee and Other Measures to Ensure Equity and Excellence) Act, 2007.

[136] *Indian Medical Association* (n. 132), para 88.

to a fundamental right effectively shielded legislation that would have been struck down in its absence, without failing the basic structure test.

The arguments of Randhawa and Jaising, which call into question the operational space available to Parliament after *Coelho*, are belied by the fact that in *Coelho* itself, the Court observed that *some* (and not all) fundamental rights (including Arts 14,[137] 15,[138] 19,[139] and 21[140]) formed a part of the basic structure.[141] Further, applying the 'rights test', not every amendment that had some effect on even those fundamental rights *pertaining to the basic structure* would be considered invalid—only those which *abridged or abrogated* the fundamental right, examined with reference to each individual case, would fail the basic structure test.[142] If this were not the case, then Art. 31B of the Constitution would become an empty provision—an outcome that the Supreme Court has been conscious to avoid.[143]

Judges in *Coelho* and in previous cases have offered examples of legislation that might be struck down for breaching Part III, but could be validly revived through the Ninth Schedule. For example, in *Coelho*, Sabharwal C.J. held that freedom might be interfered with (presumably, to a limited extent) in cases relating to terrorism without the basic structure doctrine being triggered.[144] In a previous decision, Chandrachud C.J. observed: 'If by a constitutional amendment, the application of articles 14 and 19 is withdrawn from a defined field of legislative activity, which is reasonably in public interest, the basic framework of the Constitution may remain unimpaired.'[145] Krishna Iyer J. expressed the argument: '[W]hat is a betrayal of the basic feature [sic] is not a mere violation of Article 14 but a shocking, unconscionable or unscrupulous travesty of the quintessence of equal justice ... the constitutional

---

[137] The right to equality before the law and equal protection of the laws.

[138] Prohibition of discrimination on the grounds of religion, race, caste, sex, or place of birth.

[139] Protection of certain freedoms including the freedom of speech.

[140] The right to life and personal liberty.

[141] *Coelho* (n. 124), paras 48, 57, 59, and 60.

[142] *Coelho* (n. 124), para 58. See also *Indian Medical Association* (n. 132), para 84.

[143] *Glanrock Estate* (n. 110), para 8.

[144] *Coelho* (n. 124), para 78.

[145] *Minerva Mills* (n. 78), para 70.

fascination for the basic structure doctrine [cannot] be made a Trojan horse to penetrate the entire legislative camp fighting for a new social order.'[146] These quotations comprise judicial confirmation of the space available to Parliament to invoke the Ninth Schedule as a response mechanism to judgments striking down primary legislation for breaching fundamental rights.[147]

Overall, it can be concluded that the exercise of the power to strike down statutes has not necessarily constituted the last word on rights-based questions. Judicial interpretation of rights under the old model has not been as determinative as proponents of the new model seem to suggest. Two parliamentary response mechanisms have, individually or in conjunction, channelled political responses to the striking down of legislation. As Pratap Bhanu Mehta puts it (albeit in a slightly broader context), an 'iterative game of action-response-rejoinder' is in motion.[148] The important point to bear in mind is that political actors in India retain the space to respond to the striking down of legislation (an articulation of judicial rights reasoning) through fundamental rights amendments and Ninth Schedule amendments.

## Response Mechanisms Not Requiring Supermajorities

Even though the Indian Constitution is amongst the more frequently amended codified constitutions in the world,[149] constitutional

---

[146] *Maharao Singhji v. Union of India*, AIR 1981 SC 234, para 21. Of course, the opposite may not be true: the Supreme Court has sympathized with the argument that every violation of the basic structure would also constitute a violation of specific fundamental rights. See *Supreme Court Advocates on Record* (n. 131), para 221 (Khehar J.).

[147] Randhawa herself acknowledges that cases after *Coelho* have exhibited judicial restraint and reopened the parliamentary space under the Ninth Schedule. My argument is that this is a misreading of *Coelho*, as that case itself (along with decisions before it) recognized the space available to Parliament. The approach of the Supreme Court in subsequent cases has been consistent with *Coelho*.

[148] Mehta (n. 36), p. 112.

[149] On an average, the Indian Constitution is amended more than once a year. See Chintan Chandrachud, 'Constitutional Interpretation' in Sujit Choudhry, Madhav Khosla, and Pratap Bhanu Mehta (eds), *The Oxford Handbook of the Indian Constitution* (Oxford University Press 2016), p. 73.

amendments are not always easy to enact. The proliferation of regional political parties[150] coupled with fractured electoral mandates has meant that securing a two-thirds majority in Parliament requires support cutting across party lines. It is unsurprising, then, that Indian governments have also attempted to invoke response mechanisms that do not require parliamentary supermajorities. Amongst these is the strategy of enacting ordinary legislation, or promulgating an 'ordinance', that effectively detracts from the court's judgment.

Ordinances are temporary statutory instruments that may be promulgated by the president at the federal level, or governors at the state level.[151] Quite remarkably, they have the 'same force and effect' as ordinary legislation.[152] Ordinances can only be promulgated when the relevant legislature is not in session, need to be laid before the legislature during its next session, and if not enacted as law, expire within six weeks after the start of the legislative session.[153] Since the president and the governors act on the advice of the Cabinet of Ministers of the relevant (Union or state) government, in practice, it is the relevant government which decides whether or not an ordinance should be enacted. This provides the government with a way of revising judicial decisions that does not even require a simple legislative majority until the ordinance is laid before the relevant legislature.

Legislation or ordinances may either attempt to reject a court's judgment striking down legislation outright, or instead, respond to it in

---

[150] The rise of regional political parties has shifted political power away from the Union to the states. See Manjeet S. Pardesi and Sumit Ganguly, 'The Rise of India and the India-Pakistan Conflict' (2007) 31 Fletcher Forum of World Affairs 131, p. 142.

[151] Shubhankar Dam is the leading scholar on ordinances in India. See Subhankar Dam, 'Constitutional Fiat: Presidential Legislation in India's Parliamentary Democracy' (2010) 24 Columbia Journal of Asian Law 96; Shubhankar Dam, 'President's Legislative Powers in India: Two and a Half Myths' (2011) 11 Oxford University Commonwealth Law Journal 53; Shubhankar Dam, *Presidential Legislation in India: The Law and Practice of Ordinances* (Cambridge University Press 2013); Shubhankar Dam, 'An Institutional Alchemy: India's Two Parliaments in Comparative Perspective' (2014) 40 Brooklyn Journal of International Law (forthcoming), p. 613.

[152] Constitution of India, Arts 123(2), 213(2).

[153] Constitution of India, Arts 123(2), 213(2).

a more nuanced, subtle way. One highly publicized effort to do the former failed to materialize. In *Lily Thomas* v. *Union of India*,[154] the petitioners challenged the constitutional validity of a statutory provision[155] that protected sitting MPs from immediate disqualification on the grounds of conviction for a criminal offence. The statutory provision allowed them a period of three months before the disqualification operated, within which they could appeal against their conviction to a higher court. The Indian Supreme Court struck down the provision on the basis that it discriminated between sitting parliamentarians and potential parliamentarians.[156] Given that this judgment would have affected many existing MPs, the government led by the Congress party swiftly introduced a bill in the Rajya Sabha (Upper House)[157] and later, sought to promulgate an ordinance[158] that would have reversed the effects of the Supreme Court's judgment.[159] However, the government's efforts came to a grinding halt after Rahul Gandhi, the vice president of the Congress party, publicly derided the attempt—much to the embarrassment of the government.[160]

---

[154] AIR 2013 SC 2662.

[155] Representation of the People Act, 1951, section 8(4).

[156] The Supreme Court held that the statutory provision was contrary to Arts 102(1)(e) and 191(1)(e) of the Constitution, which, in its view, required the disqualifications for sitting parliamentarians and potential parliamentarians to be coextensive.

[157] The Representation of the People (Second Amendment and Validation) Bill, 2013.

[158] 'Cabinet Overrules Supreme Court, Clears Ordinance to Protect Convicted MPs' *The Indian Express* (New Delhi, 25 September 2013).

[159] It appears that the bill did not seek to restore the status quo entirely. It did impose some restrictions on the rights of convicted parliamentarians awaiting appeal, but nonetheless went against the substance of the Supreme Court's judgment. For a useful comparison of the bill with the statutory provision that was struck down by the Supreme Court, see PRS Legislative Research, 'Legislative Brief: The Representation of the People (Second Amendment and Validation) Bill 2013' <http://www.prsindia.org/uploads/media/Representation/Brief-%20 RoPA%202nd%20(A)%20Bill%202013.pdf> accessed 13 November 2014.

[160] Gandhi said that the ordinance was 'complete nonsense' and should be 'torn up and thrown away'—see 'Rahul Gandhi: Ordinance on Convicted Politicians Is Complete Nonsense' *The Times of India* (New Delhi, 27 September

In a another prominent case,[161] the Supreme Court struck down a statutory ban imposed by the government of Maharashtra on dance performances in bars, except in certain establishments, such as hotels rated three-stars and above. The Supreme Court adopted two lines of reasoning. First, it was impermissible for the state to distinguish between 'posh' hotels and other establishments seeking licences for dance performances. Second, the ban had proven to be counterproductive, resulting in the unemployment of over 75,000 women, many of whom were forced by circumstances to engage in prostitution. Unhappy with the Court's decision, the state government almost instantly began exploring legal options to override the judgment and decided to pass a bill imposing a blanket ban on dance performances in all bars.[162] The bill effectively sought to reject the judgment outright and failed to address the issues concerning the loss of livelihood and large-scale unemployment that were raised in the Court's judgment. It waits to be tested in a second round of litigation, though it is almost certain to be struck down again.

We do not have the benefit of 'sequel' judgments to these responses that have attempted to reject outright Indian Supreme Court judgments striking down legislation. But all indications are that responses of this nature are, at best, likely merely to postpone the legislature's defeat. This is because, unlike fundamental rights amendments, amendments through ordinary legislation or ordinances encounter the same constitutional hurdles as the original legislation did, and fail to comply with the court's original judgment to an extent that would prompt the court to allow the legislative response to pass constitutional muster. As the Supreme Court said in a slightly different context: 'A court's decision

---

2013). This episode led to widespread calls for the resignation of Prime Minister Manmohan Singh on the basis that his authority had been undercut by a member of his party—see 'Manmohan Singh Should Resign over Rahul Gandhi's Remarks on Ordinance: Shivraj Singh Chouhan' *DNA* (Bhopal, 28 September 2013); 'Rahul's Opposition to Ordinance a "Farce", PM Should Quit: BJP' *The Indian Express* (Allahabad, 2 October 2013).

[161] *State of Maharashtra* v. *Indian Hotel and Restaurants Association*, AIR 2013 SC 2582.

[162] Priyanka Kakodkar, 'Maharashtra Passes Bill Banning Dance Bars' *The Hindu* (Mumbai, 14 June 2014).

must always bind unless the conditions on which it is based are so fundamentally altered that the decision could not have been given in the altered circumstances.'[163] And unlike Ninth Schedule amendments, they are not insulated from judicial review in any way.

However, more nuanced responses through ordinary legislation or ordinances, which take into account the court's reasoning at least partially, stand a better chance in the second round of litigation. For instance, in *Nandini Sundar* v. *State of Chhattisgarh*,[164] the Supreme Court was called upon to decide the constitutional validity of the establishment of a state-sponsored armed civilian vigilante group, going by the name of Salwa Judum, which was intended to counter insurgent militant groups in the state.[165] Untrained and poorly paid tribal youth were appointed as 'special police officers', participating in anti-insurgency operations. It was widely reported that the Salwa Judum itself was involved in widespread human rights violations and atrocities.[166] The Court held that the mobilization of Salwa Judum violated the right to equality before the law under Art. 14 of the Constitution. According to the Court, subjecting untrained, poorly educated members of the tribal communities to the same dangers as the regular state police force was discriminatory. Moreover, the right to life under Art. 21 was breached on account of the fact that, as experience had shown, employing such persons in counter-insurgency operations endangered the lives of others in society. The Court therefore disbanded the Salwa Judum and directed the state to recall firearms provided to its members.[167]

[163] *Shri Privthi Cotton Mills* v. *Broach Borough Municipality*, AIR 1970 SC 193, para 4 (Hidayatullah C.J.).

[164] AIR 2011 SC 2839.

[165] For a brief background of the Naxalite insurgency in the context of which the Salwa Judum was established, see Ramachandra Guha, 'Adivasis, Naxalites and Indian Democracy' (2007) 42 Economic and Political Weekly 3305; Priyanka Vora and Siddhant Buxy, 'Marginalization and Violence: The Story of Naxalism in India' (2011) 6 International Journal of Criminal Justice Sciences 358.

[166] *Nandini Sundar* (n. 164), para 59.

[167] It should be noted, however, that the Supreme Court did not strike down the provisions of primary legislation in this case. In that respect, the case differs from most of the other cases discussed in this chapter. However, the state could have adopted a similar response, had the provisions of the primary legislation been struck down by the Supreme Court to the same effect.

Soon after the judgment, Chhattisgarh's governor promulgated an ordinance[168]—later to become legislation[169]—that sought to address some of the Supreme Court's concerns. This was done by increasing the pay scales of the members of the force, mandating greater training of officers, and providing that members of the force would be eligible to be recruited as part of the regular state police. The state undoubtedly enacted legislation in the hope that it would have allayed the Supreme Court's concerns and would no longer need to disband the force altogether. Presumably, the argument to be made on behalf of the state is that by 'regularizing' the Salwa Judum, the mobilization of the force could no longer be labelled as discriminatory,[170] and that by providing greater training and benefits, its establishment was 'fair, just, and reasonable' and hence would not violate the right to life under Art. 21.[171]

Another way in which the government can respond to judgments striking down legislation is by filing a 'review petition' in the Supreme Court, seeking reconsideration by the Court of its own judgment.[172] At first, it may seem somewhat odd to characterize a review petition as a political response mechanism to the striking down of legislation. But what it effectively constitutes is the government telling the court that in its opinion, the court had got its rights reasoning wrong and should therefore reconsider its judgment. Although review petitions are filed quite frequently, they rarely ever succeed—making it safe to say that this is

---

[168]   Chhattisgarh Auxiliary Armed Police Force Ordinance, 2011.

[169]   Chhattisgarh Auxiliary Armed Police Force Act, 2011.

[170]   The state could argue that they were no longer 'arming civilians because these civilians are now part of a legal force'. See Nandini Sundar, 'Public–Private Partnerships in the Industry of Insecurity' in Zeynep Gambetti and Marcial-Godoy Anativia (eds), *Rhetorics of Insecurity* (NYU Press 2013) 153, pp. 163–4.

[171]   Petitions, claiming that the state government acted in contempt of the Supreme Court's judgment, were filed. See Nandini Sundar, 'For the Love of Justice' *Hindustan Times* (New Delhi, 4 July 2013). The outcome of these proceedings is awaited, but the state's response is more likely to withstand scrutiny than the 'outright rejection' response of Maharashtra following the judgment in *Indian Hotel and Restaurants Association* (n. 161).

[172]   See Constitution of India, Art. 137 and Supreme Court Rules, 1966, Order XL, Rule 1.

a particularly low-yield response mechanism.[173] The Supreme Court only allows review petitions if the petitioner (for our purposes, the government) is able to prove that the court committed an 'error apparent on the face of the record'.[174] This means that the government must not only show that the Court got it wrong, but that its rights reasoning was glaringly and quite obviously mistaken. The Indian Supreme Court has even established a second review petition (or a 'curative petition') jurisdiction, but the burden that needs to be discharged in order to successfully invoke this jurisdiction is even higher.[175]

## Declarations of Incompatibility and Political Responses in the UK

Having considered the space for political responses to striking down of legislation in India, this section analyses the space for political responses to declarations of incompatibility under the HRA. Three central arguments are developed here: First, that the space for political responses to declarations of incompatibility is much narrower than that which is assumed in the existing scholarship. Second, that expected political reactions to declarations of incompatibility are an important element in the courts' process of choosing between the remedial routes offered by sections 3 and 4 of the HRA. Third, that given these and other relevant factors, it is unlikely that governments will (or at the least it is very onerous for governments to) ignore or reject declarations

---

[173] The author has not come across a single case in which the Supreme Court, in exercise of its review jurisdiction, has upheld a provision of primary legislation which was previously struck down. However, there have been cases in which the Supreme Court has reconsidered its decision to reinterpret provisions of primary legislation so as to render them compliant with fundamental rights. Chapter 4 discusses at length one of these cases, *Union of India* v. *Namit Sharma*, (2013) 11 SCALE 85.

[174] See Constitution of India, Art. 137 and Supreme Court Rules 1966, Order XL, Rule 1. See also *Kerala State Electricity Board* v. *Hitech Electrothermics*, [2005] Supp. (2) SCR 517, para 10.

[175] In *Rupa Hurra* v. *Ashok Hurra*, AIR 2002 SC 1771, the case which established the curative petition jurisdiction, the Supreme Court held that the jurisdiction was necessary to 'cure a gross miscarriage of justice' (para 47).

of incompatibility. Nevertheless, the argument that this power may atrophy or be politically neutralized through a constitutional convention over time requires qualification.

Commentators often engage in arguments concerning the 'space' available to the Westminster Parliament and government in responding to declarations of incompatibility without defining that protean word. For the sake of clarity, the word 'space' is defined in two different senses. The first is *decisional* space, which addresses the question about whether Parliament and the government are obliged to accept declarations of incompatibility to begin with. In theory, when a declaration of incompatibility is made, the government has several options available, in terms of its decisional space. This includes (a) announcing that the declaration will be fully addressed; (b) announcing that it will not be addressed at all (such an announcement may take two forms—the government may assert either that the provisions of primary legislation are compliant with Convention rights and that the court was *wrong* to make a declaration of incompatibility, or that the court was *right* in making the declaration of incompatibility, but Parliament nevertheless wishes to retain the legislation); (c) announcing that a declaration of incompatibility will be addressed to a certain extent, but not fully; and (d) completely ignoring or refusing to acknowledge the declaration of incompatibility—part of the reason for which the declaration was considered a 'masterful' way of preserving parliamentary sovereignty.

The second is *remedial* space, which focuses on the legal mode and the substantive means by which a declaration of incompatibility will be addressed. Primary legislation passed by Parliament and remedial executive orders under section 10 of the HRA comprise the methods by which declarations of incompatibility can be addressed. The substantive means by which a declaration of incompatibility may be dealt with concern the options available to Parliament and government in addressing such declarations. For instance, an incompatibility may be addressed by introducing a fresh statutory regime, making changes to the existing system, introducing legislative safeguards, redrawing lines of institutional authority, etc.

The argument that developed in this section is that the remedial space available to Parliament and government is narrower than that assumed by the existing scholarship. Further, the decisional space is limited not only because it is politically difficult to reject declarations of incompatibility, but also because in practice, courts are mindful of expected political reactions to declarations of incompatibility.

## Declarations of Incompatibility in Practice

Section 4(2) of the HRA reads: 'If the court is satisfied that [a provision of primary legislation] ... is incompatible with a Convention right, it may make a declaration of that incompatibility.' As stated in the introduction, section 4 empowers higher courts, when satisfied that a provision of primary legislation is incompatible with a Convention right, to make a declaration of incompatibility. The decision to make a declaration of incompatibility is at the discretion of the court,[176] and the government is entitled to notice and hearing when the court considers making such a declaration.[177] A declaration under section 4 does not affect the 'validity, continuing operation or enforcement' of the provision in respect of which it is given.[178] It is also not binding on the parties to the proceedings in which it is made.[179] One scholar usefully describes it as an 'open remedy', which leaves it formally open to the other branches of government to decide what remedial action to take, if any.[180]

An examination of the declarations of incompatibility that have been made thus far reveals many interesting features. As Appendix B shows, 20 declarations of incompatibility were final declarations that were not overturned on appeal[181] and eight declarations were overturned

---

[176] This discretion is narrow, and courts have rarely found an incompatibility without declaring it—see Helen Fenwick, *Civil Liberties and Human Rights* (4th edn, Routledge 2007), p. 200. However, for an example in which this has been done, see the judgments of Lords Neuberger, Mance, and Wilson in *Nicklinson* (n. 35).

[177] HRA, section 5.

[178] HRA, section 4(6)(a).

[179] HRA, section 4(6)(b).

[180] Aruna Sathanapally, *Beyond Disagreement: Open Remedies in Human Rights Adjudication* (Oxford University Press 2012), pp. 15–16.

[181] The report of the Ministry of Justice to the Joint Committee on Human Rights contains a mistaken figure. This is attributable to the fact that the decision in *R (Hooper and Others) v. Secretary of State for Work and Pensions*, [2002] EWHC 191 (Admin), [2003] 1 WLR 2623, [2005] 1 WLR 1681, is treated as a case in

at an appellate stage. Remarkably, almost all the cases in which declarations of incompatibility were issued concerned marginalized groups at the fringes of society, including patients with mental disorders, illegal immigrants, and international terrorist suspects.[182]

By virtue of its formally non-binding status, the declaration of incompatibility is looked upon by some commentators as the 'unwanted remedy' for parties—litigants in search of an instant remedy urge the court to invoke the interpretive power under section 3 of the HRA, whereas the government seeks judgment that the impugned provisions are, on the face of it, compatible with Convention rights.[183] Although this is the paradigm scenario, it is certainly not true in every case. Section 4 may be the only remedial course sought by the claimant in cases where she acknowledges the need for systemic legal change or recognizes that it is impossible to employ section 3 to interpret the statutory provisions in a Convention-compliant manner.

There have accordingly been cases in which claimants have sought a declaration of incompatibility alone.[184] For instance, in *Nasseri*,[185] the claimant sought a declaration that paragraph 3 of Schedule 3 to the Asylum and Immigration (Treatment of Claimants, etc.) Act, 2004, applied by section 33 of that statute, was incompatible with Art. 3 of the Convention, since it authorized the removal of the claimant to another state without substantive consideration of whether the removal would

---

which the declaration of incompatibility became final. See Ministry of Justice, *Responding to Human Rights Judgments: Report to the Joint Committee on Human Rights on the Government Response to Human Rights Judgments 2012–13* (Cm 8727, 2013), pp. 44, 52. As a matter of fact, the House of Lords saw 'no point' in issuing a declaration of incompatibility in that case, since the impugned statutory provisions had already been repealed ([2005] 1 WLR 1681, para 52).

[182] Sathanapally (n. 180), p. 133.

[183] Justice Gerard Hogan, 'Declarations of Incompatibility, Inapplicability and Invalidity: Rights, Remedies and the Aftermath' (Lecture at the University of Oxford, Oxford, 1 February 2013).

[184] *McR's Application for Judicial Review*, [2002] NIQB 58; *R (M) v. Secretary of State for Health*, [2003] EWHC 1094 (Admin); *R (Nasseri) v. SSHD*, [2008] 2 WLR 523; *R (T) v. Chief Constable of Greater Manchester Police*, [2012] EWHC 147 (Admin).

[185] See *Nasseri* (n. 184).

violate the prohibition on torture, inhuman or degrading treatment or punishment. In that case, it was fairly clear that it would not be possible to read the statutory provisions compatibly with the Convention, and therefore section 3 was ruled out of the picture.

## The Nexus between Declarations of Incompatibility and Expected Responses

It emerges from the case law that the courts have made two kinds of declarations of incompatibility. The first is a declaration that particular statutory provisions are incompatible with one or more Convention rights (specific declarations). For example, in A v. SSHD,[186] the House of Lords declared section 23 of the Anti-Terrorism, Crime and Security Act, 2001 (ATCSCA) to be incompatible with Arts 5 and 14 of the Convention, insofar that it permitted detention of suspected international terrorists in a way that was disproportionate and discriminatory on the grounds of nationality and immigration status. The second category includes declarations that consider a statutory scheme or regime incompatible with Convention rights (general declarations). In International Transport Roth GmbH v. SSHD,[187] the Court of Appeal declared the penalty regime under Part II of the Immigration and Asylum Act, 1999 (which penalized unknowing carriers of illegal entrants into the UK) incompatible with Art. 6 and Art. 1 of the Protocol 1 to the Convention. In that case, Brown L.J. observed that the 'troubling features of the scheme' were 'all inter-linked'.[188]

Sathanapally argues that in some cases, declarations of incompatibility have been made (in preference over rights-compliant interpretations under section 3 of the HRA) in conditions where a complex scheme needs to be developed or difficult policy-based choices need to be made.[189] This, according to her, has been done in order to avoid 'pre-empting changes to the law through the legislative process'[190] by identifying standards by which the incompatibility may be remedied.

---

[186] [2004] UKHL 56 (Belmarsh Prison case).

[187] [2003] QB 728.

[188] International Transport Roth (n. 187), para 66.

[189] Sathanapally (n. 180), p. 98.

[190] Sathanapally (n. 180), p. 98.

The first part of her argument is correct and is discernible in the case of specific declarations and general declarations. In fact, both the cases discussed above were followed by comprehensive changes to legislative policy. The detention scheme for suspected international terrorists under the ATCSA, which was at issue in the Belmarsh Prison case, was replaced by the 'control order' regime under the Prevention of Terrorism Act, 2005. The penalty scheme under the Immigration and Asylum Act, 1999, which was declared incompatible in *International Transport Roth*, was replaced by a new regime for carriers' liability under the Nationality, Immigration and Asylum Act, 2002.

The second part of her argument—that declarations of incompatibility in such cases avoid pre-empting changes to the law—stands on a more tenuous footing. In many cases where declarations of incompatibility are issued, courts nonetheless make obiter dicta suggestions about how remedial law on the issue might be framed and which legal method (primary legislation or a remedial executive order) could be used to bring about that change. These will be referred to as 'soft suggestions'. It is now worth considering a few examples.

In *R (T) v. Chief Constable of Greater Manchester Police*,[191] the primary question before the Court of Appeal was whether the statutory scheme under the Police Act, 1997, which required enhanced criminal record certificates to be issued by the Criminal Records Bureau to those working with people under 18, was compliant with Convention rights. The Court found the scheme disproportionate and declared it incompatible with Art. 8 of the Convention.[192] The Court's observations accompanying the declaration of incompatibility are of particular interest. It first stated that a proportionate scheme that Parliament may seek to introduce would not require the individual consideration of every case. It then endorsed some of the recommendations made by an expert in a recent Criminal Records Review on the manner in which offences should be filtered for the purposes of disclosure. However, the Court stated thereafter that it would not 'prescribe the solution that should be adopted'[193] and that it would be left to Parliament to decide 'what

---

[191] [2013] EWCA Civ 25.
[192] The declaration of incompatibility was later confirmed by the Supreme Court in *R (T) v. Chief Constable of Greater Manchester Police*, [2014] 3 WLR 96.
[193] *T* (n. 192), para 69.

amendments to make'.[194] This disclaimer merely reiterates an obvious fundamental principle: if courts prescribed the specific remedial course that Parliament should pursue, that would overstep their role under the HRA and comprise a usurpation of parliamentary authority.

In *R (Clift)* v. *SSHD*,[195] the House of Lords was faced with determining the compatibility of certain provisions of the Criminal Justice Act, 1991, under which the home secretary retained the power to determine the release on parole of prisoners serving determinate terms of 15 years or more. Since the parties agreed that a Convention-compatible interpretation would not be possible, the Court made a declaration that sections 46(1) and 50(1) of the statute were incompatible with Art. 14 (read with Art. 5). Lord Brown observed that, given the Court's decision, the home secretary needed to consider whether 'the time [had] ... not now come to leave all future decisions as to release on licence exclusively to the Parole Board'.[196]

On comparable lines, in *R (Baiai)* v. *SSHD*,[197] Buxton L.J. in the Court of Appeal issued guidance of what a Convention-compatible regime for controlling sham marriages might look like, after declaring the existing statutory regime incompatible. He observed: 'To be proportionate, a scheme ... must either properly investigate individual cases, or at least show that it has come close to isolating cases that very likely fall into the target category. It must also show that the marriages targeted do indeed make substantial inroads into the enforcement of immigration control.'[198]

To identify a fourth example, in *R (Thompson)* v. *SSHD*,[199] statutory provisions that imposed unreviewable notification requirements on certain classes of sexual offenders under the Sexual Offences Act, 2003 (SOA) were at issue before the Supreme Court. While making a declaration of incompatibility, Lord Phillips clarified that Parliament could impose an 'appropriately high threshold for review' to avoid opening the floodgates to review applications.[200] He confirmed the Court of

---

[194]   *T* (n. 192), para 75.
[195]   [2007] 1 AC 484.
[196]   *Clift* (n. 195), para 69.
[197]   [2008] QB 143.
[198]   *Baiai* (n. 197), para 58.
[199]   [2011] 1 AC 331.
[200]   *Thompson* (n. 199), para 57.

Appeal's prognosis that Parliament could make it difficult to secure a review through controls such as the time at which an application can first be made, the general frequency at which applications can be made, and what applicants need to prove for notification requirements to be varied or discharged.

The soft suggestions made by the courts in these cases have performed one of two distinct functions. In *Clift*, Lord Brown's statement had the effect of acting as a guiding influence on Parliament and government, indirectly indicating that any role for the home secretary in decisions for release on licence might face further compatibility issues. In *T, Baiai,* and *Thompson*, the Court's suggestions operated as assurances that not much needed to be done in order to remedy the incompatibility, clarifying the minimum—an incentive, of sorts, to do so. In *T*, it was suggested that an appropriate system of filtering could be introduced in the criminal record certificates regime, without having to establish a system of individual consideration of every case.

In *Baiai*, the Court of Appeal said that in order to be proportionate, the scheme for controlling sham marriages should 'at least show' that it has come close to isolating cases that are very likely to fall into the target category.[201] In *Thompson*, the Supreme Court's observations constituted an assurance that establishing a high threshold for review of indefinite notification requirements would be compatible with the Convention. These suggestions constitute a form of carrot dangling to the government—'change the law only in a certain way or up to a certain extent, and you have fixed the incompatibility without compromising too much on your original legislative policy'.

In another case before the Court of Appeal, the question was whether sections 72 and 73 of the Mental Health Act, 1983, imposing a 'reverse burden of proof' on patients applying for discharge from detention in hospital, were compatible with the Convention.[202] The Court declared these provisions as incompatible with Arts 5(1) and 5(4) of the Convention. However, Lord Phillips said that only rarely would sections 72 and 73 constrain a Mental Health Review Tribunal to refuse an order of discharge where the continued detention of the

---

[201] *Baiai* (n. 197), para 58.

[202] *R (H) v. London North and East Region Mental Health Review Tribunal,* [2002] QB 1.

patient infringes Art. 5. It was a matter which, in the opinion of the Court, the secretary of state had to bear in mind while determining whether to take remedial action under section 10 of the HRA. Thus, in this decision, the Court made a subtle suggestion about the means that could be employed (in the form of a section 10 remedial order) in responding to the declaration of incompatibility. The incompatibility was later removed through a remedial order under section 10 of the HRA.[203] Thus, whereas in *Clift*, the Court exerted guiding influence on how the incompatibility might be addressed, in this case, it focused on the means by which this might be done.

Some scholars might disagree with this analysis of strategic adjudication under the HRA, citing Baroness Hale's judgment in *R (Wright)* v. *Secretary of State for Health*[204] in support of their argument. Part VII of the Care Standards Act, 2000 established a scheme for the creation and maintenance of a statutory list of persons who were unsuitable to work with vulnerable adults. The relevant question before the Court in this case was whether the provisions of Part VII were compatible with the Convention rights of care workers. After declaring section 82(4) of the Care Standards Act to be incompatible with Arts 6 and 8 of the Convention, Baroness Hale observed that she 'would not make any attempt to suggest ways in which the scheme could be made compatible'.[205]

Two reasons were provided for this. First, the issue involved striking a delicate balance between the rights of care workers and the rights of the vulnerable people with whom they work. The legislature was in a better position to strike this balance in the first instance. Second, the statute in question was likely to be replaced by a fresh statutory regime, and she did not want her judgment to cast light on the incompatibility of that regime. Baroness Hale's reasoning does not constitute a rejection, *in principle*, of courts providing subtle suggestions of how an incompatibility might be remedied. From these observations, it seems clear that it was grounded in the specific circumstances of the case. In fact, her decision to provide two pointed case-specific reasons for not making

---

[203] Mental Health Act 1983 (Remedial) Order, 2001.
[204] [2009] 1 AC 739.
[205] *Wright* (n. 204), para 39.

such suggestions in *Wright* reflects that she may not have exercised the restraint that she did in the absence of those reasons—a conclusion that is confirmed by her opinion in *Nicklinson*.[206]

Strong approval of the practice of courts offering soft suggestions of how incompatibilities with Convention rights may be addressed came from the UK Supreme Court's judgment in *Nicklinson*. The question before the nine-member panel in that case was whether the English law criminalizing assisted suicide[207] violated the right to privacy under Art. 8 of the Convention, and whether a code published by the Director of Public Prosecutions,[208] on the prosecution of those who assisted suicide, was lawful. Three of the judges (Lords Neuberger, Mance, and Wilson) acknowledged that even if the law, as it stood, was incompatible with Convention rights and could not be given a rights-compliant interpretation, no declaration of incompatibility would be issued. Lord Neuberger justified this position on several grounds, one of which was: '[T]his is not a case … where the incompatibility is simple to identify and simple to cure: whether, and if so how, to amend section 2 [of the Suicide Act, 1961] would require much anxious consideration from the legislature; this also suggests that the courts should, as it were, take matters relatively slowly.'[209]

These observations seem to suggest that making soft suggestions to accompany a declaration of incompatibility is part of the prevailing orthodoxy under the HRA. But Lord Neuberger went even further than this, indicating that doing so was not merely a matter of convention, but judicial duty:[210]

> [I]t is for Parliament to decide how to respond to a declaration of incompatibility, and in particular how to change the law. However, at least in a case such as this, the Court would owe a duty, not least to Parliament, not to grant a declaration without having reached and *expressed some idea of how the incompatibility identified by the court could be remedied*. (Emphasis added)

---

[206] See n. 35.

[207] Suicide Act, 1961, section 2(1).

[208] Policy for Prosecutors in Respect of Cases of Encouraging or Assisting Suicide, 2010.

[209] *Nicklinson* (n. 35), para 116.

[210] *Nicklinson* (n. 35), para 127.

Lord Mance's opinion in the same case indicates that the soft suggestions made by courts could be part of a broader project of constitutional collaboration between Parliament and the courts:[211]

> [A declaration of incompatibility] affords to the courts of the U.K., no
> doubt uniquely, an opportunity to collaborate to some extent with
> Parliament in the amendment of the statutory provision which is dis-
> covered to have overridden human rights. I do not regard a degree of
> collaboration as objectionable or, in particular, as compromising judicial
> independence. But a court will be of maximum assistance to Parliament
> in this regard if it *not only identifies the factors which precipitate the infringe-
> ment but articulates options for its elimination*. (Emphasis added)

Baroness Hale was one of the judges who would have made a declaration of incompatibility. In another example of the issuance of soft
suggestions to guide Parliament's remedial options, she prescribed four
requirements that could be put in place to identify people who should
be allowed help to end their lives.[212]

There is an interesting nexus between these soft suggestions
offered by British courts and the legislative history of the HRA. The
Conservative Party had proposed an amendment to what was then
Clause 4 of the Human Rights Bill, which would have required courts
to set out the 'nature and extent' of a declaration of incompatibility 'in
so far as arises from the nature of the case before the court'.[213] As one

---

[211]  *Nicklinson* (n. 35), para 204.

[212]  *Nicklinson* (n. 35), para 314 (Baroness Hale):

> It would not be beyond the wit of a legal system to devise a process for iden-
> tifying those people, those few people, who should be allowed help to end
> their own lives. There would be four essential requirements. They would firstly
> have to have the capacity to make the decision for themselves. They would
> secondly have to have reached the decision freely without undue influence
> from any quarter. They would thirdly have had to reach it with full knowl-
> edge of their situation, the options available to them, and the consequences
> of their decision.... And they would fourthly have to be unable, because of
> physical incapacity or frailty, to put that decision into effect without some
> help from others.

See also Lord Wilson's prescription of factors that courts may be required to
take into account when deciding whether or not to allow assisted suicide in
*Nicklinson* (n. 35), para 205.

[213]  HC Deb 3 June 1998, vol. 313, col. 437.

Conservative MP (who was later to become attorney general during the prime ministership of David Cameron) explained, this amendment was intended to require courts to provide guidelines on how an incompatibility might be complied with.[214] The amendment was rejected on the basis that it would cause confusion and require courts to certify the precise extent of an incompatibility with Convention rights, which was not feasible.[215] Have the soft suggestions offered by courts been prompted by this particular debate in the House of Commons, or are they simply obiter dicta statements that one might expect to see in judgments of this nature? It is very hard to tell, especially since British courts explicitly cite parliamentary debates sparingly.

## The Impact of Section 4 on the Legislative Process

It is also worth flagging the nexus between declarations of incompatibility and expected responses in the case law. In a relatively early decision under the HRA, Lord Nicholls confirmed that extrinsic evidence extending beyond the statute being examined might need to be relied upon in deciding the compatibility of a statutory provision.[216] Evidence of this kind includes ministerial statements in Parliament, explanatory notes published with a statute, government white papers, etc. But extrinsic evidence has performed two different functions in the case law under the HRA. The first is to decide whether a statutory provision may be incompatible to start with, given its 'practical effect' and with regard to the 'complete picture' of rights protection.[217] This would precede the inquiry as to whether the provision may be read compatibly, relying on section 3 of the HRA. The second use of extrinsic evidence, which is more interesting in the context of this chapter, is in the choice between the remedial routes offered by sections 3 and 4 of the HRA after an incompatibility has been found. This use of extrinsic evidence is explored further.

Extrinsic evidence from the political arena and judgments of the Strasbourg Court have influenced the courts' decisions about whether

---

[214] HC Deb 3 June 1998, vol. 313, col. 454 (Dominic Grieve).

[215] HC Deb 3 June 1998, vol. 313, col. 459 (Geoff Hoon).

[216] *Wilson* v. *First County Trust (No 2)*, [2004] 1 AC 816, paras 62–7. See also *R (Morris)* v. *Westminster City Council*, [2006] 1WLR 505, para 39.

[217] *Wilson* (n. 216), para 61.

or not to issue a declaration of incompatibility. For instance, in *Bellinger* v. *Bellinger*,[218] the failure of the Matrimonial Causes Act, 1973 to recognize the marriage of a post-operative male-to-female transsexual with a man was at issue before the House of Lords. Given that the Court found the relevant statutory provision prima facie incompatible with Convention rights, it could have either stretched the meanings of the words 'male' and 'female' under the statute so as to include persons who were born with one sex but had later become, or were regarded as, persons of the opposite sex, or issued a declaration of incompatibility.

In his judgment, Lord Nicholls (with whom all the other judges agreed) took account of a number of factors in choosing to make a declaration of incompatibility. The Strasbourg Court had already determined that the barring of transsexuals from marrying in the UK was unjustified.[219] The Interdepartmental Working Group on Transsexual People had been reconvened in the UK, with a mandate to examine the implications of granting full legal status to transsexual people. The Labour government had expressed a commitment to enact primary legislation allowing transsexuals to marry in such situations. A draft outline bill on the issue was expected to be published in due course. Lord Nicholls avoided the section 3 route and made a declaration of incompatibility, on the premise that these matters were for Parliament to determine, 'especially when the government, in unequivocal terms ... already announced its intention to introduce comprehensive primary legislation on this difficult and sensitive subject'.[220] Thus, the Court kept a close eye on the government's expected response while deciding which remedy to invoke between section 3 and section 4.

Phillipson criticizes the House of Lords' reliance on the expected response from Parliament while determining whether or not to issue a declaration of incompatibility in *Bellinger*.[221] He makes three arguments: First, that the issue should not have been treated as one to be considered either by the Court or by Parliament: both institutions

---

[218] [2003] 2 AC 467.

[219] *Goodwin* v. *UK*, [2002] 35 EHRR 18.

[220] *Bellinger* (n. 218), para 37.

[221] Gavin Phillipson, 'Deference, Discretion, and Democracy in the Human Rights Act Era' (2007) 60 CLP 40, pp. 66–7.

could have played a valuable role in the circumstances. The Court could have reinterpreted the section to the benefit of Mrs Bellinger and Parliament could have introduced a comprehensive legislative scheme thereafter. A similar point is made by Tom Hickman, who posits that invoking section 3 would not have precluded legislative intervention in any event.[222] Second, the Court could not have been certain that the relevant legislation would actually be passed. The proposed legislation could, amongst other things, be outweighed by 'more pressing business' and the government could change its mind.[223] Third, the new legislation may not have been retrospective, leaving the litigant in the same position as before.

These arguments are problematic. Perhaps the House of Lords could have chosen to reinterpret the relevant statutory provisions in *Bellinger*. But exercising this option could itself easily have invoked Phillipson's second concern, as immediate judicial redress could have led to the issue being placed on the political backburner. The Court would justifiably have been concerned that intervention through section 3, as opposed to a 'headline-grabbing'[224] declaration of incompatibility, would risk pushing the matter lower down on the government's priority list, rather than inviting 'prompt parliamentary action'.[225] This also explains the reason owing to which the Court may have consciously eschewed granting immediate redress to Mrs Bellinger, in the apprehension that doing so might alleviate the pressure for systemic change in the law. Further, as Kavanagh argues, the decisional space available to the government for changing its mind was limited, since the government's intention to bring about legal reform was not a purely voluntary decision, but was considered an international law obligation in the light of the judgment from Strasbourg.[226]

---

[222] Tom Hickman, *Public Law after the Human Rights Act* (Hart 2010), p. 92.

[223] Phillipson (n. 221), p. 67. Hickman (n. 222) articulates this concern as well (p. 93).

[224] Danny Nicol, 'The Human Rights Act and the Politicians' (2004) 24 LS 451, p. 469. See also Kent Roach, *The Supreme Court on Trial: Judicial Activism or Democratic Dialogue* (Irwin Law 2001), p. 288.

[225] Hickman (n. 222), p. 93.

[226] Aileen Kavanagh, *Constitutional Review under the UK Human Rights Act* (Cambridge University Press 2009), p. 142.

The case of $M$[227] illustrates a similar point. The important question was whether sections 26 and 29 of the Mental Health Act, 1983, under which a patient could not seek review of the person who was appointed as his/her 'nearest relative' under the statute, were incompatible with Art. 8 of the Convention. According to the statutory definition, the claimant patient's allegedly abusive father would have been her nearest relative. The government accepted the incompatibility. However, citing a number of factors seeking to establish its intention to change the law, it argued that a formal declaration of incompatibility was unnecessary. These factors included a draft bill to amend the law, statements of MPs, a statement by a minister in the Department of Health, and a friendly settlement entered into by the government in a case[228] that was pending in the Strasbourg Court, in which it committed to amending the law.

Highlighting that immediate change was not forthcoming and that it would be difficult to 'predict with accuracy when or how' the incompatibility would be rectified, Kay J. made a declaration of incompatibility.[229] It is instructive to notice from the tenor of the judgment of the Administrative Court that the fact that the incompatibility would, in principle, be remedied was beyond question. What motivated the Court to make the declaration of incompatibility was, inter alia, that the remedy was not immediately forthcoming. In other words, the Court looked upon its declaration as a further catalyst for a remedy that was already in the pipeline.

A similar justification was partially the basis for the House of Lords' decision to make a declaration of incompatibility in *R (Anderson)* v. *SSHD*.[230] The only question in that case was whether the Home Secretary's power to set the 'tariff'[231] for mandatory life sentence prisoners was compatible with Art. 6 of the Convention. Mindful of the two recent Strasbourg Court decisions[232] declaring the power incompatible

---

[227] See *M* (n. 184).

[228] *JT* v. *UK*, 2000 ECHR 133.

[229] *M* (n. 184), para 19.

[230] [2003] 1 AC 837; Kavanagh (n. 226), pp. 133–4.

[231] How long a prisoner sentenced to life should actually spend in prison, given the aims of retribution and deterrence.

[232] *Stafford* v. *UK*, (2002) 35 EHRR 1121; *Benjamin and Wilson* v. *UK*, (2002) 36 EHRR 1.

and evidence from parliamentary debates that these decisions would be acted upon,[233] the Court chose to make a declaration of incompatibility.

It should be clarified that the argument developed thus far does not necessarily imply that courts will issue a declaration of incompatibility whenever the government seeks one in preference to a Convention-compatible interpretation under section 3 of the HRA. The case of *SSHD* v. *MB*[234] offers a good example. The case concerned the compatibility of the 'non-derogating control order' regime under the Prevention of Terrorism Act, 2005 with Art. 6 of the Convention. Finding the regime incompatible, the majority chose to interpret the relevant statutory provisions in a Convention-compliant manner, in spite of the plea of the Secretary of State that section 4 be invoked in preference to section 3. As Baroness Hale's opinion demonstrates, the Court was clearly concerned that a declaration of incompatibility would not actually be positively addressed.[235] A finding that the regime was non-compliant with Art. 6 would likely prompt the government to derogate from that provision of the Convention, thereby permitting it to conduct the proceedings in a way that it 'knew to be incompatible'.[236] Thus, the majority chose section 3 over section 4 in the belief that the government's remedial preference was not backed by a genuine commitment to address the incompatibility with Convention rights.

Some commentators are troubled by courts' application of consequentialist reasoning in deciding whether or not to make a declaration of incompatibility. Jowell, for instance, says that judges should not be influenced by the fact that Parliament may disregard their pronouncements.[237] But this plea seems far removed from reality—judicial consciousness about the aftermath of decisions is so intrinsic to the judicial process that if judges are to take criticism for doing so seriously, they would likely continue to take political reactions into account without actually saying that they do so. As Justice Hogan of the High Court of

[233] *Anderson* (n. 230), para 45 (Lord Steyn).

[234] [2008] 1 AC 440.

[235] Aileen Kavanagh, 'Special Advocates, Control Orders and the Right to a Fair Trial' (2010) 73 MLR 836, p. 851.

[236] *MB* (n. 234), para 73.

[237] Jeffrey Jowell, 'Judicial Deference: Servility, Civility or Institutional Capacity?' [2003] PL 592.

Ireland argues extrajudicially, judges consider it important to be able to have some control on the aftermath of their decisions, so as to avoid 'social and political chaos', and arrive at a consensus in favour of a solution that avoids controversy.[238] Judges' willingness to make findings of incompatibility is hampered by the possibility that uncontrolled or devastating consequences would follow their decisions. Some prominent theories of judicial decision-making also posit that judges take into account the extent to which political actors are willing and able to overcome judicial decisions.[239]

In the context of the HRA, explanations for making declarations of incompatibility whose consequences are predictable extend beyond the avoidance of chaos and promotion of consensus building. Judges could well be deeply conscious of preserving the legitimacy and authoritative nature of the declaration of incompatibility.[240] This argument rests on the fear that ignorance or rejection of a few declarations of incompatibility would open the floodgates or establish an adverse constitutional precedent. Another explanation could be that judges are anxious for justice to be served to individual litigants in cases under the HRA. Therefore, when a remedy through government is not imminent, they would be inclined to invoke section 3. However, this explanation is less persuasive, since legislation addressing declarations of incompatibility may not be retrospective and does not necessarily benefit the litigants in the case.[241] In any event, it is discernible that courts in the UK have

---

[238]   Hogan (n. 183). See also Kavanagh (n. 235), p. 135.

[239]   Christine Bateup, 'Reassessing the Dialogic Possibilities of Weak Form Bills of Rights' (2009) 32 Hastings International & Comparative Law Review 529. As Bateup argues, judges 'adjust their rulings' in anticipation of the responses of political actors. Friedman also discusses the literature on the influence of anticipated political reactions on judicial decision-making, Barry Friedman, 'The Politics of Judicial Review' (2005) 84 Texas Law Review 257. Vermeule describes this as the 'law of anticipated reactions', Adrian Vermeule, 'The Atrophy of Constitutional Powers' (2012) 32 OJLS 421. See also Lee Epstein and Jack Knight, *The Choices Justices Make* (CQ Press 1998), p. 82; Georg Vanberg, *The Politics of Constitutional Review in Germany* (Cambridge University Press 2005), pp. 14, 175.

[240]   Bateup (n. 239); Kavanagh (n. 226), p. 136.

[241]   Phillipson (n. 221).

made decisions on whether to issue declarations of incompatibility with a close eye on expected political consequences.

This argument should not be taken to mean that Parliament is unable to reject a judicial invocation of the interpretive obligation under section 3 of the HRA.[242] It may do so, for example, by re-enacting the statute in the same terms or amending the statutory provision to clarify its meaning. The important difference between section 3 and section 4 is that in the case of the former, the burden of legislative inertia is on Parliament.[243] In other words, the government needs to provide the impetus for change through Parliament and would have to bear the additional social and political costs associated with doing so. But when a declaration of incompatibility is made, simply doing nothing is enough to retain the incompatibility on the books.[244] Other things being equal, it is easier to ignore, or at the least, delay responses to, declarations of incompatibility than override Convention-compatible interpretations under section 3.[245]

In both situations, the government would need to pay the political price (including the loss of public confidence, a breach of international

[242] Ian Leigh and Roger Masterman, *Making Rights Real: The Human Rights Act in Its First Decade* (Hart 2008), p. 116; Stephen Gardbaum, 'Reassessing the New Commonwealth Model of Constitutionalism' (2010) 8 International Journal of Constitutional Law 167; Timothy Endicott, *Administrative Law* (Oxford University Press 2011), p. 83.

[243] Bateup (n. 239). Phillipson (n. 221) fails to consider this point in his criticism of courts' consideration of expected political responses to declarations of incompatibility. Gardbaum (n. 242), p. 194, makes the same point in different language, stating that section 3 'places the default position in favour of the courts'.

[244] Roach (n. 224), p. 63; Kahana (n. 89); Michael J. Perry, 'Protecting Human Rights in a Democracy: What Role for Courts?' (2003) 38 Wake Forest Law Review 635; David Feldman, 'Standards of Review and Human Rights in English Law' in David Feldman (ed.), *English Public Law* (Oxford University Press 2009), p. 317.

[245] The only reason why overriding an interpretation under section 3 could be easier for the government is because declarations of incompatibility usually receive wider and more prominent coverage in the media, and thus funnel public pressure more effectively. Equally, however, it could be argued that the more modest press coverage of section 3 interpretations would make them less likely to be high on the political agenda in the first place.

obligations under the Convention, and the possibility of an adverse ruling from Strasbourg)[246] for rejecting the court's understanding of Convention rights. In the case of the declaration of incompatibility, however, it would need to bear the additional costs accompanying the introduction of fresh legislation. As Michael Perry posits, there is a presumption (in the form of the burden of legislative inertia), carrying institutional force, in favour of the status quo of the law.[247] Those seeking to change the law would be tasked with overcoming that presumption.

Further, the parties contending that statutory provisions should be read in a Convention-compatible manner are certain to benefit from the reinterpretation of a statutory provision under section 3, and this benefit is unlikely to be withdrawn by subsequent legislation.[248] Thus, courts can invoke section 3 with the knowledge that Parliament is virtually powerless, even with the enactment of fresh legislation, to deprive benefits conferred upon specific parties by the court.

## Responses to Declarations of Incompatibility

### The Limited Decisional Space and Remedial Space of Parliament and Government

Judges have been quite conscious in asserting the formal position under the HRA—that the consequences of declarations of incompatibility are political rather than legal. As Lord Scott put it in the Belmarsh Prison case, the court only draws attention to the incompatibility and provides ammunition to people to agitate for change through the democratic process.[249] In another case, Kay J. observed that it was for the 'the

---

[246] Mark Tushnet, *Weak Courts, Strong Rights: Judicial Review and Social Welfare Rights in Comparative Constitutional Law* (Princeton University Press 2009), pp. 30–1.

[247] Michael J. Perry, *Morality, Politics and Law* (Oxford University Press 1988), pp. 176, 304.

[248] Paul Gewirtz, 'Legislative Supervision of Court Cases' (International Symposium on Judicial Fairness and Supervision, Beijing, January 2004).

[249] Belmarsh Prison case (n. 186), para 145. See also the opinion of Baroness Hale in the same case, para 220.

Government to decide what, if anything, to do' about a declaration of incompatibility.[250]

However, in practice, as Appendix B indicates, responses to declarations of incompatibility have been made either through remedial orders or primary legislation in almost every instance. Amongst the 20 declarations that attained finality, 13 were remedied through primary legislation. Amendments were largely made either by introducing special legislation or by inserting provisions into a bill that was already before Parliament at the time.[251] The fast-track remedial power under section 10 of the HRA was invoked on three occasions.[252] In two cases, the impugned provisions had already been amended by primary legislation before the filing of the claim.[253] One final declaration of incompatibility, concerning the restrictions on the voting rights of prisoners, is still under consideration.[254] Even in this case, the Conservative–Liberal Democrat coalition government introduced a draft bill for pre-legislative scrutiny, in which two out of three options laid out by the government sought to purge the incompatibility, while the third restated the existing ban.[255]

Governments across the political spectrum have focused more on the imperative question of *how* to act, rather than whether to take any remedial action to begin with.[256] Thus, since the enactment of

[250]   *M* (n. 184), para 17.

[251]   Vernon Bogdanor, *The New British Constitution* (Hart 2009), p. 61.

[252]   *H* (n. 202); *Baiai* (n. 197); *Thompson* (n. 199). On one occasion—to address the Court of Appeal's judgment in *T* (n. 191)—a declaration of incompatibility was remedied by executive order, The Police Act 1997 (Criminal Record Certificates: Relevant Matters) (Amendment) (England and Wales) Order, 2013.

[253]   *R (Wilkinson) v. Inland Revenue Commissioners*, [2005] 1 WLR 1681; *Wright* (n. 212).

[254]   *Smith* v. *Scott*, [2007] CSIH 9. In *R (Chester)* v. *Secretary of State for Justice*, [2010] EWCA Civ 1439, the Court of Appeal declined to make another declaration of incompatibility on the same issue, highlighting that the Court had no role to 'sanction government' for delays in responding to declarations of incompatibility.

[255]   Ministry of Justice, *Voting Eligibility (Prisoners) Draft Bill* (Cm 8499, 2012).

[256]   Sathanapally (n. 180), p. 131.

the HRA, the norm during the two Labour governments and the Conservative–Liberal Democrat coalition government has been to positively address declarations of incompatibility.[257] Parliamentary debates are also replete with statements to the effect that the government is generally expected to amend the law in some way following a declaration of incompatibility.[258] This is particularly the case after all avenues of appeal are exhausted. A peer in the House of Lords put the point quite succinctly: 'Our constitutional arrangements are such that when the highest court of the land identifies an incompatibility with the European Convention on Human Rights, the Government of the day, whoever is in power, take remedial action.'[259]

Considerable academic debate has surfaced about whether the government has any remedial space in responding to declarations of incompatibility. Some scholars claim that in elongating the response time for legislative response to a declaration and through the strategic technique of making minor alterations without fully addressing the declaration, the legislature has considerable remedial space in engaging with such declarations.[260] While conceding that 'judicial reasoning leading to a finding of incompatibility' will imply that 'certain legislative options are precluded', others contend that Parliament will have 'room for legislative manoeuvre' in deciding how to remedy an incompatibility.[261] But none of them has considered the extent to which

---

[257] The Labour Government addressed 15 declarations of incompatibility, whereas the Conservative–Liberal Democrat coalition government addressed four declarations of incompatibility. See Appendix B.

[258] See, for example, HL Deb 11 April 2002, vol. 633, col. 604 (Lord Clement-Jones): 'The court having made its decision [issuing a declaration of incompatibility] in March last year in Regina (H) v. Mental Health Review Tribunal, North and East London Region, it was right to remove the requirement that the burden of proof should be placed upon the patient'; HL Deb 18 December 2003, vol. 655, col. 1301 (Lord Carlile, Lord Bishop of Winchester); HC Deb 28 February 2005, vol. 431, cols 778–9 (Mr Denham): 'The law that we would have to renew in March, but which we cannot because of the Law Lords' judgment, applies solely to foreign nationals.'

[259] HL Deb 5 July 2012, vol. 738, col. 875 (Baroness Stowell of Beeston).

[260] Sathanapally (n. 180), pp. 149–52.

[261] Kavanagh (n. 226), p. 281. Similarly, David Feldman argues that Parliament retains the 'political freedom' to fashion a response to declarations

judicial reasoning does in fact narrow the options of Parliament and government.

Commentators have failed to factor in other important elements that limit the remedial space available to the government in responding to declarations of incompatibility. To begin with, such declarations are sometimes made in respect of a narrow, transitional group of cases where the law has already been changed prospectively. This is what happened in *Clift*, which was discussed earlier. In these situations, the government is deprived of the discretion of deciding whether a remedy should be retrospective, since the failure to adopt a retrospective remedy would constitute ignorance of the declaration and bear attendant political costs.[262]

Further, it was argued earlier that declarations of incompatibility are accompanied by soft suggestions explaining how the incompatibility might be remedied. These suggestions, as already expounded upon, could perform three distinct functions. First, they may exercise a guiding influence on the government by narrowing the government's substantive options in deciding how to remedy the incompatibility, limiting its remedial space. The House of Lords' judgment in *Clift* was used to demonstrate this.

Second, they may constitute an incentive to remedy the incompatible provisions, by indicating that only limited change is required to remove the incompatibility. Such declarations operate as assurances to Parliament that an amendment providing a certain floor of rights protection is all that is required to comply with the court's decision. Here, Parliament is not prevented from providing for a higher level of rights protection, but would not be *required* to do so in order to 'fix' the incompatibility. Thus, the remedial space available to Parliament and government for deciding the level of rights protection that should be granted in order to eliminate the incompatibility is effectively attenuated.

---

of incompatibility. See David Feldman, 'The Impact of the Human Rights Act 1998 on English Public Law' (Lecture at BIICL, London, 7 October 2005).

[262] It should be noted, however, that the associated political costs in such cases might be slightly lower than in cases where laws in force are declared incompatible, since in these situations, the existing law is not incompatible with Convention rights.

Political developments following the Supreme Court's declaration of incompatibility in *Thompson* confirm this claim. The incompatibility identified in that case was rectified through a remedial order,[263] which incorporated the Court's suggestions of imposing a high threshold for review for those subjected to indefinite notification requirements under the SOA. It appears that the soft suggestions made by the Supreme Court in this case enabled the Conservative Party–led coalition government to address the incompatibility without alienating an important part of their political constituency. As the parliamentary under-secretary of state for the home department said in the House of Commons:[264]

> We have also brought forward the draft Sexual Offences Act 2003 (Remedial) Order 2012, which will ensure that strict rules are put in place and a robust review is carried out on a case-by-case basis before any sex offender placed on the register for life can be removed. This will remove the legislative incompatibility identified by the Supreme Court in the case.... We are clear that we have developed a process that is robust, workable and makes public protection a central factor, while at the same time preventing sex offenders being able to waste taxpayers' money by repeatedly challenging our laws. Sex offenders who continue to pose a risk will remain on the register and will do so for life if necessary.

The minimalist approach of the government to addressing the incompatibility was exemplified by the then home secretary's, Theresa May's, statement to Parliament that the government would make the 'minimum possible changes to the law' that would be necessary to comply with the Supreme Court's judgment.[265]

This claim was also confirmed by developments following the Court of Appeal's judgment in *T*.[266] The secretary of state amended the statutory provisions declared incompatible by an executive instrument,[267]

---

[263] Sexual Offences Act 2003 (Remedial) Order, 2012.

[264] HC Deb 5 March 2012, vol. 541, cols 52WS, 53WS (James Brokenshire).

[265] Alan Travis, 'David Cameron Condemns Supreme Court Ruling on Sex Offenders' *The Guardian* (London, 16 February 2011). See also HL Deb 5 July 2012, cols 875–6 (Baroness Stowell of Beeston).

[266] See n. 191.

[267] The Police Act 1997 (Criminal Record Certificates: Relevant Matters) (Amendment) (England and Wales) Order, 2013. This instrument was made in spite of the fact that an appeal against the Court of Appeal's judgment was pending in the Supreme Court. The Supreme Court later confirmed the declaration of incompatibility in *T* (n. 192).

based on the suggestions of the Court of Appeal that an appropriate filtering mechanism, which would not require the individual consideration of every case, could be introduced.[268] Once again, the soft suggestions offered by the Court made it more politically plausible for the government to address the incompatibility, whilst assuring their constituents that 'important safeguards for public protection' would be maintained.[269] While discussing the amendments to the law in Parliament, the under-secretary of state for the Ministry of Justice thus emphasized the government's 'commitment to maintaining public protection and national security'.[270] The claim that soft suggestions have incentivized addressing declarations of incompatibility remains politically untested in relation to the other case in which such suggestions were made: *Baiai*. A soft assurance of this nature accompanied Buxton L.J.'s declaration of incompatibility in the Court of Appeal. However, the declaration of incompatibility was varied in appeal to the House of Lords.[271]

Third, courts may on some occasions even go to the extent of suggesting the means by which an incompatibility may be addressed. The case of *H*[272] provides a good example of this. The Court of Appeal's subtle suggestion of making a remedial order was acted upon by the secretary of state.

These arguments indicate that the remedial space available to Parliament and the government varies, both in terms of content and form, and is often more limited than one might expect. It would be going much too far to say that Parliament has 'unfettered discretion'[273] to determine the manner of its response to a declaration of incompatibility. These soft suggestions should not be mistaken as exerting an

---

[268] The Court's suggestions were based on a Criminal Records Review. See Sunita Mason, 'A Common Sense Approach: A Review of the Criminal Records Regime in England and Wales—Report on Phase 1' <https://www.gov.uk/government/uploads/system/uploads/attachment_data/file/97894/common-sense-approach.pdf> accessed 11 November 2014.

[269] HC Deb 20 May 2013, cols 3–4 (Jeremy Wright).

[270] HC Deb 20 May 2013, cols 3–4 (Jeremy Wright).

[271] *R (Baiai) v SSHD* [2009] 1 AC 287.

[272] See n. 202.

[273] Roger Masterman, 'Interpretations, Declarations and Dialogue: Rights Protection under the Human Rights Act and Victorian Charter of Human Rights and Responsibilities' [2009] PL 112.

insuperable normative force on the government. They are obiter dicta statements, but function as conduits through which broader messages are conveyed from the judiciary to Parliament.[274] The suggestions, along with a failure to adhere to them would, however, like (but to a lesser extent than) the declaration of incompatibility, form an important part of the political discourse. As Tushnet argues, in weak-form systems, legislative deliberations are 'informed but not controlled' by what courts have said, since the legislature recognizes that courts have some advantages over them in constitutional interpretation.[275] Evidence from parliamentary debates about declarations of incompatibility also indicates that MPs not only consider the bare text of these declarations, but also judicial observations accompanying them.[276] Judicial observations are sometimes even cited or paraphrased to understand the scope of the incompatibility, as well as the possible options to remedy it.[277]

Closely related to these points is the fact that the Westminster Parliament is conscious of the possibility of sequel judgments resulting in further declarations of incompatibility, in the event that legislation addressing an earlier declaration does not do so adequately. While discussing the government's proposed response to the judgment in the Belmarsh Prison case (declaring provisions of the ATCSA incompatible with Convention rights), some MPs expressed scepticism about whether the response would itself withstand future judicial scrutiny. As

[274] Danny Nicol, 'Law and Politics after the Human Rights Act' [2006] PL 722.

[275] Mark Tushnet, 'Weak-form Judicial Review and "Core" Civil Liberties' (2006) 41 Harvard Civil Rights–Civil Liberties Law Review 1. See also Tom Hickman's analysis of the political response following the judgment in Belmarsh Prison case (n. 186), in which the political debate 'took place within' the parameters of principle set out in the judges' speeches in Hickman (n. 222), p. 345.

[276] HL Deb 3 February 2003, vol. 644, col. 3 (Lord Filkin); HC Deb 28 March 2003, vol. 402, col. 604 (Tony Clarke).

[277] A good example of this is from the debates following the declaration of incompatibility made by the House of Lords in Bellinger (n. 218). See HL Deb 13 January 2004, vol. 657, col. 5GC (Lord Filkin); HL Deb 13 January 2004, vol. 657, col. 13GC (Lord Moynihan); HL Deb 29 January 2004, vol. 656, col. 365 (Lord Filkin).

Lord Donaldson, the former Master of the Rolls, observed in the House of Lords:[278]

> If the Government are to persist [with its current response] ... in the very near future someone will ask the courts to set the matter aside. That will go to the House of Lords, no doubt, where I should be very surprised if the Law Lords did not say, 'No—this won't do.' Where they will draw the line, I do not know, but it will not be where the Government have drawn it.

It thus becomes sensible for a government seeking to avoid a second declaration of incompatibility to address the (original) declaration based on the soft suggestions of the court making it, as a kind of insurance policy against future challenge. So far, the only sequel judgment to have resulted in a declaration of incompatibility was in *Royal College of Nursing* v. *SSHD*,[279] where the Administrative Court declared that provisions of a statute[280] that replaced a law that was declared incompatible,[281] as itself being incompatible with Convention rights.

These arguments are consistent with the 'court-centric' approach to pre-enactment political rights review under the HRA in practice. Ministerial statements of compatibility under section 19 tend to focus on whether proposed legislation will withstand challenge in domestic courts and the Strasbourg Court as opposed to whether such legislation is, in the government's own view, compatible with Convention rights.[282] The Cabinet Office's Guide to Making Legislation also requires the relevant government departments to 'consider any risk of legal challenge and ensure that the way the bill is drafted reduces the risk as far as possible'.[283] Further, a memorandum setting out the impact of a bill on Convention rights, containing a 'frank assessment by the department of the vulnerability to challenge in legal and policy terms', is required to be provided to the Parliamentary Business and

---

[278] HL Deb 1 March 2005, vol. 670, col. 175 (Lord Donaldson).

[279] [2011] PTSR 1193.

[280] Safeguarding Vulnerable Groups Act, 2006, Schedule 3, Part 2, para 8.

[281] Care Standards Act, 2000, section 82(4). See *Wright* (n. 204).

[282] Janet Hiebert, 'Parliamentary Bills of Rights: An Alternative Model?' (2006) 69 MLR 7.

[283] Cabinet Office, *Guide to Making Legislation* (June 2012), p. 98.

Legislation Committee before the bill can be approved for introduction or publication in draft.[284]

## The Strasbourg Court Dimension

One important aspect influencing political responses to declarations of incompatibility remains to be discussed. Section 2(1) of the HRA requires courts in the UK determining questions in relation to Convention rights to take Strasbourg Court jurisprudence into account. British courts have adopted the 'mirror' principle in their consideration of case law of the Strasbourg Court. According to this principle, which was first articulated in *R (Alconbury Developments)* v. *Secretary of State*[285] and has been cited in several cases thereafter,[286] a strong presumption—that clear and constant Strasbourg jurisprudence will be followed—operates.

This presumption can be displaced only for very good reasons,[287] for instance, if the Strasbourg decision is 'fundamentally at odds with the distribution of powers under the British constitution'[288] or misunderstands some aspect of English law.[289] The transformation of Convention rights into domestic law is meant to function as a floor rather than a ceiling: whereas domestic courts can provide augmented rights protection, they cannot fall below the minimum standard set by Strasbourg.[290] As Lord Bingham famously put it, the national courts would 'keep pace with the Strasbourg jurisprudence as it evolves over time: no more, but certainly no less'.[291]

The failure to address a domestic declaration of incompatibility could result in a case being taken to the Strasbourg Court, with a high

---

[284]  Cabinet Office (n. 283), p. 92.

[285]  [2003] 2 AC 295.

[286]  See, for example, *R (Al Skeini)* v. *Secretary of State for Defence*, [2008] 1 AC 153; *Pinnock* v. *Manchester, City Council* [2011] 2 AC 104.

[287]  Philip Sales, 'Strasbourg Jurisprudence and the Human Rights Act: A Response to Lord Irvine' [2012] PL 253.

[288]  *Alconbury Developments* (n. 285), para 76 (Lord Hoffman).

[289]  *R* v. *Lyons*, [2003] 1 AC 976 [46].

[290]  Feldman (n. 261).

[291]  *R (Ullah)* v. *Special Adjudicator*, [2004] UKHL 26, para 20.

probability that the Court would find a breach of Convention rights.[292] This is because of the fact that the Strasbourg Court accords a margin of appreciation to decisions of national authorities, including courts. Thus, the political sanction underlying a declaration of incompatibility transforms into a legal one through the Strasbourg Court,[293] and the UK falls under an international obligation to amend its domestic law. As one MP had put it (rather bluntly) in the House of Lords: 'We have no choice but to respond to a judgment of the European Court of Human Rights. We have obligations under human rights law.'[294] The possibility of an aggrieved claimant making an application to the Strasbourg Court makes the declaration of incompatibility a potent remedy—a matter which Chapter 5 discusses at length .

## A Constitutional Convention or Atrophy of Constitutional Power?

Has the expectation that Parliament or the government of the day will address declarations of incompatibility transformed into a constitutional convention? Sir Ivor Jennings famously set out a (now familiar) three-part test for establishing that a practice had transformed into a constitutional convention. The three necessary conditions are: the existence of a precedent, belief on the part of political actors that they are bound by the precedent, and a reason for the rule.[295] Jaconelli added a self-evident, but sometimes overlooked, fourth condition: that the rule must be constitutional in character (that is, it must 'regulate the manner in which the business of government is to be conducted').[296]

Many scholars believe that a convention of compliance with declarations of incompatibility is emerging, but has not yet fully

---

[292] Anthony Lester and Kate Beattie, 'Human Rights and the British Constitution' in Jeffrey Jowell and Dawn Oliver (eds), *The Changing Constitution* (6th edn, Oxford University Press 2007), p. 59.

[293] Nicol (n. 274).

[294] HL Deb 29 January 2004, vol. 656, col. 383 (Baroness Buscombe).

[295] Ivor Jennings, *The Law and the Constitution* (5th edn, University of London Press 1959), pp. 134–6.

[296] Joseph Jaconelli, 'The Nature of Constitutional Convention' (1999) 19 LS 24.

crystallized.[297] The Strasbourg Court, tasked with determining whether the declaration of incompatibility was an effective domestic remedy for the purposes of Art. 35(1) of the Convention,[298] adopted a similar position in *Burden* v. *UK*.[299] Although there is no legal obligation to address declarations of incompatibility, the Court observed that it was possible that in the future, evidence of a 'long-standing and established practice' of giving effect to declarations of incompatibility 'might be sufficient to persuade [it] ... of the effectiveness of the procedure'.[300] The implication is that while the practice has a constitutional character (since it has deep implications on the functioning of the government) and is supported by underlying reasons (varying from the special status of courts in determining the meaning of Convention rights to the protection of minorities), sufficient precedent is not yet available and political actors' beliefs on the binding nature of this expectation are not firmly developed.

Adrian Vermeule argues that some constitutional powers tend to 'atrophy' over time.[301] Powers that remain unexercised for long periods gradually become un-exercisable, as their exercise would seem to run contrary to the rules of the political game. The other way of looking at his argument is that on account of political precedent heuristics, a constitutional convention against the use of such powers develops as the power falls into desuetude. In the context of the declaration

---

[297] Feldman (n. 261); K.D. Ewing, 'The Continuing Futility of the Human Rights Act' [2008] PL 668; Kavanagh (n. 226), p. 289; Vermeule (n. 239). Writing in 2010, Gardbaum (n. 242), p. 197, argued that it was too early to say that the fact that Parliament had not ignored a declaration of incompatibility meant that section 4 of the HRA was 'practically irrelevant'.

[298] Article 35(1) of the Convention reads: 'The [Strasbourg] Court may only deal with the matter after all domestic remedies have been exhausted, according to the generally recognised rules of international law, and within a period of six months from the date on which the final decision was taken.'

[299] (2007) 44 EHRR 51.

[300] *Burden* (n. 299), para 39. However, it should be noted that since conventions are rooted in practice, a judicial declaration of their existence is not decisive.

[301] Vermeule (n. 239). The author of this book benefited from attending the Oxford–Harvard teleconference in April 2012, at which a previous draft of this paper was discussed.

of incompatibility, he claims that Parliament's compliance may 'unintentionally be preparing the ground for a day in which Parliament will be thought to violate a constitutional convention if it refuses to comply'.[302]

Vermeule provides the following examples to demonstrate his argument: the royal veto in the UK, the notwithstanding clause under section 33 of the Canadian Charter, the 'disallowance' power (also of Canadian heritage), the power to 'pack' the Supreme Court, and the Congressional power to impeach executive officers (both from the US). However, it is not merely coincidental that all the examples he gives refer to powers where the burden of legislative inertia is on the body that seeks to exercise its constitutional power. Thus, for instance, in order to invoke the notwithstanding clause under section 33 of the Canadian Charter, the relevant legislature needs to do so expressly through statute. Similarly, to pursue a 'court-packing' agenda, the US Congress would need to assemble the political capital to pass appropriate legislation. In these examples, the position after the power has atrophied is the default case. As explained earlier, the declaration of incompatibility is subtly different. Under the HRA, the default case is that primary legislation remains valid *unless* the government or Parliament addresses the declaration that it is incompatible with Convention rights.

Evaluating the atrophy of powers where the burden of legislative inertia is on the legislature or government is fairly straightforward and can be expressed in terms of a binary. Hence, in the case of the notwithstanding clause and the court-packing power, we can say that required legislation has either been enacted or not. The prisoners' voting rights story following the declaration of incompatibility in *Smith*[303] demonstrates that this is not quite as easy to discern with the declaration of incompatibility. Eight years after the Scottish Registration Appellate Court declared section 3 of the Representation of People Act, 1983 incompatible with Art. 3 of Protocol 1 to the Convention, the incompatibility remains on the statute books. In some official statements, governments have expressed an intention to remove the

[302] Vermeule (n. 239), p. 443.
[303] See n. 254.

incompatibility.[304] However, individuals in government, including the prime minister,[305] have expressed strong disagreement with the decision.

How is such a case to be considered in the context of a constitutional convention or atrophy analysis? If we were to argue that only express rejection of a declaration of incompatibility constitutes a refusal to comply, then this would be treated as compliance. On the other hand, the incompatible law still remains the law of the land. The evaluation of compliance with declarations of incompatibility is not conducive to a binary analysis, but fits more comfortably with the idea of a gradient, requiring a nuanced approach.

It may, of course, be possible for a constitutional convention to develop to the effect that all declarations of incompatibility will be addressed by the government or Parliament. The important point to be made is that by virtue of the unique design of the HRA, the crystalliza-tion of a constitutional convention that declarations of incompatibility will be addressed is likely to be a slower and more arduous process than it would be for powers where the burden of legislative inertia is on the body possessing the power. Two factors justify this argument: First, it is simpler to exercise a power by maintaining the status quo rather than to exercise a power by assembling the political capital required to alter it. Second, it is difficult to evaluate the atrophy of the power to reject declarations of incompatibility in binary terms, thereby neces-sitating a longer frame of reference before any definitive constitutional conclusion can be drawn.

Thus, the following conclusions emerge from the foregoing analysis. Declarations of incompatibility are very likely to be remedied by the government or Parliament. Courts sometimes issue a declaration of incompatibility where extrinsic evidence and Strasbourg Court deci-sions make it fairly clear that the declaration will be acted upon. In such cases, the government is in any event likely to address the incom-patibility, limiting its decisional space. On other occasions, courts

---

[304] C.R.G. Murray, 'We Need to Talk: "Democratic Dialogue" and the Ongoing Saga of Prisoner Disenfranchisement' (2011) 62 Northern Ireland Law Quarterly 57.

[305] 'I Won't Give Prisoners the Vote, Says David Cameron' *The Guardian* (London, 24 October 2012).

have made soft suggestions, as a form of carrot dangling, about how incompatible provisions might be remedied with minimal change to the existing statutory scheme. These suggestions assume the form of incentives to address the declaration and influence the decisional space available to Parliament and the government. Finally, the failure to address a declaration of incompatibility is likely to result in an adverse ruling from Strasbourg, transforming the government's domestic political obligation to act into an international legal obligation. This would be accompanied by political and public pressure both domestically and internationally, leaving the government in a position where it has little to gain, but much to lose in refusing to remove the incompatibility.[306] This renders the decisional space politically difficult to enjoy.

The menu of political options available to the government when a declaration of incompatibility is made (or the remedial space, as described) is narrower than that assumed in the existing scholarship. Some declarations of incompatibility are so narrowly framed that they leave little room to the government for manoeuvre. Suggestions made in judgments declaring primary legislation incompatible with Convention rights exercise a guiding influence on the manner and the mode by which an incompatibility may be addressed.

Finally, the power to ignore or reject declarations of incompatibility may atrophy in the future through disuse. But the road towards a constitutional convention that all declarations of incompatibility will be addressed is a difficult one, on account of the fact that when section 4 is invoked, the burden of legislative inertia remains on the person that seeks the removal of the incompatibility. Therefore, declarations of incompatibility have greater coercive force than we might imagine at first glance—in practice, they not only tell Parliament and the government what to do, but often also advise them on how to go about doing it.

\*\*\*

Despite India having been formally categorized as a jurisdiction with judicial supremacy in which courts have the power to strike down primary legislation (the old model of judicial review), judicial decisions

---

[306] Mark Elliott, 'Parliamentary Sovereignty and the New Constitutional Order: Legislative Freedom, Political Reality and Convention' (2002) 22 LS 340.

have not necessarily comprised the 'last word' on questions about rights. The Indian Parliament has sometimes responded to judgments through two kinds of constitutional amendments, embracing the opportunity to offer its alternative interpretation of rights to that of the courts. Conversely, even though the HRA is categorized under the new model labels, in which courts do not have the power to strike down primary legislation, legislative rejection of declarations of incompatibility has proven a very difficult option to invoke in practice. Moreover, the space available to the Westminster Parliament for political responses is narrower than that assumed in the existing scholarship.

# 3 Comparing Political Responses in India and the United Kingdom

Chapter 2 considered the responses to the striking down of legislation in India and declarations of incompatibility in the UK separately. This chapter will link the two, in order to determine whether it is genuinely more difficult for the Indian Parliament to respond to judicial review decisions than the Westminster Parliament. This brings us to the crux of the question—whether the new model of judicial review genuinely engenders a more balanced allocation of powers for the reasons offered in the existing scholarship.

The last chapter drew a distinction between two kinds of space available in responding to declarations of incompatibility—decisional space and remedial space. This chapter will invoke the two concepts of space in the context of both India and the UK. Thereafter, the chapter will examine parliamentary debates in both jurisdictions to consider the role that MPs believe they are playing when addressing declarations of incompatibility and judgments striking down legislation in the UK and India respectively. Finally, the chapter will consider the swiftness of responses to these remedies in both jurisdictions. Even if it is equally easy (or difficult) for legislatures in both jurisdictions to offer their rights-based reasoning in response to that of the courts, is this process undertaken faster under the HRA, as proponents of the new model claim?

## Comparing Decisional Space in India and the UK

What is the difference between the capacity of the UK Parliament and government to reject declarations of incompatibility compared with that of the Indian Parliament and government to reject the judgments striking down legislation? At the outset, it is worth flagging the distinction between the design of the HRA and the Indian Constitution. The former, as explained in Chapter 2, places the burden of inertia on the person seeking to remove the incompatibility. In other words, a declaration of incompatibility does not *automatically* result in a change of the law—it still requires remedial action (in the form of an executive remedial order or legislative change) in order for the application of the law to be affected in any way. As long as Parliament and the government choose not to act, the expectation is that the law will continue to be enforced as it was before the declaration of incompatibility was made. In India, the burden of inertia is on Parliament and the government, since a judgment striking down legislation automatically results in disapplication and non-enforcement of the law.[1] The political capital in the form of a two-thirds majority in Parliament needs to be assembled before fundamental rights amendments or Ninth Schedule amendments can be made in order to nullify an Indian court's judgment.

The decisional space available in the UK is less than that assumed in the existing literature. This is for a number of reasons. First, governments' record of consistently addressing declarations of incompatibility is not simply about 'inductive reliance on a given pattern of behaviour';[2] it is often the result of calculated attempts by the courts to issue such declarations in conditions favourable to change. In many cases, courts make declarations of incompatibility knowing that there is either an intention to amend the law in any event, or a strong likelihood that the law will be amended if the declaration of incompatibility is made. This

---

[1] However, there may be exceptions—for instance, where the court order requires some explicit action to be taken by the government. See Chintan Chandrachud, 'Dance Bars, Dialogue, and the Indian Supreme Court' (UK Constitutional Law Blog, 13 July 2014) <https://ukconstitutionallaw.org/2014/07/13/comment-on-india-chintan-chandrachud-dance-bars-dialogue-and-the-indian-supreme-court/> accessed 13 July 2014.

[2] Gavin Phillipson, 'Deference, Discretion, and Democracy in the Human Rights Act Era' (2007) 60 CLP 40, p. 68.

often makes the question of 'decisional space' hollow, since neither Parliament nor the government harbours a desire to reject the declaration of incompatibility in the first place. Further, the failure to address a declaration of incompatibility (even when Parliament wishes to reject it) is likely to result in an adverse ruling from the Strasbourg Court, placing the government in breach of its international obligations. Finally, soft suggestions made by courts indicating that only minimal change is required in order to address the incompatibility influence the decisional space available to Parliament and the government.

Conversely, the decisional space available to the Indian Parliament and government when primary legislation is struck down for violating fundamental rights is wider than that which is ascribed to them in the existing scholarship. Parliament has two principal methods of repudiating judgments striking down legislation: fundamental rights amendments and Ninth Schedule amendments. Whether the judgments in the Basic Structure case[3] and Coelho[4] have circumscribed these response mechanisms to such an extent that they are rendered non-exercisable or virtually non-exercisable has remained a controversial question. It was argued earlier, based on an analysis of these two judgments as well as other decisions of the Indian Supreme Court, that Parliament still retains some amount of space to respond to judgments through these two response mechanisms.

While the Westminster Parliament and government have less space for response than that often assumed, its Indian counterparts have greater space for response than that attributed by scholars after the judgments in the Basic Structure case and Coelho. The decisional space for responding to judgments in both jurisdictions cannot be described with surgical precision. However, it can at least be said that the decisional space available in India and the UK is comparable, and provides for a much closer similarity than a bare juxtaposition of the scholarship in both jurisdictions seems to suggest. As we will see later, what becomes lucid from an analysis of the practice in both jurisdictions is that in India as well as in the UK, pronounced disagreement by some (or even a majority of) political representatives with a judgment striking down legislation or making a declaration of incompatibility has not proven

---

[3] *Kesavananda Bharati* v. *State of Kerala*, AIR 1973 SC 1461.
[4] *I.R. Coelho* v. *State of Tamil Nadu*, AIR 2007 SC 861.

sufficient to reject the judgment. The political fallout of the judgment in the Belmarsh Prison case[5] (declaring a part of UK's erstwhile anti-terrorism law[6] incompatible with Convention rights), which was initially opposed by sections of the government and Parliament but eventually led to a repeal of the law and its replacement by a fresh anti-terrorism regime,[7] exemplifies this.[8]

In India and the UK, extraordinary impetus is required in order to reject judgments striking down legislation and declarations of incompatibility respectively. Of course, the hurdles that this impetus needs to overcome in both jurisdictions are distinct. In the UK, these hurdles include the public and political pressure when a declaration of incompatibility is made and the risk of a finding from the Strasbourg Court that the government is in breach of its international obligations. In India, the most significant hurdle is the fact that these response mechanisms need to be invoked through a two-thirds majority vote in Parliament. Unless the ruling government has a particularly strong parliamentary mandate, this would necessitate considerable support cutting across political party lines. The other hurdle that governments in India would be tasked with overcoming is the pressure of public opinion, particularly given the surge in the institutional legitimacy of the Supreme Court and high courts since the early 1980s.

However, these arguments should not be taken so far as to say that Parliament and the government in India and the UK have virtually no decisional space. It is not inconceivable to think of situations where Parliaments in both jurisdictions gather the impetus to reject a judgment holding that primary legislation, which is a political 'hot potato' or high on the political agenda, is incompatible/unconstitutional. There is ample evidence in support of this claim with regard to property rights cases in India. Since agrarian reform was a cornerstone of the political agenda after independence, several judgments striking down land redistribution legislation on fundamental rights grounds were nullified through fundamental rights amendments and Ninth Schedule amendments.

---

[5] *A v. SSHD*, [2004] UKHL 56.

[6] Anti-terrorism, Crime and Security Act, 2001.

[7] Prevention of Terrorism Act, 2005.

[8] Aruna Sathanapally, *Beyond Disagreement: Open Remedies in Human Rights Adjudication* (Oxford University Press 2012), pp. 189–93.

In the UK, the developments surrounding the declaration of incompatibility issued in *Smith* v. *Scott*[9] concerning the restrictions on prisoners' right to vote provides a good example of the prospect of rejecting declarations of incompatibility. The draft bill[10] introduced by the government for pre-legislative scrutiny contemplates, as one of its options, rejecting the declaration outright. It remains to be seen whether and how the government chooses to address the incompatibility. But the side on which the scales eventually tip will not affect the argument made here. Even if the Westminster Parliament chooses to address the incompatibility, the aftermath of the case would demonstrate that the impetus for rejecting the declaration, although considerable, was not eventually sufficient to overcome the considerable difficulties faced by Parliament and the government confronting the declaration.

## Remedial Space in India and the UK

Comparing the remedial space available in India and the UK is slightly more complicated. Once again, an important difference between the HRA and the Indian Constitution bears implications for the manner in which remedial space should be understood in these jurisdictions. In the UK, remedial space has been referred to as the legal mode (a remedial order under section 10 of the HRA or fresh primary legislation) and substantive means (the replacement of an entire legislative regime, minor changes to existing legislation, etc.) available for addressing declarations of incompatibility. In other words, it refers to the room for legislative manoeuvre after Parliament or the government has *decided to address the declaration of incompatibility in some way* (rather than simply to ignore it or reject it outright—an option which is, theoretically, on the table).

In the Indian context, remedial space refers to the legal mode (fundamental rights amendments and Ninth Schedule amendments) and substantive means available to Parliament and the government in responding to judgments striking down legislation. This refers to the room for manoeuvre available to the Indian Parliament and government *once they have decided to respond to a judgment striking down legislation.*

---

[9] [2007] CSIH 9.

[10] Ministry of Justice, *Voting Eligibility (Prisoners) Draft Bill* (Cm 8499, 2012).

At first glance, this looks like a comparison between unequals, on the footing that it is implausible to compare responses to declarations of incompatibility which seek to *comply* with human rights decisions of courts in the UK, with responses to legislation being struck down in India, which *detract* from (rather than advance) judicial decisions striking down legislation. But this approach fails to appreciate the nuances of what actually takes place when a declaration of incompatibility is made. In the UK, although the remedial order or legislation addressing a declaration of incompatibility seeks to put the court's judgment into effect, it may also provide the opportunity for Parliament and the government to calibrate their response to the court's judgment, by addressing the incompatibility in a way that does not fully give effect to the judgment or does so in a limited way.[11]

The Westminster Parliament's response to the declarations of incompatibility made in *Morris*[12] and *Gabaj*,[13] which declared section 185(4) of the Housing Act, 1996 incompatible with the anti-discrimination provision under Art. 14 of the Convention, offers an example. In spite of the remedial law amending the incompatible statutory provision, by retaining elements of discrimination in the social housing regime, the government was seen as not fully complying with the two judgments.[14] Thus, in practice, remedial orders or legislation act both as a way of complying with, and a mode of sidestepping or detracting from, the court's judgment.

It has been argued earlier in the book that the remedial space available to Parliament and the government in the UK is narrower than that often assumed by scholars. Two principal reasons were provided. First, some declarations of incompatibility are so narrowly framed that they leave little room for manoeuvre. Second, soft suggestions made in judgments declaring primary legislation incompatible exercise a guiding influence on the manner and the mode by which an incompatibility may be addressed. In India, Parliament has employed two response mechanisms to reject judgments striking down legislation: fundamental rights amendments and Ninth Schedule amendments.

---

[11]  See Sathanapally (n. 8), pp. 149–52.

[12]  *R (Sylviane Pierrette Morris)* v. *Westminster City Council*, [2006] 1 WLR 505.

[13]  *R (Gabaj)* v. *First Secretary of State*, (Administrative Court, 28 March 2006).

[14]  See Sathanapally (n. 8), pp. 149–52.

Both these response mechanisms can themselves be subjected to judicial review, but the test for reviewing them varies. While fundamental rights amendments are subjected to the 'essence of rights test', Ninth Schedule amendments are subjected to the 'rights test'. In being able to select which of these response mechanisms to invoke after primary legislation is struck down, Parliament is also in a position to decide which test for review should be applicable to its response. It would, of course, be likely to choose the test that is expected to withstand challenge in court. Parliament may also, as it has done in the past,[15] invoke both response mechanisms in conjunction to give the amendment the best chance of withstanding judicial review.

Another important factor strategically influences the Indian Parliament's choice between these two response mechanisms. By definition, the Ninth Schedule insulates statutes from judicial review and thus has an impact exclusively vis-à-vis the law that is protected through a Ninth Schedule amendment. Fundamental rights amendments, on the other hand, have broader implications on the constitutional landscape. In the process of nullifying judgments through a fundamental rights amendment, Parliament also risks having an impact on other statutes and transactions affected by the amendment. In this sense, Ninth Schedule amendments are more narrowly targeted and foreseeable in their effects than fundamental rights amendments. Thus, Parliament has room for manoeuvre in choosing between these two response mechanisms, particularly bearing in mind the different standards of judicial review that apply to them and the differences in the influence of the response mechanisms on the constitutional system as a whole.

The substantive options before the Indian Parliament in responding to judgments striking down legislation are more limited. Ninth Schedule amendments are not particularly conducive to making measured responses to judgments striking down legislation. This is because of the fact that Art. 31B of the Indian Constitution is not based on any underlying legal logic[16]; it simply removes the substratum of the

---

[15] See the Constitution (Fourth Amendment) Act, 1955.

[16] There are of course shades of political logic that, it may be argued, apply to Art. 31B. For example, when Art. 31B and the Ninth Schedule were being debated in the Provisional Parliament, Jawaharlal Nehru argued that it was a

judgment by insulating a previously invalidated statute from judicial review for violating fundamental rights. It is for this very reason that at the time of the Ninth Schedule's introduction, some MPs criticized it on the basis that it was not a transparent way of nullifying judgments.[17]

In practice, the Ninth Schedule has represented an 'all or nothing' tool, presenting the government with the binary choice of either accepting a judicial decision striking down legislation or rejecting it altogether by inserting the whole statute into the Ninth Schedule (that is, if it has the political capability of securing the passage of a constitutional amendment in Parliament). This is what happened, for example, in *Balmadies Plantations* v. *State of Tamil Nadu*,[18] where the Supreme Court's invalidation of a few provisions of the Gudalur Janmam Estates (Abolition and Conversion into Ryotwari) Act, 1969 led to the insertion of the whole statute into the Ninth Schedule, nullifying the effect of the Supreme Court judgment in its entirety.

The second response mechanism, fundamental rights amendments, has represented a similarly blunt tool. Since such amendments pull the rug from under the court's judgment by altering the fundamental right on which it was based, they have also tended to assume the form of absolute reversals of judgments striking down legislation.[19] The First Amendment

---

safety valve against the colonial mindset of courts which distrusted the capacity of Indians to govern themselves. See Arudra Burra, 'Arguments from Colonial Continuity: The Constitution (First Amendment) Act, 1951' (*SSRN*, 7 December 2008) <http://papers.ssrn.com/sol3/papers.cfm?abstract_id=2052659> accessed 30 July 2013.

[17] Lok Sabha Debates, 1951, vol. XII, no. II, col. 8937 (Syamnandan Sahay). See also Lok Sabha Debates, 1974, vol. XLIII, col. 307 (P.K. Deo).

[18] AIR 1972 SC 2240.

[19] In theory, it would sometimes be possible for Parliament to meet courts halfway using the two response mechanisms described. For instance, Parliament may only insert some (and not all) of the statutory provisions that have been struck down into the Ninth Schedule. Similarly, if different provisions of a statute are struck down for violating different fundamental rights, only one of the fundamental rights may be amended to preserve the specific statutory provisions that violated it. However, calibrated responses of this kind have not been seen in practice and, as these hypothetical examples bear out, are contingent on several factors.

to the Constitution, through which the constitutionally permissible restrictions on the freedom of speech were expanded in order to revive a statutory provision[20] invalidated by the Patna High Court in *Shaila Bala Devi* v. *Chief Secretary*,[21] is an example. Having said that, other response mechanisms (not requiring parliamentary supermajorities), such as ordinary legislation, ordinances, or review petitions, may fill part of the remedial gap in India by offering the government a more subtle method of responding to judgments striking down legislation, similar to that of the British government.

Overall, governments in both the UK and India have some remedial space in deciding how to respond to declarations of incompatibility or judgments striking down legislation (whether through remedial orders or legislation in the UK and fundamental rights amendments or Ninth Schedule amendments in India). In the UK, this remedial space may be subject to the guiding influence of the court's opinion about which remedial measure should be employed to address the incompatibility. With regard to the substantive options available to Parliament and the government, the menu of possibilities available to respond to a declaration of incompatibility in the UK is wide, but may be partly narrowed by the soft suggestions made by the court in its decision. In India, on the other hand, both fundamental rights amendments and Ninth Schedule amendments tend to eliminate the substratum of judgments altogether, either restoring the statute in question to the state that it was in before the court's judgment or paving the way for the fresh enactment of an identical or substantially similar statute. Indian governments may turn to the other response mechanisms to offer more nuanced responses to judgments striking down legislation.

## Constitutional Convention of Compliance

The question of whether the ability to reject declarations of incompatibility or judgments striking down legislation has atrophied or has been effectively neutralized through constitutional convention arises in both jurisdictions. In the UK, this claim, which Chapter 2 examined, is based on the fact that no declaration of incompatibility has been rejected

---

[20] The Indian Press (Emergency Powers) Act, 1931, section 4(1)(a).
[21] AIR 1951 Pat 12.

outright in the years since the HRA came into effect. The chapter cautioned against concluding that a constitutional convention against the power to reject declarations of incompatibility has developed, based on two reasons. First, the declaration of incompatibility is subtly different from many other constitutional remedies in that it places the burden of inertia on the person seeking to remove the incompatibility. Second, evaluating the atrophy of power is more complex in a system where the burden of inertia is not on Parliament or the government. Thus, a much larger timeframe is required in order to establish that the power to reject a declaration of incompatibility has atrophied.

In India, the atrophy analysis may be premised on the basis that the last fundamental rights amendment and Ninth Schedule amendment entered into force in 1972[22] and 1990[23] respectively.[24] Does the nonuse of these powers for over two decades imply that they have been rendered extinct by constitutional convention? It would be misconceived to arrive at this conclusion. In 2007, Sabharwal C.J., speaking for a unanimous Supreme Court in *Coelho*, was awake to the possibility of the Ninth Schedule being employed as a response mechanism to nullify judgments striking down legislation.[25]

There is a complex set of reasons for which fundamental rights amendments and Ninth Schedule amendments have not been employed by Parliament in recent years. These include the following: First, a large amount of controversial government policy has been implemented through delegated legislation.[26] This has sometimes resulted in judgments striking down such delegated legislation and subsequent constitutional

[22] The Constitution (Twenty-fifth Amendment) Act, 1971.

[23] The Constitution (Sixty-sixth Amendment) Act, 1990.

[24] This should not be confused with the invocation of the Ninth Schedule and the power to amend the Constitution in general. These two powers have been invoked thereafter, hence the question of their atrophy does not arise. The plausible atrophy argument relates to the distinctive use of these powers to nullify judgments striking down legislation for violating fundamental rights. The author's response is to this discrete argument, assuming that it is possible for the specific use of a power (rather than a power in general) to atrophy through disuse.

[25] *Coelho* (n. 4), para 78.

[26] This has been partially caused by the increase in plenary bottlenecks in Parliament (which is addressed below). P. Rajeev, 'Parliamentary Supremacy under Attack' *The Hindu* (Chennai, 7 August 2013).

amendments to nullify the effects of these judgments.[27] Hence, political responses have continued, but to some extent, the battleground has shifted away from primary legislation to delegated legislation.

Second, the Congress party enjoyed large parliamentary majorities in the first few decades after independence. However, no single political party was able to secure a simple majority in the Lok Sabha between 1989 and 2014, necessitating rule by coalition governments composed of a number of political parties.[28] In many cases, more than eight political parties have formed part of a ruling coalition government.[29] This has made mobilizing the two-thirds majority required to pass fundamental rights amendments and Ninth Schedule amendments politically difficult (but not impossible, since other constitutional amendments have been enacted between 1989 and 2014).[30] Responses to judgments striking down legislation for violating fundamental rights through these mechanisms could see some resurgence with the ascendancy of a single party in Parliament,[31] as was the case with Bharatiya

---

[27] See, for example, the Constitution (Eighty-fifth Amendment) Act, 2001 (which nullified the effects of *Union of India* v. *Virpal Singh Chauhan*, AIR 1996 SC 448 and *Ajit Singh* v. *State of Punjab*, AIR 1996 SC 1189). The Constitution (Seventy-sixth Amendment) Act, 1994, the Constitution (Seventy-seventh Amendment) Act, 1995, the Constitution (Eighty-first Amendment) Act, 2000 and the Constitution (Eighty-second Amendment) Act, 2000 nullified some of the effects of *Indra Sawhney* v. *Union of India*, AIR 1993 SC 477.

[28] Since the Lok Sabha follows the 'first past the post' electoral system, an absolute majority of seats in the house does not necessarily translate into a majority of the total number of votes cast.

[29] The United Front government under H.D. Deve Gowda (1996–7), the United Front government under I.K. Gujral (1997), and the National Democratic Alliance government under A.B. Vajpayee (1999–2004) are examples.

[30] The last addition to the Ninth Schedule (speaking generally, and not referring to 'Ninth Schedule amendments' as a term of art that is used in this book) was in 1995. Since then, political parties have threatened or lobbied to use the Ninth Schedule from time to time. See, for example, M.R. Venkatesh, 'DMK Manifesto Wants Quota Laws Protected' *Hindustan Times* (Chennai, 3 April 2009); Special Correspondent, 'BJP Promises Reservation to Gujjars and Seven Other Tribes' *The Hindu* (Jaipur, 21 November 2013).

[31] Pratap Bhanu Mehta, 'India's Judiciary: The Promise of Uncertainty' in Pran Chopra (ed.), *The Supreme Court Versus the Constitution: A Challenge to Federalism* (SAGE Publications 2006) 155, p. 163.

Janata Party, led by Narendra Modi (who became the prime minister), in the general election of 2014.

Third, the increase in the Supreme Court's perceived institutional legitimacy has made it more difficult for governments to justify nullifying courts' decisions. As Baxi famously put it, by relaxing rules of standing and opening its doors to the destitute and oppressed, the Supreme Court began to transform itself from the 'Supreme Court of India' to the 'Supreme Court for Indians' in the 1980s.[32] Almost simultaneously, Parliament's reputation saw a general decline.[33] Fourth, recent years have seen an increase in plenary bottlenecks due to obstructionism in Parliament.[34] This has resulted in an overall decrease in Parliament's plenary time and legislative output,[35] giving it a smaller window of opportunity to consider matters beyond its most pressing business.

Thus, the argument that the power to reject strike-downs in India or declarations of incompatibility in the UK has atrophied is unfounded in both jurisdictions. Responding to such judgments in India and the UK remains a political option, albeit one which is very difficult to exercise.

## Parliamentary Debates

A glimpse into parliamentary debates provides us with valuable commentary on responses to judgments striking down legislation in India and declarations of incompatibility in the UK. Debates concerning the constitutional amendments in India indicate that several MPs, particularly from the Congress party, believed that they had a special claim

---

[32] Upendra Baxi, 'Taking Suffering Seriously: Social Action Litigation in the Supreme Court of India' (1985) 4 Third World Legal Studies 107.

[33] Devesh Kapur and Pratap Bhanu Mehta, 'The Indian Parliament as an Institution of Accountability' (2006) UNRISD Democracy, Governance and Human Rights Programme Paper No. 23, p. 16.

[34] Tarunabh Khaitan, 'The Real Price of Parliamentary Obstruction' (2013) 642 Seminar 37.

[35] The statistics published by PRS Legislative Research reflecting the amount of time lost due to obstruction in Parliament are available at <http://www.prsindia.org/parliamenttrack/vital-stats/> accessed 30 July 2013. See also Kapur and Mehta (n. 33), p. 16.

to understanding and interpreting constitutional rights, because they had also been members of the Constituent Assembly. Prime Minister Jawaharlal Nehru, in particular, laboured on the significance of this overlap in personnel between the body that drafted the Constitution and the elected representatives of newly independent India. To Nehru, it seemed implausible for the Supreme Court and high courts to read constitutional text legalistically based on imputed intentions, when MPs at the time represented the 'real intentions' of the framers of the Constitution.[36]

An excerpt from Nehru's speech during the Lok Sabha debates on the First Amendment to the Constitution provides evidence of this:[37]

[N]early all the members who are present here in this House were framers of this Constitution and they will remember the long debates we had about various matters. We spent many months over this. That does not mean, of course, that everything we did was perfect. No doubt we shall learn by experience and try to remedy. But the fact remains that *we have a good, general broad idea of what we intended.* (Emphasis added)

In an interesting exchange during the same debates, one MP questioned whether it was legitimate to amend the Constitution so soon after it had been drafted by the best brains in the country. P.S. Deshmukh, who was later to become Union minister in Nehru's government, swiftly retorted: 'The same brains are changing it.'[38] Of course, as any student of constitutional law knows, attributing intention to the decision of a collective body is an exercise fraught with danger. This point was not overlooked. As one of Nehru's Congress colleagues observed, '[Y]ou were not the only maker of the Constitution.'[39]

Naturally, the overlap in membership between Parliament and the Constituent Assembly could not last long. Nevertheless, this justification continued to hold sway in a slightly different form. It was said that

---

[36] Lok Sabha Debates, 1951, vol. XII, no. II, col. 9083 (Jawaharlal Nehru).

[37] Lok Sabha Debates, 1951, vol. XII, no. II, col. 9074 (Jawaharlal Nehru).

[38] Lok Sabha Debates, 1951, vol. XII, no. II, col. 8939 (P.S. Deshmukh).

[39] Lok Sabha Debates, 1951, vol. XII, no. II, cols 10040–1 (S.L. Sakshena). See also Lok Sabha Debates, 1955, vol. II, col. 2173 (Raghavachari): 'Do you expect any court to interpret the language, in which you have clothed the subject, or in the light of the intentions of the framers of the law, when the language is not capable of yielding those intentions?'.

it was Parliament's predecessor that had made the Constitution, and thus it was Parliament, rather than the courts, that was best placed to understand the intentions behind the text.[40] As Prime Minister Indira Gandhi explained on the floor of the Lok Sabha, Parliament believed that it not only *understood* the Constituent Assembly better than the courts, but also that it better *represented* the Assembly.[41]

Most significantly, the Indian Parliament did not conceive of the Supreme Court and high courts as being the exclusive or final interpreters of constitutional rights. During many of the debates, MPs discussed and criticized the courts' interpretation of constitutional provisions threadbare, and offered what they considered more plausible alternatives. While discussing the first amendment, Nehru pointed out that by amending the Constitution, Parliament was doing what 'in the normal course judicial interpretation might have done'.[42] Opposition leaders who disagreed with Nehru questioned the timing of the amendment,[43] but agreed that it was legitimate for Parliament to offer an alternative interpretation of the Constitution to that of the courts.[44] Similarly, B.R. Ambedkar disagreed with the Supreme Court's reading of the exceptions to the freedom of speech and expression, observing that they were not to be read as though they were 'matters of straight jacket [*sic*]'.[45]

The Fourth Amendment, through which Parliament responded to judgments of the Supreme Court on the right to property, reflected similar interpretive disagreement. Analysing the judgments in detail, some MPs considered the Court's mistaken interpretation to be based on an over-reliance on foreign precedent.[46] That it formed part of Parliament's role to offer competing interpretations of the Constitution was made categorical:[47]

---

[40] Lok Sabha Debates, 1971, vol. IX, no. XII, col. 291 (N. Shivappa).

[41] Lok Sabha Debates, 1971, vol. IX, no. XIII, col. 346 (Indira Gandhi).

[42] Lok Sabha Debates, 1951, vol. XII, no. II, col. 8818 (Jawaharlal Nehru).

[43] Specifically, the amendment sought to nullify a judgment of the Patna High Court, which had been appealed to the Supreme Court. Dr S.P. Mookherjee claimed that the better course of action would have been to wait for the Supreme Court decision before amending the Constitution.

[44] Lok Sabha Debates, 1951, vol. XII, no. II, col. 8818 (S.P. Mookherjee).

[45] Lok Sabha Debates, 1951, vol. XII, no. II, col. 9014 (B.R. Ambedkar).

[46] Lok Sabha Debates, 1955, vol. II, cols 2008, 2011 (H.V. Pataskar).

[47] Lok Sabha Debates, 1955, vol. II, col 2053–4 (C.C. Shah).

An attempt is being made sometimes to represent as if [*sic*] the judiciary is the only guardian of the rights and liberties of the people and that if the judiciary is not there, probably the legislatures would run amuck and encroach upon the rights and liberties of people at any time or any cost. I submit it is a wrong approach. *The legislatures, as I have said, have a very important place.* (Emphasis added)

Interpretive disagreement was also evident in the parliamentary debates on the Twenty-fifth and Thirty-fourth Amendments to the Constitution. The Bank Nationalization case,[48] discussed in the previous chapter, was nullified through the Twenty-fifth Amendment to the Constitution. MPs observed that the Supreme Court had 'misinterpreted' the constitutional provisions in its judgment,[49] and that the Court's interpretation had rendered previous amendments to the Constitution otiose.[50] When discussing the Thirty-fourth Amendment, a cabinet minister pointed out that the amendment did not actually modify the Constitution in any way—it only gave concrete expression to the Constitution as it existed, before it was misconstrued by the Supreme Court.[51]

Most often, MPs did not skirt around the issue of why these amendments were being enacted. That judgments striking down legislation were seeking to be nullified was made unequivocal. As Ambedkar observed, 'A question was asked as to what was the necessity for introducing three new heads [under Art. 19(2) of the Constitution]. The necessity has arisen out of certain judgments which have been delivered by the Supreme Court as well as the Provincial High Courts.'[52]

---

[48] *R.C. Cooper* v. *Union of India*, AIR 1970 SC 564.

[49] Lok Sabha Debates, 1971, vol. IX, no. XIII, col. 309 (V.K. Krishna Menon).

[50] Lok Sabha Debates, 1971, vol. IX, no. XII, cols 220–1 (H.R. Gokhale); Lok Sabha Debates, 1971, vol. IX, no. XII, col. 240 (N.K.P. Salve).

[51] Lok Sabha Debates, 1974, vol. XLIII, col. 263 (C. Subramanium). See also Lok Sabha Debates, 1955, vol. XXXII, cols 380–1 (N.C. Chatterjee); Lok Sabha Debates, 1964, vol. XXXII, col. 631 (A.P. Jain); Lok Sabha Debates, 1964, vol. XXXII, col. 709 (A.K. Sen).

[52] Lok Sabha Debates, 1951, vol. XII, no. II, col. 9008 (B.R. Ambedkar); Lok Sabha Debates, 1972, vol. XVI, no. 54, col. 360 (C.K. Chandrappan). See also Lok Sabha Debates, 1971, vol. IX, no. XII, cols 287–8 (Shankerrao Savant): '[A]ll along, during the last 22 years, Parliament had been proposing its theories of private property in one way and the Supreme Court has been disposing of them in another way. It is to make the law both fool-proof and knave-proof that the present amendment has been brought forward.'

Nevertheless, these amendments gave rise to different kinds of political positioning vis-à-vis the judgments. MPs did not always suggest that the courts simply interpreted the constitutional text incorrectly. Another common response was to acknowledge that the courts' interpretation of the text was correct, but that the amendment was necessary to uphold the spirit of the Constitution or the intentions of the founding fathers.[53] A third strategy was to label the courts' judgment as a 'technical fetter' that needed to be removed in order to achieve the constitutional provision's true purpose.[54] During the politically volatile period in the 1970s, it was also said that constitutional amendments were being enacted not to defy the courts, but to protect them from the public censure and controversy that their judgments had evoked.[55]

Another interesting factor to note is that, as discussed in Chapter 1, even though the Indian Constitution is designed in a way that seems to espouse judicial supremacy, the doctrine of parliamentary supremacy was commonly invoked in the debates concerning constitutional amendments. As H.R. Gokhale, the law minister during the first term of the Indira Gandhi government, commented: 'It is the Parliament that is a supreme body. It can enact any law that is suitable for the country and that is suitable for the people ... the High Courts or the Supreme Court ... must forget that they have any superiority over the Parliament.'[56] These statements are hard to dismiss offhand as political

[53] Lok Sabha Debates, 1951, vol. XII, no. II, cols 8885–6 (Pandit Thakur Das Bhargava); Lok Sabha Debates, 1955, vol. II, cols 1947–9 (Jawaharlal Nehru);

[54] Lok Sabha Debates, 1964, vol. XXXII, col. 102 (A.K. Sen); Lok Sabha Debates, 1972, vol. XVI, no. 54, col. 347 (H.R. Gokhale).

[55] Lok Sabha Debates, 1971, vol. IX, no. XII, col. 225 (H.R. Gokhale); Lok Sabha Debates, 1971, vol. IX, no. XII, col. 238 (N.K.P. Salve); Lok Sabha Debates, 1971, vol. IX, no. XIII, col. 298 (Siddhartha Shankar Ray).

[56] Lok Sabha Debates, 1971, vol. IX, no. XII, col. 301 (H.R. Gokhale). See also Lok Sabha Debates, 1971, vol. IX, no. XII, col. 220 (H.R. Gokhale). In contrast, see Lok Sabha Debates, 1964, vol. XXXII, cols 429–30 (J.B. Kripalani):

> Every time a law is considered to be invalid and unconstitutional by the Supreme Court, Government comes here with an amendment of the Constitution, and it wants to change the fundamental law. Why not then make this Parliament as supreme as the Parliament of England? Bring one all comprehensive amendment, a universal amendment that the judiciary cannot declare any law passed by Parliament *ultra vires* of the Constitution.

rhetoric or a failure to understand the sophistication of the Indian constitutional scheme. Rather, they seem to signify that the notion that courts enjoyed the 'last word' on rights-based questions—which scholars argue necessarily accompanies models of judicial supremacy—did not go uncontested.

Moving to the UK, parliamentary debates indicate that the declaration of incompatibility is particularly conducive to political positioning. This is especially because when such a declaration is made, it remains unclear whether the case has resulted in a 'win' or a 'loss' for the government. Also, would this position change if the government specifically agreed to—or did not oppose—the issuance of a declaration of incompatibility, as is sometimes the case?[57] MPs often claim in Parliament that the court did not hold that the statutory regime was unlawful—a point which is technically correct, but overlooks the fact that the court found the regime to be inconsistent with human rights obligations. For instance, in the aftermath of the declaration of incompatibility in *International Transport Roth*,[58] the under-secretary of state for the home department stated on the floor of the House of Lords that the statutory regime in question was 'not found to be unlawful' and that all penalties under it were therefore 'lawfully imposed'.[59] But while discussing the same issue, another MP said that the government had 'lost' their case in the Court of Appeal, which made a declaration of incompatibility.[60]

This also has an impact upon how MPs address declarations of incompatibility when debating legislation that seeks to amend the incompatible law. It appears that when MPs wish to secure political

---

[57] See, for example, *McR's Application for Judicial Review*, [2002] NIQB 58.

[58] *International Transport Roth GmbH* v. *SSHD*, [2003] QB 728.

[59] HL Deb 3 February 2003, vol. 644, col. 1 (Lord Filkin).

[60] HL Deb 24 June 2002, vol. 636, col. 1131 (Lord Berkeley):

It has seemed sometimes in recent years that the Government's only concern was to turn transport operators—road, rail or sea operators—into unpaid frontier guards of fortress Britain, fining anyone who failed even if he or she were not at fault; and there was no real appeal. The Government lost on that point in the case of Roth in the Court of Appeal earlier this year.

For further examples, see HL Deb 25 November 2002, vol. 641, col. 18WA (Lord Filkin); HC Deb 28 March 2003, vol. 402, col. 602 (Stephen McCabe).

capital from the amendments, they situate the declaration of incompatibility as being only one of the reasons, or perhaps an additional impetus, to change the law. This is demonstrated by what was said by a Conservative Party MP following *Blood and Tarbuck*[61] (in which the failure of a statutory regime to permit a father's name to be entered on the birth certificate of a child, when the father had died and the child was conceived as a result of fertility treatment, was declared incompatible with Convention rights):[62]

> We have heard talk of the 28 February court case and the ruling that the Human Fertilisation and Embryology Act 1990 is incompatible [with Art. 8 of the Convention].... That has clearly made the issue all the more urgent. However, although the courts have made a ruling, the measure should be not a response to decisions taken there, but a statement by the House on what is the right thing to do. That is the way forward for it.

On the flip side, when MPs are anxious about the political ramifications of changing the law, the declaration of incompatibility is portrayed as a binding obligation, with which Parliament has no choice but to comply. For example, the declaration of incompatibility made against the 'indefinite notification' regime under the SOA[63] received an acrimonious reception from the government. MPs emphasized that they had no option but to address the incompatibility, although they would follow the path of minimal compliance with the Supreme Court's judgment.[64]

In this vein, similar to the Indian system sometimes being depicted as one where the doctrine of parliamentary supremacy held sway, the British system—characterized by the 'new model' labels set out in Chapter 1—has been depicted as a jurisdiction where judicial supremacy prevails. MPs have often described the declaration of incompatibility in terms resembling a power to strike down legislation—observing

---

[61] *Blood and Tarbuck* v. *Secretary of State for Health* [Administrative Court], 28 February 2003 (unreported).

[62] HC Deb 28 March 2003, vol. 402, col. 609 (Chris Grayling). See also HL Deb 4 July 2003, vol. 650, col. 1150 (Baroness Kitpeathley).

[63] *R (Thompson)* v. *Secretary of State*, [2011] 1 AC 331.

[64] HL Deb 5 July 2012, vol. 738, cols 875–6 (Baroness Stowell of Beeston).

for instance, that the courts 'struck down'[65] or 'overturned'[66] provisions of primary legislation.[67] Once again, it is hard to dismiss these statements as merely a failure to understand the UK's constitutional arrangements. Rather, they reinforce that in practice, the Westminster Parliament does not enjoy the kind of space for political responses that scholars expected, following the HRA's enactment.

## The Time Factor

The discussion thus far has not fully established the claim that responses to judgments striking down legislation in India and responses to declarations of incompatibility in the UK are equally difficult. In order to establish this claim, it is also necessary, recalling what was said in Chapter 1, to examine the 'time factor' cited by Tushnet and other scholars as a key benefit of the new commonwealth model over judicial supremacy. The new commonwealth model, scholars have argued, is superior to judicial supremacy because it enables the legislature to revise judicial understanding of rights in the short run, rather than in the long run.[68] If we were to accept that political responses to declarations of incompatibility and political responses to judgments striking down legislation are equally difficult, can it be still be argued that the model of rights protection under the HRA is nevertheless superior because the Westminster Parliament can revise judicial understandings of rights more swiftly than the Indian Parliament? Political practice simply fails to hold up this claim.

---

[65] HL Deb 8 March 2005, vol. 670, col. 715 (Lord Stoddart); HL Deb 18 December 2003, vol. 645, col. 1301 (Lord Bishop of Winchester); HC Deb 22 February 2005, vol. 669, cols 158–9 (Charles Clarke); HC Deb 23 February 2005, vol. 431, cols. 778–9 (John Denham).

[66] HC Deb 23 February 2005, vol. 431, col. 417 (William Cash).

[67] Sathanapally and Kavanagh also make this point. See Sathanapally (n. 8) 154; Aileen Kavanagh, 'What's So Weak About "Weak-form" Judicial Review? The Case of the UK Human Rights Act 1998' (2015) 13 International Journal of Constitutional Law 1008.

[68] Mark Tushnet, *Weak Courts, Strong Rights: Judicial Review and Social Welfare Rights in Comparative Constitutional Law* (Princeton University Press 2008), p. 34.

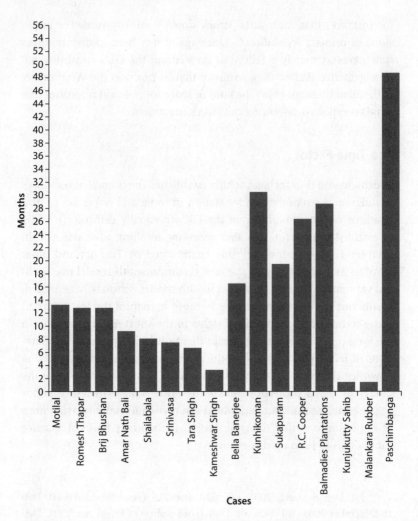

**Figure 3.1**   Speed of Political Responses to Strike-downs in India

Figure 3.1 shows the time taken by the Indian Parliament to respond to judgments striking down primary legislation through fundamental rights amendments and Ninth Schedule amendments.

On an average, the Indian Parliament has taken 15 months to respond to judgments striking down primary legislation. Within this sample, there are, of course, examples of responses that are much swifter and slower than this. For instance, the Ninth Schedule amendment following the Supreme Court's judgments in *Malankara Rubber*[69] and *Kunjukutty Sahib*[70] took barely one and a half months to enact. The explanation for the prompt parliamentary response to these cases was that a high court judgment[71] that formed the subject of appeal in one of the cases was delivered more than 20 months before the Supreme Court judgment, enabling the government of the day to prepare the ground for the Ninth Schedule amendment even before the case reached the corridors of the Supreme Court. On the other hand, it took Parliament over two and a half years to reject the Supreme Court's judgment in *Kunhikoman* v. *State of Kerala*[72] (striking down parts of the Kerala Agrarian Relations Act, 1961) through a fundamental rights amendment, and over four years to reject the judgment in *Paschimbanga* v. *State of West Bengal*,[73] through a Ninth Schedule amendment.

As Figure 3.2 demonstrates, Westminster Parliament's responses to declarations of incompatibility have been slower.

In the early years following the enactment of the HRA, the expectation was that Parliament would not only positively address declarations of incompatibility, but would do so quite swiftly.[74] When it comes to addressing declarations of incompatibility, time is particularly of the essence because litigants secure no direct or immediate benefit when such a declaration is made. In other words, a violation of rights—such as in the case of a prisoner who is incarcerated based on statutory provisions that are held to be incompatible with Convention rights— endures despite the declaration. The first declaration of incompatibility that survived appeal was in respect of provisions of the Mental Health Act, 1983 that placed a reverse burden of proof on patients applying to a review tribunal to be discharged from detention in hospital.[75] The

---

[69] *Malankara Rubber* v. *State of Kerala*, AIR 1972 SC 2027.

[70] *Kunjukutty Sahib* v. *State of Kerala*, AIR 1972 SC 2097.

[71] *Narayanan Nair* v. *State of Kerala*, AIR 1971 Ker 98.

[72] AIR 1962 SC 273.

[73] MANU/WB/0564/1986.

[74] See HC Deb 16 February 1998, vol. 306, col. 778 (Jack Straw): '[I]t is likely that the Government and Parliament would wish to respond to such a situation [a declaration of incompatibility] and would do so rapidly.'

[75] *R (H)* v. *London North and East Region Mental Health Review Tribunal*, [2002] QB 1.

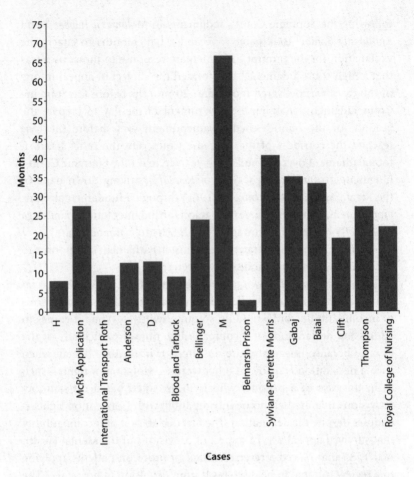

**Figure 3.2**    Speed of Political Responses to Declarations of Incompatibility in the UK

government took a few months to respond, prompting some peers to voice dissatisfaction with its failure to do so promptly. One of them said:[76]

> Whether it was the ordinary or the urgent [remedial order] procedure it seems rather a slow process. The court decided on the case in March. Yet, here we are a year later faced with an order of this kind. In the meantime,

[76] HL Deb 11 April 2002, vol. 633, col. 604 (Lord Clement-Jones).

we do not know but it may well be that patients have been prejudiced.... Some response is required about future earnest as to whether or not in the future this can be achieved rather more quickly, as a year seems to be rather excessive for what was then regarded as a fairly urgent matter.

Similar concerns were articulated in Parliament in the aftermath of *Anderson*,[77] in which the House of Lords declared that the secretary of state's statutory power to set the tariff (how long a convicted murderer should actually spend in prison, given the aims of retribution and deterrence) for mandatory life sentence prisoners was incompatible with Art. 6 of the Convention. As one MP noted, 'There are about 600 prisoners who have been convicted but have not yet received a tariff, so as a result of the Anderson judgment, this substantial number must be dealt with quickly and efficiently.'[78]

Ironically, the responses to the declarations of incompatibility in these cases turned out to be amongst the swiftest since the HRA was enacted. The average response time in the UK has been 23 months,[79] compared to 15 months in India—as indicated in Figure 3.3.

There are outliers on both ends of the spectrum in the UK as well. For instance, it took Parliament only three months to address the declaration of incompatibility made in the Belmarsh Prison case. But Parliament took as long as five-and-a-half years to address the declaration of incompatibility made by the Administrative Court in respect of sections 26 and 29 of the Mental Health Act, 1983 in *R (M)* v. *Secretary of State for Health*.[80]

Once again, the declaration of incompatibility made in the prisoner voting rights litigation,[81] over which Parliament has dragged its feet for

[77] *R (Anderson)* v. *SSHD*, [2003] 1 AC 837.

[78] HL Deb 14 October 2003, vol. 653, col. 860 (Baroness Scotland of Asthal).

[79] The response time excludes the following cases, where the declaration of incompatibility was addressed before the final judgment: *R (Wilkinson)* v. *Inland Revenue Commissioners*, [2005] 1 WLR 1718; *R (Wright and Others)* v. *Secretary of State for Health*, [2009] 1 AC 739; *R (T)* v. *Chief Constable of Greater Manchester Police*, [2014] 3 WLR 96.

[80] [2003] EWHC 1094 (Admin).

[81] *Smith* (n. 9).

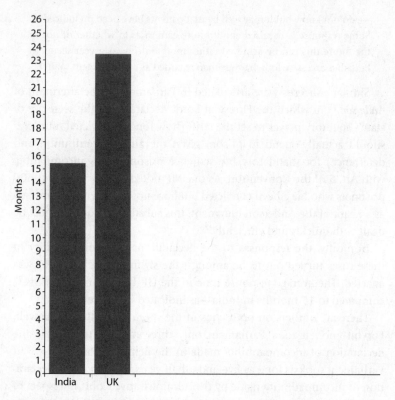

**Figure 3.3**  Comparison of Speed of Political Responses in India and the UK

over eight[82] years, presents a challenge. On account of the way in which
burdens of inertia are distributed following a declaration of incompatibility, the case is one which is hard to classify. Messages from the
government about whether the declaration will be addressed have been
mixed, leaving open many possibilities—that the declaration will be
addressed in some way, that it may be expressly rejected, or that it will,
as far as possible, be ignored. If we were to argue that the declaration of
incompatibility has still not been responded to properly and the time
taken by the government to respond (considered up to 1 June 2015)
should be taken into account, the UK's average response time increases
from 23 months to 28 months.

---

[82] Counted until 1 June 2015.

A more sceptical reading of the prisoner voting rights litigation is possible: it might be suggested that, given the institutional bite of the HRA (a matter examined in Chapter 5), seeking to reject outright a declaration of incompatibility takes a much longer time than complying with a declaration of incompatibility, even if it means doing so in a minimalist way or in a manner that does not fully comport with the court's reasoning. However, this would probably amount to drawing too much inference from a single case. Future declarations of incompatibility in respect of which outright rejection is a sustained and serious option would provide us with further insights on this question.

Once we move beyond the form of the remedies and examine the political practice, it is not hard to understand why the Indian Parliament's response time is slightly quicker than the Westminster Parliament's response time. Governments in Britain may not consider it such a bad thing for responses to declarations of incompatibility to be delayed. So long as the status quo is maintained, the law originally enacted by Parliament and declared incompatible by the court continues to remain in force. Coupled with the fact that the beneficiaries of declarations of incompatibility are often from 'discrete and insular minorities'[83]—terrorist suspects, former sexual offenders, and the like—it becomes increasingly easy to explain the delays in addressing such declarations. This is the reason why, when the HRA was being debated in Parliament, some MPs proposed the introduction of a statutory timetable for addressing declarations of incompatibility[84]—an idea that was shot down by the Home Secretary at the time on the basis that it would impinge upon Parliament's sovereignty.[85]

In contrast, an Indian government which commands the political dominance to be able to respond to judgments through fundamental rights amendments or Ninth Schedule amendments is likely to want to do so quickly, since the judicial decision would have effectively halted the implementation of the relevant statute with immediate effect. Moreover, declarations of incompatibility are responded to in every case, whereas fundamental rights amendments and Ninth Schedule amendments are invoked in India in only a small fraction of the cases

---

[83] See *United States* v. *Carolene Products*, (1938) 304 US 144.

[84] HC Deb 16 February 1998, vol. 306, col. 772 (Kevin McNamara).

[85] HC Deb 16 February 1998, vol. 306, col. 772 (Jack Straw).

in which primary legislation is struck down for violating fundamental rights.

We should, therefore, remember that the most common reaction of the Indian Parliament and government to a judgment striking down primary legislation is to do nothing at all (whether in acceptance of the judgment, or disagreement without the political capacity or will to act, or indifference). Other factors—such as the level of publicity of the judgment, reputational ramifications for the government, and capacity of the issue to capture the public imagination—are also likely to influence governments in both jurisdictions to hasten or delay the response, as the case may be.

Thus, the claim that the Westminster Parliament is able to revise judicial understandings of rights more quickly than the Indian Parliament is belied by political practice. Available evidence suggests that when it wishes to do so, the Indian Parliament responds more swiftly to judgments striking down legislation than the Westminster Parliament responds to declarations of incompatibility.

\*\*\*

This chapter concludes the negative claim made in the book. Although a bare comparison of the scholarship in both jurisdictions suggests otherwise, a careful study of the case law and political practice reflects that the Westminster Parliament and the Indian Parliament have a very similar degree of space in responding to declarations of incompatibility and exercises of the power to strike down legislation, respectively. In other words, the Westminster Parliament holds no advantage over the Indian Parliament in being able to assert its conception of rights following judicial review. This holds true of decisional space—or the ability to reject altogether judicial rights reasoning, and remedial space—the ability to fashion responses to exercises of judicial review.

Parliamentary debates confirm that MPs in the UK do not enjoy the kind of rights-assertive role vis-à-vis declarations of incompatibility that new model scholars might have expected, and correspondingly, that MPs from India have sometimes taken the opportunity to offer interpretations of rights that differ from those of courts. The time factor, which was expected to weigh in favour of the Westminster Parliament, since it can respond to declarations of incompatibility through ordinary legislative procedures, does not fall in its favour in practice. Even though they require greater than simple parliamentary majorities, responses to judgments striking down legislation in India have been faster than responses to declarations of incompatibility in the UK.

# 4 Judicial Review in the Shadow of Remedies

Chapters 2 and 3 sought to establish the negative claim made by this book. The argument that the new Commonwealth model of constitutionalism is superior to the old model of judicial supremacy because it facilitates relatively easy and swift political responses to judicial review has turned out to be a misconception in reference to India and the UK. Constitutional practice has shown that political responses are equally difficult in both jurisdictions and the evidence reflects that judicial supremacy in India actually allows for swifter political responses than the new model in Britain. This chapter, along with Chapter 5, will shift focus to the positive claim: that the remedial scheme established by the new Commonwealth model enables courts in the UK to assert their true understanding of rights more freely than Indian courts.

The chapter begins by arguing that courts in India and the UK adopt a similar three-stage approach in reviewing legislation for compliance with substantive constitutional rights or rights under the Convention. They first examine whether the legislation is compliant with rights, based on ordinary methods of interpretation. If not, then they determine whether the legislation can be upheld based on special interpretive techniques. In the UK, these techniques are specifically sanctioned by section 3 of the HRA, which requires courts to give effect to legislation in a manner compliant with Convention rights, 'so far as it is possible' to do so. In India, these special interpretive techniques have no specific textual grounding and have developed through case law. Finally, if legislation cannot be protected in this way, Indian courts strike it down and courts in the UK may choose to issue a declaration of incompatibility under section 4 of the HRA.

In the context of this three-stage process of review, Indian courts have a smaller range of interpretive tools at their disposal than courts in the UK to interpret primary legislation in a manner compliant with human rights. Since Indian courts have a smaller interpretive toolbox, one would imagine that ceteris paribus, Indian courts' power to strike down legislation would be triggered earlier than the power to issue a declaration of incompatibility arises in the UK. Conversely, this proposition should also imply that in similar cases, declarations of incompatibility in the UK should correspond with exercises of the power to strike down legislation in India.

Case law, however, seems to narrate a different story. Faced with legislation that cannot be read compatibly with rights, Indian courts sometimes rethink their initial view that a statute is unconstitutional before choosing to strike it down, in situations in which British courts would make a declaration of incompatibility. Indian courts, therefore, make their decisions about the rights implications of statutes in the shadow of the power to strike down legislation, withholding their genuine understanding of rights from time to time.

This chapter relies upon three pairs of examples, consisting of one case each from India and the UK, as evidence of this claim. There are many cases reflecting the withholding of true rights reasoning by Indian courts, and equally, the expression of genuine rights reasoning by British courts. However, the six cases discussed in this chapter have been selected and compared based on the existence of analogous features—although they may not be immediately apparent—which, in the case of Indian courts, influenced the judges to not express their genuine understanding of rights and strike down the statutory provisions that formed the subject of judicial review.

The first pair of cases involved judicial review of recently enacted legislation with a strong democratic mandate the Indian Supreme Court's judgments in the *Sharma* cases.[1] These cases, reviewing India's law governing access to information, are compared with the UK Supreme Court's judgment in *Thompson*[2] (which concerned the

---

[1] *Namit Sharma* v. *Union of India*, (2013) 1 SCC 745 (or *Sharma I*); *Union of India* v. *Namit Sharma*, 2013 (11) SCALE 85 (or *Sharma II*).

[2] *R (Thompson)* v. *SSHD*, [2011] 1 AC 331.

law on sexual offences in the UK). The second pair of cases involved judicial review of legislation whose (potential) invalidation would have produced serious collateral consequences in other areas of the law—the Indian Supreme Court's controversial decision effectively re-criminalizing homosexuality in *Naz Foundation*[3] is compared with the UK House of Lords' judgment in *Bellinger*,[4] on the rights of trans-sexuals to marry. The third pair of cases, dealing with emergency anti-terrorism legislation, consists of the Indian Supreme Court's judgment in *Kartar Singh*[5] and the House of Lords' judgment in the Belmarsh Prison case.[6]

These examples demonstrate that Indian courts' decision-making process takes place in the shadow of the power to strike down legislation. The robust nature of the power (compared with the softer power to make a declaration of incompatibility) sometimes influences Indian courts not to exercise it, but to think again about the constitutional validity of statutes under review. In this way, the nature of the remedy under the old model of judicial review sometimes prevents courts from expressing their genuine understanding of rights in order to avoid having to invoke the power to strike down legislation. How do we know that the Indian courts in these cases withheld their genuine understanding of rights? In each of them, there is an obvious disjunction between the proclivities of the court and its ultimate decision. This disjunction, it will be argued, is a consequence of the reluctance to invoke the power to strike down legislation, which would have entailed the court taking its genuine rights reasoning the full way.

The final section of this chapter argues that textual and institutional constraints indicate that the Indian Supreme Court would be unwilling to exercise remedial discretion to issue 'intermediate remedies' seen frequently in many other jurisdictions, such as suspended declarations of invalidity or informal declarations of incompatibility, in cases such as *Sharma*, *Naz Foundation*, and *Kartar Singh*.

---

[3] *Suresh Kumar Koushal* v. *Naz Foundation*, (2014) 1 SCC 1.
[4] *Bellinger* v. *Bellinger*, [2003] 2 AC 467: [2003] UKHL 21.
[5] *Kartar Singh* v. *State of Punjab*, (1994) 3 SCC 569.
[6] *A* v. *SSHD*, [2004] UKHL 56 (the 'Belmarsh Prison case').

## The Three-stage Process of Review

### Stage One: Ordinary Methods of Interpretation

The first stage in reviewing legislation for compliance with rights entails an examination of whether the statutory provisions, according to ordinary principles of interpretation, are consistent with the rights in question. This involves a relatively straightforward process of statutory interpretation based on settled common law principles. In both jurisdictions, if ordinary principles of interpretation render the legislation compliant with rights, the inquiry ends at this stage without the need to advance to stage two.

In India, courts deciding cases involving a challenge to legislation presume, as a starting point, that the impugned legislation is constitutionally valid. This presumption takes different forms. The Supreme Court has frequently acknowledged that it must presume that the legislature, on account of its institutional position, understands and appreciates the needs of its people, that its laws are directed to problems made manifest by experience, and that even its discrimination and classifications are based on adequate grounds.[7] In order to avoid a 'doctrinaire approach' which might 'choke all beneficial legislation',[8] courts have placed the burden of showing that there has been a clear transgression of fundamental rights on the litigant that challenges the statute.[9]

The court can consider matters of common knowledge, matters of common report, and the history of the times at which the statute was enacted in order to sustain the presumption of constitutionality.[10] It may also assume every state of facts that can be considered to exist at the time of enactment of the statute.[11] The presumption of constitutionality holds greater influence in the review of economic and social legislation as against statutes that affect civil liberties.[12] According to

[7] See, for example, *State of Kerala* v. *N.M. Thomas*, AIR 1976 SC 490; *Municipal Corporation of Ahmedabad* v. *Usmanbhai*, AIR 1986 SC 1205.

[8] *Harman Singh* v. *Regional Transport Authority*, AIR 1954 SC 190.

[9] *Chiranjit Lal Chowdhuri* v. *Union of India*, AIR 1951 SC 41.

[10] *R.K. Dalmia* v. *Justice Tendolkar*, AIR 1958 SC 358.

[11] *Dalmia* (n. 10).

[12] *Government of Andhra Pradesh* v. *Laxmi Devi*, (2008) 4 SCC 720, paras 73, 88.

the Indian Supreme Court, there is much to learn from the Lochner era in the US and courts should be slow to interfere with legislative decisions on economic policy.[13]

In India, the presumption of constitutionality influences the interpretation of legislation under constitutional challenge. Where multiple interpretations of a statute are possible, courts have the functional flexibility to adopt the interpretation that complies with the constitutional mandate.[14] The presumption of constitutionality can be rebutted with prima facie evidence that a statutory provision transgresses fundamental rights. It is then left to the state to establish that the provision falls within constitutional limits. Moreover, the Indian Supreme Court has on some occasions leaned in favour of negating the presumption of constitutionality and employing the 'strict scrutiny' standard to test the validity of legislation, although the circumstances in which this standard may be invoked are unclear.[15]

Similarly, in the UK, courts begin their analysis by interpreting legislation that is being reviewed under the HRA in the ordinary way. In other words, they seek to discern the intention of Parliament through a prima facie interpretation in order to determine whether the legislation is proportionate and compliant with Convention rights.[16] Section 3 of the HRA is ignored unless the legislation would, adopting these traditional methods of interpretation, breach Convention rights.[17]

---

[13] *Laxmi Devi* (n. 12). See also *P.N. Tiwari v. Union of India*, [2004] 265 ITR 224 (All).

[14] *Sunil Batra* v. *Delhi Administration*, AIR 1978 SC 1675; *Bhanu Athaiya* v. *Commander Kaushal*, 1980 (82) Bom LR 12, para 10; *Chettiar* v. *Narsimhalu*, AIR 1980 Mad 305 [10]; *Githa Hariharan* v. *Reserve Bank of India*, AIR 1999 SC 1149, para 9.

[15] Raag Yadava, 'Taking Rights Seriously: The Supreme Court on Strict Scrutiny' (2010) 22 NLSIR 147.

[16] Aileen Kavanagh, Constitutional Review under the UK Human Rights Act (Cambridge University Press 2009), p. 23; Mark Elliott and Robert Thomas, *Public Law* (Oxford University Press 2011), p. 737.

[17] *Poplar Housing and Regeneration* v. *Donoghue*, [2001] EWCA Civ 595; *Wardle* v. *Leeds Crown Court*, [2002] 1 AC 754 [79]; *S* v. *L*, [2012] UKSC 30, para 15. Phillipson argues that the first stage of this analysis is based on convenience—'to discourage the courts from wasting time trying to apply section 3(1) to statutes which were Convention-compliant in the first place' rather than

These methods of interpretation include looking to the context of the legislation where its plain meaning is not clear.[18] Further, courts apply the presumption that the legislature did not intend to place the UK in breach of its international obligations.[19]

## Stage Two: Special Methods of Interpretation

In India, the next stage arises when courts conclude that legislation, on ordinary principles of interpretation, is not compliant with fundamental rights. Courts have held that at this stage, where statutory language permits, the impugned provisions should be read down or interpreted restrictively to make them fall within constitutional limits.[20] This is called the doctrine of 'reading down' or 'severability in application', which allows courts to restrict the application of a statutory provision to those areas in which it would be constitutionally permissible, omitting its application to areas in which it would transgress constitutional limits. In other words, the application of an overbroad statute can be narrowed down to fit within constitutional limits so long as the constitutionally valid spheres of application can be separated from the unconstitutional spheres of application, even if the language of the statute does not consider these spheres of application separately.

If, on the other hand, the unconstitutional spheres of application are in separate and distinct textual provisions from the constitutionally valid spheres of application, the court may sever or disapply the former, without affecting the operation of the latter. This is called 'severability in form'. Thus, for both kinds of severability, the principal question

---

principle; see Gavin Phillipson, '(Mis)-reading Section 3 of the Human Rights Act' (2003) 119 LQR 183. However, subsequent case law suggests otherwise. Lord Reed points out that there are constitutional grounds for determining whether ordinary construction of the statutory provision gives rise to an incompatibility before invoking section 3; see S (above), para 15.

[18] S (n. 17), para 16.

[19] S (n. 17), para 16.

[20] *Kedar Nath* v. *State of Bihar*, AIR 1962 SC 955: 1962 Supp (2) SCR 769, paras 26–7; *Commissioner of Sales Tax* v. *Radhakrishnan*, (1979) 2 SCC 249, para 15; *B.R. Enterprises* v. *State of Uttar Pradesh*, AIR 1999 SC 1867 [87]; *Indra Das* v. *State of Assam*, (2011) 3 SCC 380, para 24.

is whether the invalid portion of a statute can be separated from the valid portion (either textually or in terms of the breadth of its application). Severability is based on the presumed intention of the Indian Parliament that when a part of a statute is void, that should not affect the rest of the statute.[21]

In the UK, after courts decide that primary legislation is prima facie incompatible with Convention rights, they are tasked with deciding whether it can be read compatibly with Convention rights. Section 3 of the HRA directs courts to read and give effect to primary and subordinate legislation in a manner that is compatible with Convention rights, 'so far as it is possible to do so'. It applies to existing legislation and legislation passed after the enforcement of the HRA.[22] Section 3 enhanced the influence of Convention rights in the process of interpretation—rather than simply having to take them into account while interpreting ambiguous legislative provisions, courts would be required to interpret legislation so as to uphold Convention rights unless the legislation was so clearly incompatible that it would be impossible to do so.[23]

In the early years of the HRA, some scholars argued that on a proper understanding, section 3 marked a shift in the focus of courts from upholding parliamentary intention to interpreting legislation in a Convention-compliant manner, even if doing so was artificial and went

[21] *RMDC* v. *Union of India*, AIR 1957 SC 628.

[22] Section 3(2)(a) specifies that section 3 of the HRA 'applies to primary legislation and subordinate legislation whenever enacted'. There is an emerging body of judicial opinion and academic scholarship that suggests that common law and the HRA/Convention share a symbiotic relationship. See *R (Osborne)* v. *Parole Board*, [2013] 3 WLR 1020; T.R.S. Allan, *The Sovereignty of Law: Freedom, Constitution, and Common Law* (Oxford University Press 2013), p. 242; Conor Gearty, 'Theresa May's Human Rights Stunt' *The Guardian* (London, 4 May 2013); Lord Justice Laws, 'The Common Law and Europe' The Hamlyn Lecture Series: Lecture III (Exeter, 27 November 2013) <https://www.judiciary.gov.uk/wp-content/uploads/JCO/Documents/Speeches/laws-lj-speech-hamlyn-lecture-2013.pdf> accessed 22 September 2016. Therefore, it is unsafe to assume that courts would return to the pre-HRA position if section 3 (or, more likely, the HRA itself) were to be repealed.

[23] Home Office, *Rights Brought Home: The Human Rights Bill* (Cm 3782, 1997), para 2.7.

beyond the intent of lawmakers.[24] This argument requires qualification. There are two intentions at play in section 3 cases: the intention of Parliament in enacting the impugned statute and the intention of Parliament in enacting section 3 of the HRA.[25] Thus, the shift in focus, if at all, is in the selection of the second intention over the first. Others also highlight that section 3 is aimed at identifying the intention of Parliament with the rebuttable presumption that the legislature does not intend to breach Convention rights, given the 'new constitutional setting' created by that provision.[26] According to Samuels, the judge must search for a 'legitimate, justified, reasonable, and proportionate interpretation', based on a broad rather than narrow legalistic approach.[27]

British courts have adopted the interpretive techniques of 'reading down'[28] and 'reading in'[29] in order to protect legislation from transgressing Convention rights.[30] As Lord Steyn observed in R v. A (No 2),[31] section 3 permits the courts to strain statutory language, read down express language, and imply provisions to promote compliance with Convention rights. However, courts cannot depart from a fundamental feature of a statute[32] or radically alter its effect[33] as this breaches the boundary between interpretation and amendment. Nor can courts, through an act of 'judicial vandalism', squarely contradict parliamentary intent.[34] In the House of Lords' seminal judgment in Ghaidan, it was emphasized by the majority that the limits of the application of

---

[24] Dawn Oliver, Constitutional Reform in the UK (Oxford University Press 2003), p. 114.

[25] Aileen Kavanagh, 'Unlocking the Human Rights Act: The "Radical" Approach to Section 3(1) Revisited' (2005) 3 EHRLR 259.

[26] Philip Sales and Richard Ekins, 'Rights-consistent Interpretation and the Human Rights Act 1998' (2011) 127 LQR 217, p. 138.

[27] Alec Samuels, 'Human Rights Act 1998 Section 3: A New Dimension to Statutory Interpretation?' (2008) 29 SLR 130.

[28] R v. Keogh, [2007] EWCA Crim 528.

[29] Ghaidan v. Godin-Mendoza, [2004] UKHL 30.

[30] Oliver (n. 24), p. 114.

[31] [2002] 1 AC 45.

[32] Ghaidan (n. 29); In re S, [2002] 2 AC 291.

[33] Poplar Housing and Regeneration v. Donoghue, [2001] EWCA Civ 595.

[34] R (Anderson) v. SSHD, (2003) 1 AC 837.

section 3 extend up to the conceptual scheme of the statute rather than the precise language used by parliamentary draftsmen to give effect to that scheme.[35] Moreover, courts are not required to make decisions for which they are not institutionally equipped.[36]

What is discernible from the case law is that courts in the UK remain context sensitive when determining the extent to which they are willing to mould statutory language and purpose.[37] This was made clear by Lord Hoffman's observation in *Wilkinson* that section 3 was not intended to 'have the effect of requiring the courts to give the language of statutes acontextual meanings'.[38] Thus, developing a self-standing test independent of context would probably be a futile exercise.[39]

### Stage Three: Striking Down Legislation and Declarations of Incompatibility

In India, courts approach the third stage after concluding that it is not possible, based on available interpretive techniques, to read legislation in compliance with rights. At the third stage, courts exercise their power to strike down legislation. The statute (or statutory provision) is disapplied with immediate effect, and the court's judgment applies prospectively as well as retrospectively as far as the parties to the dispute are concerned.[40]

In the UK, the third stage entails the court deciding whether it should make a declaration of incompatibility under section 4 of

---

[35] Kavanagh (n. 16), p. 52.

[36] *Ghaidan* (n. 29), para 33.

[37] Roger Masterman, 'Interpretations, Declarations and Dialogue: Rights Protection under the Human Rights Act and Victorian Charter of Human Rights and Responsibilities' [2009] PL 112.

[38] *R (Wilkinson)* v. *Inland Revenue Commissioners*, [2005] 1 WLR 1681, para 17.

[39] T.R.S. Allan, 'Parliament's Will and the Justice of the Common Law: The Human Rights Act in Constitutional Perspective' (2006) 59 CLP 27.

[40] Like most other courts that enjoy the power to strike down legislation, Indian courts have some discretion in limiting the effects of exercising this power. However, on account of certain textual and institutional constraints, Indian courts do not find it easy to limit the effects of the power to strike down legislation. These constraints are discussed in the final section of this chapter.

the HRA.[41] Section 4 empowers courts[42] to issue a declaration of incompatibility when legislation,[43] which cannot be interpreted in a Convention-compliant manner, is inconsistent with a Convention right. As explained in earlier chapters, a declaration of incompatibility is not binding on the parties to the proceeding and 'does not affect the validity, continuing operation or enforcement of the provision in respect of which it is given'.[44] In other words, it does not give rise to an automatic legal benefit for the litigant and has no immediate effect on their legal rights.[45] However, it is an important form of political and moral sanction and invites Parliament and the government to address the incompatibility. It also triggers a statutory power to enable a minister to take fast-track remedial action. Under section 10 of the HRA, a minister of the Crown may, if he finds compelling reasons to do so, make amendments to legislation as he considers necessary to remove the incompatibility identified by a declaration under section 4 of the HRA.[46] Unless it is declared urgent, a remedial order can only be made when a draft of the order has been approved by a resolution of each House of Parliament.[47]

[41] Unlike section 3, which is framed in obligatory language, section 4 gives courts discretion in choosing whether to make a declaration of incompatibility.

[42] Section 4(5) of the HRA specifies that only the following courts may issue declarations of incompatibility: the Supreme Court; the Judicial Committee of the Privy Council; the Court Martial Appeal Court; the High Court of Justiciary sitting otherwise than as a trial court or the Court of Session (Scotland); the High Court or the Court of Appeal (England and Wales or Northern Ireland); the Court of Protection, in any matter being dealt with by the President of the Family Division, the Chancellor or a puisne judge of the High Court.

[43] This encompasses primary legislation and subordinate legislation made in exercise of a power conferred by primary legislation, where such primary legislation prevents removal of the incompatibility. This chapter focuses on primary legislation.

[44] HRA, section 4.

[45] T.R.S. Allan, 'Questions of Legality and Legitimacy: Form and Substance in British Constitutionalism' (2011) 9 International Journal of Constitutional Law 155.

[46] This ministerial power is controversial, and has courted serious criticism on separation of powers and rule of law grounds. See, for example, William Wade, 'The Human Rights Act and the Judiciary' (1998) 5 EHRLR 520.

[47] HRA, Schedule 2.

## Progressing from Stage Two to Stage Three

The major distinction between the three-stage analysis conducted in India and the UK is the point at which courts progress from stage two to stage three. Two factors indicate that stage two is prolonged in the UK, since courts in the UK have a larger interpretive toolbox at their disposal than their Indian counterparts. First, unlike British courts, which are quite prepared to adopt the technique of 'reading in' to protect statutory provisions, Indian courts (which frequently 'read down' legislation) consider 'reading in' as an illegitimate interpretive technique.[48] In the absence of a section 3–type mandate, Indian courts remain unwilling to adopt this technique on account of the fact that, unlike 'reading down', 'reading in' involves extending the application of a statute to areas beyond parliamentary contemplation.[49]

Second, Indian courts consider the language of the statute a pivotal factor in determining whether a rights-complaint interpretation is possible. In a frequently cited passage, the Indian Supreme Court observed that where a statutory provision cannot be saved because its plain meaning is clear, courts should not be hesitant to strike it down.[50] Although striking down a statute is a measure of last resort,[51] Indian courts do not protect legislation from constitutional challenge by distorting or contradicting statutory language.[52] This position stands in contrast with courts in the UK, which consider the broad scheme and essential

---

[48] B.R. Kapur v. State of Tamil Nadu, AIR 2001 SC 3435, para 39.

[49] As Hogg posits, 'reading in' involves the insertion 'of words that Parliament never enacted' and is therefore 'a technique of judicial amendment'. See Peter W. Hogg, Constitutional Law of Canada (5th edn, Carswell 2007), para 40.1(g).

[50] B.R. Enterprises v. State of Uttar Pradesh, AIR 1999 SC 1867, para 87, cited in Calcutta Gujarati Education Society v. Calcutta Municipal Corporation, AIR 2003 SC 4278, para 35; Union of India v. Ind-Swift Laboratories, [2011] 2 SCR 1087, para 18.

[51] Laxmi Devi (n. 12).

[52] The Indian Supreme Court's judgment in Noor Aga v. State of Punjab, (2008) 16 SCC 417 is a notable exception. In this case, in reading down section 35 of the Narcotic Drugs and Psychotropic Substances Act, 1985, the Court went squarely against the language of the statute. Subsequent decisions have not endorsed this interpretive approach.

features (rather than the language) of the statute as decisive in determining whether it can be read in compliance with Convention rights.[53]

The fact that British courts have a larger range of interpretive tools at their disposal suggests that the power to strike down legislation triggers earlier in India than the power to make a declaration of incompatibility does in the UK. This means that, hypothetically speaking and ceteris paribus, there would be identical cases in which section 3 of the HRA is invoked to read legislation in a Convention-compliant manner in the UK but in which the legislation is struck down in India.[54] Taking this idea further, cases in which UK courts declare legislation incompatible would be expected to correspond with cases in which the power to strike down legislation is invoked in India.

It is worth considering an example reflecting the argument that stage three is triggered earlier in India than it is in the UK. The House of Lords (in *Hammond*)[55] and the Indian Supreme Court (in *Bidhannagar Welfare Association*)[56] were confronted with a common question—could a statutory provision which expressly or by necessary implication excluded the right to a pre-decisional oral hearing be interpreted to allow an oral hearing in certain circumstances? *Hammond*[57] concerned a provision[58] of the Criminal Justice Act, 2003 enabling prisoners subjected to mandatory life sentences to apply to a high court judge for reconsideration of the 'tariff'[59] set for them by the home secretary. The statutory provision categorically stated that such applications were to be determined 'without an oral hearing'.[60] However, the possibility of appealing from

---

[53] *Ghaidan* (n. 29).

[54] This claim is based on a further underlying assumption: that courts in India and the UK foster an equal commitment to protect fundamental rights or human rights.

[55] *R (Hammond)* v. *SSHD*, [2006] 1 AC 603.

[56] *Bidhannagar Welfare Association* v. *Central Valuation Board*, AIR 2007 SC 2276.

[57] *Hammond* (n. 55).

[58] Schedule 22, paragraph 11(1).

[59] This refers to the minimum period necessary to satisfy the requirements of retribution and deterrence before consideration would be given to any question of the prisoner's release on licence.

[60] Schedule 22, paragraph 11(1) of the Criminal Justice Act, 2003 read as follows: 'An application under paragraph 3 or a reference under paragraph 6 is to be determined by a single judge of the High Court without an oral hearing.'

the High Court's decision to the Court of Appeal (where the prisoner would secure an oral hearing) remained open.

The claimant contended that by denying him an oral hearing at first instance, this statutory provision was incompatible with his right to a fair trial under Art. 6 of the Convention. The House of Lords agreed, holding that notwithstanding the possibility of an appeal, the denial of an oral hearing at first instance breached Art. 6. Relying on section 3 of the HRA, it confirmed the Divisional Court's decision to read the statutory provision as permitting an oral hearing where it was necessary to meet the requirements of fairness. So even though the language of the statute contained a blanket prohibition on oral hearings, the House effectively interpreted the statutory provision so as to allow oral hearings in a narrow category of cases.[61]

On the other hand, *Bidhannagar* involved a constitutional challenge to state legislation[62] that regulated the valuation of lands for the assessment of property tax. The statute that was challenged excluded provisions in earlier legislation[63] that allowed an oral hearing to affected parties before a draft valuation was prepared. It was thus clear that by necessary implication, the amending statute had excluded the right to a pre-decisional hearing. The statute did, however, contain provisions for review of the original decision.

Mirroring the argument advanced by the British government in *Hammond*, the state government of West Bengal contended that the possibility of review cured the breach of the rules of natural justice at

---

[61] The House of Lords provided a disclaimer that since the parties to the proceeding accepted that this exercise of reinterpretation was possible, its decision should not be taken as authorizing such a bold exercise of interpretation under section 3 of the HRA; see *Hammond* (n. 55), paras 17, 29, 30. However, this disclaimer has a limited impact on the argument that is made here, for two reasons. First, the House of Lords did accept that its decision was only achievable by virtue of section 3 and that it was possible to interpret a statute prohibiting oral hearings as allowing an oral hearing where fairness required it; see Timothy Endicott, *Administrative Law* (2nd edn, Oxford University Press 2011), p. 136. Second, the Divisional Court's judgment considered this remarkable interpretation of the statutory provision as a legitimate application of section 3 of the HRA; see *R (Hammond)* v. *SSHD*, [2004] EWHC 2753 (Admin), para 33.

[62] West Bengal Central Valuation Board (Amendment) Act, 1994.

[63] West Bengal Central Valuation Board Act, 1978.

first instance. The Indian Supreme Court rejected this contention, holding that generally, any order entailing civil consequences would need to be preceded by an opportunity of being heard.[64] It cited precedent to the effect that a statutory provision could be construed so as require the observance of rules of natural justice as long as it was silent on the matter.[65] However a statute that expressly or by necessary implication *excluded the rules of natural justice* could not be read as *including the rules of natural justice* to protect it from being struck down. As a result, the Indian Supreme Court moved from stage two to stage three of the analysis to strike down the statute. Thus, in similar situations, the House of Lords relied on section 3 of the HRA and remained at stage two of the analysis *in spite of* contrary statutory language, whereas the Indian Supreme Court moved to stage three and struck down the statutory provision *because of* contrary statutory language.

This analysis, however, is not always borne out in practice: seemingly presented with no choice but to strike down a statute, Indian courts sometimes rethink the constitutionality of the statute and uphold it without taking recourse to special interpretive techniques. In other words, at the cusp of stage two and stage three, Indian courts sometimes step back to stage one to reconsider the validity of the statute facing challenge, resulting in a situation in which courts disguise their real interpretation of rights with an alternative interpretation of rights. This unique process, and possible explanations for it, will be explored through three pairs of cases in the following section.

## Adjudication in the Shadow of the Remedy: Three Examples

An obvious issue that is worth addressing upfront is whether three examples, or three cases from each jurisdiction, are sufficient to establish the broader claims being made in this chapter. This resonates particularly in the Indian context, where the Supreme Court hears thousands of cases a year, many of which involve challenges to primary legislation. The charge of 'cherry-picking' can be rebutted with the argument that the cases considered are amongst the most salient cases that the Indian Supreme Court has decided.

---

[64] *Bidhannagar* (n. 56), para 29.

[65] *C.B. Gautam v. Union of India*, (1993) 1 SCC 78.

This is indicated by the size of the bench—comprising five judges—hearing *Kartar Singh*, suggesting that the Court was deciding a 'substantial question of law as to the interpretation' of the Constitution.[66] If newspaper reports of Supreme Court decisions can be treated as a reliable indicator of case salience, the other two—*Naz Foundation* and the *Sharma* cases—were amongst the most salient constitutional cases decided by the Supreme Court between 2010 and 2013.[67] While bench strength provides a useful endogenous marker of case salience, newspaper reports provide a useful exogenous marker of case salience.[68] This chapter relies on both.

## Recently Enacted Legislation with a Strong Democratic Mandate: *Sharma* and *Thompson*

The *Sharma* cases in the Indian Supreme Court and the UK Supreme Court's decision in *Thompson* will be considered as the first example of the impact of the power to strike down legislation on judicial rights reasoning.

### Sharma I—The First Round of Litigation

In *Namit Sharma* v. *Union of India*,[69] the petitioner, described by the Court as a public-spirited citizen, challenged the constitutional validity

---

[66]   See Constitution of India, Art. 145(3).

[67]   See Chintan Chandrachud, 'Measuring Constitutional Case Salience in the Indian Supreme Court' (2016) Journal of Indian Law and Society 42, arguing that on account of the decline in Constitution Benches consisting of five or more judges, the number of citations of a case in the *Times of India* within one year of the decision can be treated as a reliable proxy for case salience. The *Naz Foundation* case was cited a staggering 386 times in the year after the decision, whereas both the *Sharma* cases were cited nine times in that period. Close to 85 per cent of Supreme Court decisions in that period were cited on less than five occasions, while 58 per cent of Supreme Court decisions were never cited.

[68]   Media-based measures are the most common proxy for political case salience, since the views of newspaper editors, as elite actors, are likely to correspond with those of the judges. See Chandrachud (n. 67); Lee Epstein and Jeffrey A. Segal, 'Measuring Issue Salience' (2000) 44 American Journal of Political Science 66.

[69]   *Sharma I* (n. 1).

of several provisions of the Right to Information Act, 2005 (RTIA) in the Indian Supreme Court.[70] The RTIA was a revolutionary statute enacted by India's Parliament to enable citizens to access information under the control of public authorities. It fostered a variety of important objectives, including establishing a more informed citizenry and promoting transparency in the functioning of public institutions. It established complex institutional machinery to deal with complaints concerning requests for information, including a Central Information Commission for the Union and a State Information Commission for each state.

The statutory eligibility criteria for the appointment of members of the Central and State Information Commissions provided that they 'shall be persons of eminence in public life with wide knowledge and experience in law, science and technology, social service, management, journalism, mass media or administration and governance'.[71] The petitioner claimed that these criteria were arbitrary and vague and thus, violated the right to equality under Art. 14[72] of the Constitution. He also contended that since the Commissions performed judicial or quasi-judicial functions, they should consist predominantly of persons with legal qualifications and judicial experience—something that the RTIA failed to stipulate. The RTIA also detailed a set of ineligibility criteria—Commission members could not be 'a Member of Parliament or Member of the Legislature of any State or Union territory ... or hold any other office of profit or [be] connected with any political party or carrying on any business or pursuing any profession'.[73] The petitioner challenged these criteria on similar grounds of vagueness.

The Court empathized with the petitioner's arguments from the outset. However, it held that it would be reluctant to strike down a law and that doing so would be a measure of last resort. The Court claimed that the principles that had emerged from a 'consistent view' taken by the Court was that it would invoke interpretive tools such as 'reading down'

---

[70] The petition was filed under Art. 32 of the Constitution, which empowers citizens to move the Supreme Court at first instance for the violation of fundamental rights.

[71] RTIA, sections 12(5), 15(5).

[72] Article 14 of the Indian Constitution reads: 'Equality before law: The State shall not deny to any person equality before the law or the equal protection of the laws within the territory of India.'

[73] RTIA, sections 12(6), 15(6).

or 'reading into'[74] statutory provisions so as to save them from unconstitutionality.[75] Based on this putative line of authority, the Court radically reinterpreted the statutory provisions that were challenged. It held that in order to lend clarity to the eligibility provisions of the RTIA, the expression 'knowledge and experience' in specified fields would be read down to be restricted to persons who had basic educational qualifications in those fields.

Perhaps more remarkably, it held that since Information Commissions possessed the trappings of a court, they were quasi-judicial authorities that should predominantly consist of persons with experience in adjudication. Even if people without a judicial background were appointed, they should only make decisions in benches of two sitting with someone that had judicial experience. Finally, the Court held that appointment of members to the Commissions should be made in consultation with the Chief Justice of India or the Chief Justice of the relevant state. This was in spite of the statutory regime making no mention of judicial consultation in the appointments process—appointments were to be made by a 'High Powered Committee' consisting of political leaders from the government and the opposition. In fact, legislative history indicates that provisions for judicial presence on the High Powered Committee were specifically dropped.[76]

The Court's approach to the ineligibility criteria in the RTIA was equally radical. It considered the ineligibility criteria so broad and vague that it was unsure about which category of people would actually be eligible for appointment. It read down the disqualifications so as to be applicable post-appointment only. In other words, people holding positions that fell within the ineligibility criteria would be eligible for appointment, so long as they demitted office before being appointed as members of the Commissions.

Soon after it was made, the decision in *Sharma I* was subjected to widespread criticism. One scholar's remarks were particularly caustic: he described the judgment as 'rich in florid prose, disdainful of brevity' and

---

[74] It is not clear from the Court's judgment whether by 'reading into', the Court meant what is commonly described as 'reading in'.

[75] *Sharma I* (n. 1), para 47.

[76] See Rajya Sabha Debates, *The Right to Information Bill, 2005* (12 May 2005), p. 320 <http://rsdebate.nic.in/bitstream/123456789/47229/1/PD_204_1205 2005_37_p263_p350_13.pdf> accessed 22 September 2016.

'animated by a desire to legislate'.[77] The Court assumed interpretive powers that were unprecedented. It curiously said that its wide interpretive mandate 'clearly emerge[d]' from the 'consistent view' of the Court,[78] without citing a single judgment as evidence of this mandate. By insisting that members of Information Commissions should consist of (and perhaps more remarkably, be appointed by) judges, the Court undermined Parliament's intention of ensuring that a diversity of viewpoints are represented in the quest for increasing transparency and access to information.[79] Significantly aggrandizing the judicial role in the functioning of the right to information regime therefore disturbed a fundamental feature of the statute. The Indian Supreme Court's judgment went beyond even what British courts, following the majority in *Ghaidan*, would have done armed with the mandate of section 3 of the HRA.[80] If the Court remained sceptical about the lack of a robust judicial role in the RTIA, the appropriate recourse would have been to strike down the statute.

## Sharma II—Rethinking the Radical Approach in Sharma I

Unsurprisingly, the government too was dissatisfied with the Supreme Court's judgment in *Sharma I*. It soon petitioned the Court, seeking a review of its judgment, on the basis that the Court had committed 'errors apparent on the face of the record'.[81] The government argued that reinterpreting the provisions in the manner that was done in *Sharma I*

[77] A.G. Noorani, 'Judiciary's Assault on Democracy' *The Hindu* (Chennai, 12 January 2013). Andhyarujina described the judgment as effectively amending the RTIA; see T.R. Andhyarujina, 'The Unique Judicial Activism of the Supreme Court of India' (2014) 130 LQR 53, p. 61. See also Dhananjay Mahapatra, 'Judgments Should Not Read Like Monologues' *The Times of India* (17 September 2012); Seetha, 'Tough Act to Follow' *The Telegraph* (26 September 2012).

[78] *Sharma I* (n. 1), para 47.

[79] Chintan Chandrachud, 'Beyond Ghaidan and Back: The Supreme Court of India on Rights-compliant Interpretation' (*UK Constitutional Law Association*, 29 November 2013) <https://ukconstitutionallaw.org/2013/11/30/chintan-chandrachud-beyond-ghaidan-and-back-the-supreme-court-of-india-on-rights-compliant-interpretation/> accessed 24 September 2016.

[80] Chandrachud (n. 79).

[81] See Constitution of India, Art. 137 and Supreme Court Rules, 1966, Order XL, Rule 1.

was justified neither by the Court's precedent nor by the terms of the RTIA. The respondent (the original petitioner in *Sharma I*) argued that if the Court considered it an error to reinterpret the statutory provisions in the manner that it did, it would be left with no choice but to strike them down as unconstitutional.

The Indian Supreme Court accepted most of the government's arguments in its judgment in *Union of India* v. *Namit Sharma*.[82] It held that the Central and State Information Commissions did not perform judicial or quasi-judicial functions under the RTIA—they performed purely administrative functions and did not decide disputes between parties. Acknowledging that imposing a requirement that Commissions should be staffed primarily by judges was an 'encroachment in the field of legislation',[83] the Court upheld the validity of the eligibility criteria set out in the RTIA. It dispensed with the requirement imposed by the Bench in *Sharma I* that the chief justice of India or the chief justice of the relevant state be consulted in making appointments to the Commissions. The Supreme Court in *Sharma II* also overturned *Sharma I*'s reading down of the eligibility criteria, which had effectively enabled only those who had educational qualifications (rather than 'knowledge and experience') in specified fields to be appointed. The Court believed that this reading of the eligibility criteria was contrary to settled principles of statutory interpretation.[84] One segment of the judgment in *Sharma I* remained intact—the *Sharma II* bench considered that the narrow interpretation of the ineligibility criteria for Commission members (so as to apply post-appointment only) was justified.

In spite of upholding the constitutional validity of the RTIA in *Sharma II*, the Supreme Court seemed to harbour a sense of discomfort with many of its provisions and their implementation:[85]

---

[82]  *Sharma II* (n. 1).

[83]  *Sharma II* (n. 1), para 25.

[84]  The Indian Supreme Court in *Sharma II* mistakenly identified what the Court did in *Sharma I* as 'reading into' the provisions of the statute. What the Court actually had done was to read down its provisions, since it narrowed the category of persons eligible for the positions to those with knowledge and experience in certain fields having educational qualifications in those fields. The Court's interpretation excluded those with knowledge and experience, but without educational qualifications, in the specified fields.

[85]  *Sharma II* (n. 1), para 31.

Unfortunately, experience over the years has shown that the orders passed by Information Commissions have at times gone beyond the provisions of the Act and that Information Commissions have not been able to harmonise the conflicting interests [transparency and optimal utilisation of state resources] indicated in the preamble and other provisions of the Act. The reasons for this experience ... could be either that persons who do not answer the criteria mentioned [in the RTIA] ... have been appointed ... or that the persons appointed answer the criteria ... but they do not have the required mind to balance the interests indicated in the Act and to restrain themselves from acting beyond the provisions of the Act. This experience of the functioning of the Information Commissions prompted this Court to issue the directions in the judgment under review [*Sharma I*] to appoint judicial members in the Information Commissions. But it is for Parliament to consider whether appointment of judicial members in the Information Commissions will improve the functioning of the Information Commissions.

The Court thus remained sympathetic with the *Sharma I* judgment, which is evident from its comment that the experience under the RTIA had 'prompted' the Court to reinterpret the provisions of the statute.[86] While the *Sharma II* Court echoed the statutory requirement of appointing persons from diverse fields to the Commissions, it also said that it hoped that persons with wide knowledge and experience in law would be appointed. Moreover, where the chief information commissioner was of the opinion that intricate questions of law would have to be decided, he should ensure that a commissioner with legal knowledge and experience would hear the matter. In order to promote transparency in the appointments process, the Court said that the High Powered Committee established by the RTIA should mention, against the name of each candidate recommended, the facts that indicate his eminence in public life, and his knowledge and experience in a particular field.[87] In one of the case hearings, the bench is reported to have remarked that independent members needed to be appointed to the Commissions and that the government was regrettably appointing people who were in their 'good books'.[88] Thus, in spite of serious misgivings about the

---

[86] *Sharma II* (n. 1), para 31.

[87] *Sharma II* (n. 1), para 32.

[88] Press Trust of India, 'CIC, ICs Should Be Independent of Govt Influence: Supreme Court' (*The Hindu*, 22 November 2012) <http://www.thehindu.com/

RTIA, the Court chose to uphold, rather than strike down, the relevant statutory provisions.

## The UK Supreme Court in Thompson

The Westminster Parliament enacted the Sexual Offences Act, 2003 (SOA) with the objective of preventing and punishing a range of sexual offences. It contained detailed provisions as to notification requirements by sexual offenders. These notification requirements included informing authorities in advance about address changes and foreign travel plans. Every notification under the SOA had to be made in person at a police station.

The two claimants in the case had previously been convicted and sentenced for committing sexual offences and were subjected to indefinite notification requirements by virtue of section 82(1) of the SOA[89] based on the term of their sentences. No statutory mechanism was available for reviewing the indefinite notification requirements, which effectively meant that they would be burdened by these requirements for life. The claimants contended that the notification requirements were inconsistent with the right to private and family life under Art. 8 of the Convention.[90] The Divisional Court agreed, holding that lifelong notification requirements, in the absence of any review process, were disproportionate and breached Art. 8.[91] Since the Court found that an

---

news/national/cic-ics-should-be-independent-of-govt-influence-supreme-court/
article4123334.ece> accessed 11 March 2014.

[89] Section 82(1) of the SOA provides a table specifying the relevant notification period for different classes of offenders. Those imprisoned for a term of 30 months or more would be subjected to indefinite notification requirements.

[90] Article 8 of the Convention reads as follows:

1. Everyone has the right to respect for his private and family life, his home and his correspondence. 2. There shall be no interference by a public authority with the exercise of this right except such as is in accordance with the law and is necessary in a democratic society in the interests of national security, public safety or the economic well-being of the country, for the prevention of disorder or crime, for the protection of health or morals, or for the protection of the rights and freedoms of others.

[91] *R (Thompson)* v. *SSHD*, [2008] EWHC 3170 (Admin).

Art. 8–compliant interpretation of the statutory provisions was not possible without doing 'unacceptable violence to the statutory words',[92] it made a declaration of incompatibility. The Court of Appeal confirmed this conclusion on the basis that Art. 8 entitled the offender to seek a review of whether the notification requirements continued to serve any legitimate purpose.[93]

The Home Secretary appealed to the Supreme Court. While highlighting the importance of the legislative objective of preventing sexual offending, Lord Phillips (speaking for the majority) held that lifelong, unreviewable notification requirements were not a proportionate means of achieving that objective.[94] Implicit in the requirement to notify the police was the fact that the offender would have to explain the purpose of the notification to police authorities, which carried the risk of the information being inappropriately passed to third parties. His judgment also demonstrated a sense of unease with the manner in which the SOA was operating:

> If some of those who are subject to lifetime notification requirements no longer pose any significant risk … there is no point in subjecting them to supervision or management or to the interference with their article 8 rights involved in visits to their local police stations…. Indeed subjecting them to these requirements can only impose an unnecessary and unproductive burden on the responsible authorities. We were informed that there are now some 24,000 ex-offenders subject to notification requirements and this number will inevitably grow.

By the time the matter reached the Supreme Court, the claimants had accepted that in the event that the Court found the notification requirements in breach of Art. 8, a declaration of incompatibility would be the only appropriate remedy. Accordingly, Lord Phillips confirmed the declaration of incompatibility made by the Divisional Court, with a rider that it would be open to Parliament, when addressing the

---

[92] *R (Thompson)* v. *SSHD*, [2008] EWHC 3170 (Admin), para 28. This chapter does not seek to address the valid question of whether a refusal to invoke section 3 of the HRA on the ground of doing violence to statutory words is a correct representation of the case law, or, for that matter, justified in constitutional principle.

[93] *R (Thompson)* v. *SSHD*, [2010] 1 WLR 76.

[94] *Thompson* (n. 2).

incompatibility, to impose 'an appropriately high threshold' for those seeking review of their indefinite notification requirements.[95]

## The Similarities between Sharma I and Sharma II, and Thompson

The cases of *Sharma I and Sharma II* and *Thompson* were plainly different in some respects. The former concerned the review of a statute for social empowerment, the latter dealt with the compliance of provisions of a penal statute with Art. 8 of the Convention. However, there were significant similarities between the cases that are worth noticing. The legislation reviewed in both cases had a strong and relatively recent political mandate. The RTIA was mentioned both in the Congress party–led United Progressive Alliance government's 'common minimum programme'[96] and in the Congress party's election manifesto for the general elections of 2004.[97] Many commentators considered the enactment of the RTIA as a defining moment in independent India; a concerted effort to transform India into a participatory democracy.[98] The minister in charge of the bill described it in the Upper House of Parliament as a measure that would alter the existing administrative ethos and culture of secrecy in the functioning of government departments.[99]

The SOA, which replaced the Sexual Offences Act, 1956, was the culmination of a detailed review of sexual offences by the New Labour

---

[95] *Thompson* (n. 2), para 57. Lord Rodger (with whom Lord Hope agreed) clarified that he saw no reason for which the indefinite notification requirements under section 82 of the SOA breached Art. 8 in and of themselves. The incompatibility, in his view, stemmed exclusively from the absence of a review mechanism.

[96] The full text of the Common Minimum Programme is available here: <http://www.hindu.com/2004/05/28/stories/2004052807371200.htm> accessed 12 March 2014.

[97] Krishnan Srinivasan, 'Right to Know: The RTI Act 2005 Demands Transparency From All' *The Telegraph* (Calcutta, 20 March 2007).

[98] Oulac Niranjan, 'Right to Information and the Road to Heaven' (2005) 40 Economic and Political Weekly 4870; EPW Editorial, 'Power to the People' (2005) 40 Economic and Political Weekly 2115.

[99] Rajya Sabha Debates, *The Right to Information Bill, 2005* (12 May 2005), .p. 267 <http://rsdebate.nic.in/bitstream/123456789/47229/1/PD_204_1205 2005_37_p263_p350_13.pdf> accessed 22 September 2016.

government that was in office from 1997 to 2010. This review included a report[100] by the Home Office and a government white paper.[101] Thus, in the *Sharma* cases and in *Thompson*, the courts were faced with challenges to legislation of fairly recent vintage. In fact, when the two Supreme Courts decided these cases, the same government that was responsible for the legislation was still in office, having won the general election following the enactment of the legislation.[102]

Another striking similarity between *Thompson* and the *Sharma* cases was that although discrete statutory provisions were under challenge for non-compliance with fundamental rights, the provisions were closely intertwined with the statutory regime in which they subsisted. This meant that the costs of striking down were high. For the Indian Supreme Court, the challenge to the eligibility and ineligibility criteria for members of the Information Commissions was as good as a challenge to the entire institutional machinery of the RTIA. The Information Commissions, operating at the central and state levels, were the staple bodies that monitored public authorities' compliance with the provisions of the RTIA. The appointment of members to these Commissions therefore constituted a central cog in the functioning of the RTIA.[103]

---

[100] Home Office, *Setting the Boundaries: Reforming the Law on Sexual Offences* (Home Office Communication Directorate 2000).

[101] Home Office, *Protecting the Public: Strengthening Protection against Sex Offenders and Reforming the Law on Sexual Offences* (UK Government, 2002).

[102] In the UK, the New Labour government (first under Prime Minister Tony Blair and later, Prime Minister Gordon Brown) remained in office until May 2010, which was after the Supreme Court's judgment in *Thompson* (the judgment was delivered in April 2010). In India, the United Progressive Alliance coalition government under Prime Minister Manmohan Singh (of which the Congress was the single largest party) was in office at the time at which *Sharma I* and *Sharma II* were decided. The coalition government took a slightly different form at the time the cases were decided compared to the time at which the coalition government was originally formed in 2004.

[103] A possible objection to this analysis is that the Court need not have been as concerned (as this author contends) about striking down the statutory provisions, because citizens would still retain the *right* to information. This objection is misconceived because the principal purpose of the RTIA was not to establish citizens' right to information, which was a constitutionally recognized right well before the RTIA was enacted; see *Express Newspapers* v. *Union of India*, AIR

Similarly, in *Thompson*, a specific statutory provision—section 82 of the SOA—was under challenge. It formed part of a complex web of notification requirements woven together by the statute. The notification requirements in the case of offenders sentenced to imprisonment for terms of 30 months or more was one category of the several laid down in the 'notification period' table under section 82. It was, in fact, probably one of the more important categories, being open-ended in the sense that it applied equally to offenders sentenced to over 30 months' imprisonment, irrespective of the extent to which they crossed the 30-month bright line.

### Similar Leanings, Different Outcomes

In the *Thompson* and *Sharma* cases, the courts in both jurisdictions quickly made the switch from stage one to stage two of the analysis, realizing that the statutory provisions could not be saved based on ordinary principles of interpretation. Both courts also contemplated halting at stage two by adopting a rights-compliant interpretation of the legislation under review. The contemplation in *Thompson* was relatively short. The Divisional Court, which was the first in the hierarchy to hear the case, realized that the notification requirements under the SOA could not be reinterpreted without doing undue violence to the statute. At the level of the Court of Appeal and the Supreme Court, all the parties, and the Court, accepted that invoking section 3 was not a viable option.

The contemplation at stage two was prolonged in the *Sharma* cases. In *Sharma I*, the Indian Supreme Court used unprecedented interpretive techniques to reinterpret provisions of the RTIA in compliance with the constitutional right to equality. However, realizing its error, the Court acknowledged in *Sharma II* that it would not be possible to reinterpret the RTIA in the manner that it had done without trespassing into Parliament's domain.

---

1986 SC 872. Rather, the RTIA was enacted in order to set up a practical regime to give effect to citizens' (pre-existing) right to information. Hence, the striking down of the relevant statutory provisions would have defeated the main purpose of the statute.

What followed in both courts was most interesting. As one might have expected, the courts in the UK took the next step and moved to stage three, choosing to make a declaration that the relevant provisions of the SOA were incompatible with Art. 8 of the Convention. The Indian Supreme Court however, took a step back and veered away from its genuine understanding of rights, reluctantly holding instead that the provisions of the RTIA did not violate Art. 14 of the Constitution in the first place. That the Indian Supreme Court was uncomfortable with this conclusion is evident from many of the apprehensions expressed by the Court in its judgment, which have been set out above.

So why did the Indian Supreme Court (unlike its UK counterpart) reluctantly rethink the constitutionality of the provisions of the RTIA in *Sharma II*? The explanation can be traced back to the difference in the architecture of the HRA and the Indian Constitution. When courts in the UK consider that primary legislation violating Convention rights cannot be read compatibly, the most that they can do is to make a declaration of incompatibility. As the HRA itself affirms, the declaration does not affect the 'validity, continuing operation or enforcement' of legislation.[104] The ball is simply thrown back into Parliament and the government's court, which is left with deciding whether to (and if so, how to) eradicate the incompatibility.[105] Therefore, in spite of the declaration of incompatibility in *Thompson*, the notification requirements of the SOA remained operative until they were amended by the Sexual Offences Act (Remedial) Order, 2012, which sought to address the incompatibility by providing for review of indefinite notification requirements. In sharp contrast, when Indian courts consider that primary legislation cannot be read compatibly with fundamental rights, the remedial alternative for them is to strike down the unconstitutional legislative provisions, resulting in their immediate disapplication.

Hypothetically speaking, the invocation of the power to strike down legislation in cases such as *Thompson* and *Sharma* would have had serious implications. As pointed out above, the statutory provisions in question in both cases were deeply interwoven in the legislative

---

[104] HRA, section 4(6)(a).

[105] The question of whether Parliament chooses to respond positively to the declaration of incompatibility is a different matter, which has been dealt with at some length in Chapters 2 and 3.

regime as a whole. Striking them down would potentially short-circuit the implementation of the entire statute. How comfortable would the courts have been throwing a spanner into the works of a statutory regime that was recently approved by a democratically elected government which still commanded a legislative majority? Constitutional scholars have argued that the older the legislation challenged, the easier the courts find it to strike it down (and the more likely it is that they will do so).[106] This is because recently enacted laws place the court in the tricky position of invalidating a current expression of the majority's will by repudiating a recent legislative choice.[107] Increased time lags between the enactment of the statute and the court's judgment tend to lessen democratic and counter-majoritarian concerns held by judges.[108]

Moreover, both the SOA and the RTIA were not quite 'run-of-the-mill' legislation.[109] This is clear from parliamentary debates on the two statutes. The minister introducing the RTIA in the Upper House of the Indian Parliament described the Bill as a 'historic' piece of legislation and a 'significant landmark in the evolution of the right

---

[106] Robert A. Dahl, 'Decision-making in a Democracy: The Supreme Court as a National Policy-maker' (1957) 6 Journal of Public Law 279, p. 293; Joseph Ignagni and James Meernik, 'Explaining Congressional Attempts to Reverse Supreme Court Decisions' (1994) 47 Political Research Quarterly 353, p. 362; Michael J. Klarman, 'Rethinking the Civil Rights and Civil Liberties Revolutions' (1996) 82 Virginia Law Review 1, p. 16; Jack M. Balkin, 'Framework Originalism and the Living Constitution' (2009) 103 Northwestern University Law Review 549, p. 563.

[107] William J. Nardini, 'Passive Activism and the Limits of Judicial Self-Restraint: Lessons for America from the Italian Constitutional Court' (1999) 30 Seton Hall Law Review 1, p. 4.

[108] Chien-Chih Lin, 'Majoritarian Judicial Review: The Case of Taiwan' (2014) 9 National Taiwan University Law Review 103, p. 110.

[109] In fact, if we were to conduct the thought experiment suggested by Ernest Young of finding constitutional statutes beyond the canonical Constitution in the Indian context, the RTIA would almost certainly figure on the list; see Ernest A. Young, 'The Constitution Outside the Constitution' (2007) 117 Yale Law Journal 408.

to information'.[110] Other members described it as an 'epoch-making' statute in India's independent history,[111] a 'pacesetter',[112] and a politically bold and courageous piece of legislation.[113] In the House of Commons, the Sexual Offences Bill was described as a 'very important bill' that recognized 'changing attitudes to sex and personal relations'.[114] Thus, both statutes were considered revolutionary—measures that were intended to prompt a change in societal culture. The UK Supreme Court and the Indian Supreme Court were clearly conscious of this.[115] These factors heavily influenced the Indian Supreme Court's decision to rethink the constitutional validity of the RTIA in *Sharma II* by masking its real rights reasoning, and step back to stage one from the brink of stage three.

---

[110] Rajya Sabha Debates, *The Right to Information Bill, 2005* (12 May 2005), p. 263 (Suresh Pachouri) <http://rsdebate.nic.in/bitstream/123456789/47229/1/PD_204_12052005_37_p263_p350_13.pdf> accessed 22 September 2016.

[111] Rajya Sabha Debates, *The Right to Information Bill, 2005* (12 May 2005), p. 267 (P.C. Alexander) <http://rsdebate.nic.in/bitstream/123456789/47229/1/PD_204_12052005_37_p263_p350_13.pdf> accessed 22 September 2016.

[112] Rajya Sabha Debates, *The Right to Information Bill, 2005* (12 May 2005), p. 271 (Manmohan Singh) <http://rsdebate.nic.in/bitstream/123456789/47229/1/PD_204_12052005_37_p263_p350_13.pdf> accessed 22 September 2016.

[113] Rajya Sabha Debates, *The Right to Information Bill, 2005* (12 May 2005), p. 332 (R. Shunmugasundaram) <http://rsdebate.nic.in/bitstream/123456789/47229/1/PD_204_12052005_37_p263_p350_13.pdf> accessed 22 September 2016.

[114] HC Deb 15 July 2003, vol. 409, cols 196–7 (Sally Keeble). As Simon Hughes pointed out, until the bill came up for consideration, the UK 'had never before recognized that much of the existing law had been based on prejudices and assumptions that dated back to Victorian ages'; see HC Deb 15 July 2003, vol. 409, col. 201. Hilton Dawson noted that the Bill's importance 'cannot be overstated'; see HC Deb 15 July 2003, vol. 409, col. 213.

[115] *Thompson* (n. 2), para 18 (stating that 'the importance of the legislative objective [of the SOA] has never been in doubt' and that 'the prevention of sexual offending is of great social value'); *Sharma I* (n. 1), para 29 (stating that '[t]he Act of 2005 was enacted to radically alter the administrative ethos and culture of secrecy and control, the legacy of colonial era and bring in a new era of transparency and accountability in governance').

## The Collateral Consequences of Judicial Review:
## *Naz Foundation* and *Bellinger*

### *Naz Foundation:* —*The Challenge to the Criminalization of Homosexuality*

In *Naz Foundation* v. *Government of Delhi*,[116] a non-governmental · organization (NGO) filed a public interest litigation petition[117] in the Delhi High Court challenging the constitutional validity of section 377 of the Indian Penal Code, 1860 (IPC). The colonial era–provision, which formed part of the IPC drafted under the chairmanship of Lord Macaulay, reads as follows: 'Unnatural offences: Whoever voluntarily has carnal intercourse against the order of nature with any man, woman or animal, shall be punished with imprisonment for life, or with imprisonment of either description for a term which may extend to ten years, and shall also be liable to fine.'

Section 377 resembled the erstwhile law proscribing 'buggery' in the UK.[118] The petition challenged section 377 to the limited extent that it criminalized consensual sexual activity between adults in private. The petitioner sought for the statutory provision to be read down to exclude such consensual activity from the ambit of section 377. The underlying thrust of the petitioner's argument was that state officials used section 377 as an instrument to persecute the lesbian, gay, bisexual, and transgendered (LGBT) community in India. The statutory provision, it was argued, effectively criminalized the community, forced them underground, and impeded measures for the prevention and control of HIV/AIDS. The legal grounds for the challenge were that section 377,

---

[116]   2010 Cri LJ 94.

[117]   During the public interest litigation movement in the 1980s in India, the Supreme Court developed its jurisprudence to enable any public-spirited person or organization to approach the courts on behalf of a person or determinate class of people whose fundamental rights have been violated; see Upendra Baxi, 'Taking Suffering Seriously: Social Action Litigation in the Supreme Court of India' (1985) 4 Third World Legal Studies 107.

[118]   For details on the development of the law on buggery in the UK, see Nicola Lacey, Celia Wells, and Oliver Quick, *Reconstructing Criminal Law: Text and Materials* (3rd edn, Cambridge University Press 2003), pp. 519–31.

in its existing form, violated Arts 14,[119] 15,[120] 19,[121] and 21[122] of the Constitution.

In a widely acclaimed judgment,[123] the Delhi High Court held that section 377 violated Arts 14, 15, and 21 of the Constitution.[124] In the Court's view, the provision discriminated on the ground of sexual orientation, targeted homosexuals as a class, and was contrary to constitutional morality. The Court granted the relief sought by the petitioner, namely, that section 377 be read down so as to exclude consensual sexual activities between adults in private. The section would continue to govern 'non-consensual penile non-vaginal sex'[125] and 'penile non-vaginal sex involving minors'. According to the Court, the possibility of 'reading down' legislation in this manner had been endorsed in several previous Supreme Court judgments.[126] The Court clarified that its judgment would operate until Parliament chose to amend the law appropriately.

The Delhi High Court's judgment was appealed to the Supreme Court.[127] In its judgment, the Indian Supreme Court held that every statute in force in India, including those enacted during the British Raj, such as the IPC, would carry a presumption of constitutionality. In a questionable line of reasoning, the Court went a step further by saying that by allowing section 377 to remain on the statute book, the Union

[119] The right to equality before the law and equal protection of the laws.

[120] Prohibition of discrimination on the grounds of religion, race, caste, sex, or place of birth.

[121] Protection of seven freedoms, including the freedom of speech and expression.

[122] The right to life and personal liberty.

[123] See, for example, Vikram Raghavan, 'Navigating the Noteworthy and Nebulous in Naz Foundation' (2009) 2 NUJS Law Review 397; Tarunabh Khaitan, 'Reading Swaraj into Article 15: A New Deal for All Minorities' (2009) 2 NUJS Law Review 419.

[124] It left the issue of whether section 377 violated Art. 19 open. *Naz Foundation* v. *Government of Delhi* 2010 Cri LJ 94 [126].

[125] Non-consensual penile vaginal sex, on the other hand, was governed by the provisions for rape (IPC, sections 375 and 376).

[126] See *RMDC* (n. 21); *Kedar Nath* (n. 20); *Bhim Singhji* v. *Union of India*, AIR 1981 SC 234; *State of Andhra Pradesh* v. *NTPC*, AIR 2002 SC 1895.

[127] *Naz Foundation* (n. 3).

Parliament had effectively adopted it. Following *Sharma I*, it held that striking down a law as unconstitutional would be a measure of last resort.[128] While endorsing the general notion that a statute can be read down in order to save it from being struck down, the Supreme Court rejected the High Court's decision to read down section 377.

The Court advocated a more restrained approach in reviewing the constitutionality of legislation, stating that it was not permissible to 'change the essence of the law' and 'create a new law which in its opinion is more desirable' under the guise of interpretation.[129] It also noted that the principle of reading down should be applied bearing in mind the scheme of the statute and the intention of the legislature. The Supreme Court clarified that it was not empowered to strike down a law 'by virtue of its falling into disuse or the perception of the society having changed'.[130] Section 377, in the Court's view, did not criminalize a particular identity or orientation, but uniformly regulated sexual conduct.

The Indian Supreme Court found that the High Court was mistaken in even considering the challenge to section 377, because the petitioners had 'miserably failed' to furnish a factual foundation to support its challenge.[131] In an astonishing observation, the Supreme Court said that while reading down section 377 of the IPC, the High Court had overlooked that a 'miniscule fraction of the country's population' could be classified as LGBT.[132]

The Supreme Court ended its judgment with a couple of interesting riders, which seemed to indicate some sense of unease with the result that it arrived at. First, it held that the fact that it was claimed that section 377 was used to perpetuate harassment, blackmail, and acts of torture against LGBT persons could not be taken into account while deciding the constitutionality of the section, since it neither mandated nor condoned such acts. However, it 'might be a relevant fact for the legislature to consider while judging the desirability of section 377'.[133]

---

[128] The arguments in *Naz Foundation* concluded and the Supreme Court reserved judgment before the *Sharma II* judgment was delivered.

[129] *Naz Foundation* (n. 3), para 31.

[130] *Naz Foundation* (n. 3), para 33.

[131] *Naz Foundation* (n. 3), para 40.

[132] *Naz Foundation* (n. 3), para 43.

[133] *Naz Foundation* (n. 3), para 51.

The Court then also emphasized that notwithstanding its judgment, the legislature was free to consider deleting or amending section 377.

The judgment was justifiably met with heavy criticism from different quarters.[134] By refusing to uphold the rights of what it considered a minority of the population, the Court misconceived the nature and purpose of judicial review in a constitutional democracy. Its conclusion that Parliament had endorsed section 377 by failing to amend it was similarly flawed. There could be many explanations for Parliament's failure to amend a penal provision handed down from the colonial era, and a desire to endorse the provision is not necessarily the best one. The Court's conclusion that the petitioners' claim had no factual foundation was also misconceived—the petition was supported with affidavits submitted by several members of the LGBT community reflecting upon the persecution they had suffered at the hands of public officials. Finally, the court had misread the judgment of the Delhi High Court by labelling it as judicial legislation that changed the essence of the law. The High Court had simply restricted the application of the section to constitutionally permissible cases, a process that was grounded in existing Supreme Court jurisprudence. Having clarified that the judgment is legally untenable, the rest of this chapter will put the correctness of the Indian Supreme Court's conclusions aside, focussing instead on the reasons for which it chose to uphold section 377.

## Bellinger and Transsexual Relationship Rights

The issue before the House of Lords in *Bellinger* v. *Bellinger*[135] was whether the marriage between the claimant, a post-operative male to female transsexual, to a man, was valid. The High Court[136] and the

---

[134] See, for example, Tarunabh Khaitan, 'Koushal v Naz: The Legislative Court' (*UK Constitutional Law Association* 22 December 2013) <https://ukconstitutionallaw.org/2013/12/22/tarunabh-khaitan-koushal-v-naz-the-legislative-court/> accessed 24 September 2016; Arghya Sengupta, 'The Wrongness of Deference' *The Hindu* (16 December 2013). There is also an underlying tension between the *Naz Foundation* judgment and the Indian Supreme Court's subsequent decision in *National Legal Services Authority* v. *Union of India*, AIR 2014 SC 1863.

[135] See n. 4.

[136] *Bellinger* v. *Bellinger*, (2000) 58 BMLR 52.

Court of Appeal[137] were unable to hold in the claimant's favour by virtue of section 11(c) of the Matrimonial Causes Act, 1973, which stipulated that a marriage would be void on the ground that the parties to it were not 'respectively male and female'. Relying on existing precedent,[138] both courts held that the words 'male' and 'female' had to be judged according to fixed biological criteria, which the claimant did not satisfy. The Courts lamented their inability to provide a remedy to the claimant, but considered that the statutory provision left them with no choice.[139]

When the case went in appeal to the House of Lords,[140] the claimant advanced a new alternative claim—that section 11(c) of the Matrimonial Causes Act be declared incompatible on the basis that it was inconsistent with Art 8[141] and 12[142] of the Convention. The Court had little hesitation in getting through stage one by holding that section 11(c), based on ordinary principles of interpretation, was incompatible with Convention rights. But before making a declaration of incompatibility under section 4 of the HRA, it would need to consider whether the statutory provision could be read compatibly by invoking the interpretive obligation under section 3.[143] Each of the judges agreed that this was not a fit case to invoke section 3. Lord Nicholls said that the words 'male' and 'female' in section 11(c) could not be ascribed an extended meaning by including those who were born with one sex, but later became or were regarded as persons of an opposite sex, within its

---

[137] *Bellinger v. Bellinger*, [2001] EWCA Civ 1140.

[138] *Corbett v. Corbett*, [1970] 2 All ER 33.

[139] Johnson J. in the High Court held that he was conscious of the significance of his decision for the claimant and others in her situation (*Bellinger v. Bellinger*, (2000) 58 BMLR 52). Dame Elizabeth Butler P in the Court of Appeal held that the plight of transsexuals in the eyes of the law was 'profoundly unsatisfactory' (*Bellinger* [n. 137], para 109).

[140] *Bellinger* (n. 4).

[141] The right to respect for private and family life.

[142] The right to marry.

[143] It should be noted that in any event, invoking section 3 would not have benefited the claimant in the way that she hoped. As Lord Hope pointed out in his judgment, section 3(1) was not retrospective and hence, it would not have been possible to retrospectively validate the claimant's marriage. (*Bellinger* [n. 4], para 65.).

grasp. Moreover, taking this interpretive route would represent a major change in the law having far-reaching ramifications—something that Parliament was institutionally much better equipped to deal with. Lord Hope echoed a similar sentiment, stating that any attempt to expand the meanings of the words 'male' and 'female' in section 11(c) would lead to difficulty, as it would be challenging to narrow down on a set of criteria to determine whether and when a person belonged to a particular gender. Section 3 did not enable judges to legislate. The problems that reinterpreting section 11(c) gave rise to, in his view, were not conducive to judicial resolution, and were better left to Parliament.

The next question for the Lords' consideration was whether a declaration of incompatibility should be made.[144] The government argued that a declaration of incompatibility would serve no useful purpose, since legislation removing the incompatibility was under consideration. The Court still chose to make a declaration of incompatibility on the basis that the government was not in a position to give an assurance that remedial legislation would be enacted[145] and that it was important to record the present state of the law's incompatibility.[146]

## What Prompted the Indian Supreme Court to Avoid Exercising the Power to Strike Down Legislation?

*Naz Foundation* and *Bellinger* were different in terms of the kind of legislation that was under review. In the former, a criminal offence carrying a 10-year sentence was challenged; the latter concerned the denial to transsexuals of a basic civil right—the right to enter into a legally recognized marriage. However, there are several interesting points of convergence between the two cases. To begin with, both cases involved claims that were founded on the identity of minority social groups. Respect for their identity and the need to recognize changes in social attitudes formed the subtext of the arguments made before the Indian Supreme Court and the House of Lords.

---

[144] Unlike section 3 of the HRA, which is framed in mandatory language, section 4 is drafted in discretionary terms. So even if courts find an incompatibility, they are not legally bound to make a formal declaration under section 4.

[145] *Bellinger* (n. 4), para 79 (Lord Hobhouse).

[146] *Bellinger* (n. 4), para 55 (Lord Nicholls).

The laws that were challenged in both cases did not enjoy the fresh democratic support and political legitimacy like the laws under challenge in the *Sharma* cases and *Thompson*. Section 377 formed part of the IPC that was imposed by the British colonial government in India: the provision was enacted by an all-British Legislative Council[147] and had no grounding in Indian customs or values. The Law Commission of India had recommended the deletion of section 377 over a decade before the case challenging its validity reached the corridors of the Supreme Court.[148]

Section 11(c) of the Matrimonial Causes Act, 1973, which was at issue in *Bellinger*, was enacted about three decades before the judgment of the House of Lords. Before the Lords' decision, the European Court of Human Rights, Strasbourg (Strasbourg Court) had already declared the UK's failure to recognize the marriage of post-operative transsexuals as being contrary to the Convention.[149] After the Strasbourg Court's decision, the Lord Chancellor had accepted that those aspects of English law that failed to accord legal recognition to transsexuals were incompatible with Arts 8 and 12 of the Convention.[150] The Interdepartmental Working Group on Transsexual People had been reconvened in the UK with a mandate to examine the implications of granting full legal status to transsexual people. Finally, the New Labour government had expressed a commitment to enact primary legislation allowing transsexuals to marry and a draft outline bill on the issue was due to be published soon after the judgment of the House of Lords.

[147] Robert Wintemute, 'Same-sex Love and Indian Penal Code § 377: An Important Human Rights Issue for India' (2011) 4 NUJS Law Review 31, p. 43.

[148] Law Commission of India, *One Hundred and Seventy Second Report on Review of Rape Laws* (Law Commission, 25 March 2000). The Delhi High Court and the Supreme Court treated the report quite differently. The High Court considered the report as evidence of a heightened realization to follow global trends in the acceptance of homosexuality (*Naz Foundation* v. *Government of Delhi*, 2010 Cri LJ 94, para 86). The Supreme Court considered that the fact that the Law Commission recommendation had not been implemented by Parliament was a form of silent assent to section 377 (*Naz Foundation* [n. 3], para 32).

[149] *Goodwin* v. *UK*, (2002) 35 EHRR 447.

[150] Aileen Kavanagh, 'Statutory Interpretation and Human Rights after *Anderson*: A More Contextual Approach' [2004] PL 537.

Moreover, unlike in the *Sharma* cases and *Thompson*, the laws that were challenged were self-standing, in the sense that they did not constitute a critical cog in a network of statutory provisions.[151] Their disapplication, hypothetically speaking, would not have affected the functioning of the statutory regimes in which they operated. Section 377, forming part of the chapter on 'offences affecting the human body',[152] is independent of the other offences (concerning matters such as rape, assault, and abduction) in that chapter. Similarly, section 11(c) was a discrete ground for the voidness of marriage, autonomous of the others. So the kind of pressures that prompted the Courts in *Sharma* and *Thompson* to act as they did (upholding the constitutionality of the legislation in the case of the former, declaring it incompatible in the latter) were not in play: many governments had changed hands, independent reviews had recommended making modifications to the law so as to comply with fundamental rights, and the legislative provisions that were challenged were easily separable from their parent statutes.

But *Naz Foundation* and *Bellinger* were also similar in another important respect. In both cases, the hypothetical invalidation of the statutory provisions that were challenged would have produced profound collateral consequences or 'spillover'[153] effects. Disapplying section 11(c)

---

[151] The question of how much impact the invalidation of a statutory provision would have on the statutory regime is, of course, a matter of degree. It is difficult to imagine any statutory invalidation that will have no impact whatsoever on the statutory regime.

[152] IPC, Chapter XVI.

[153] Danny Nicol, 'Gender Reassignment and the Transformation of the Human Rights Act' (2004) 120 LQR 194. If the statutory regime is looked at as part of a grand scheme consisting of many statutes that are interrelated with one another, another way of conceptualizing these spillover effects is the impact of invalidation on the grand statutory scheme as a whole, rather than the individual statute itself (which was discussed with reference to the previous example). Just to be clear, most judgments invalidating legislation are likely to produce some kind of 'legal vacuum' in the temporary period between the court's decision and the enactment of fresh legislation; see Michael C. Dorf, 'Fallback Law' (2007) 107 Columbia Law Review 303, p. 304. The nature of the vacuum, however, is a question of degree. In both *Naz Foundation* and *Bellinger*, the vacuum that would have followed a hypothetical invalidation of the statutory provisions challenged was far too significant to leave unattended.

of the Matrimonial Causes Act, 1973 would have given rise to a series of effects across the legal system. As Lord Nicholls acknowledged,[154] changing the qualifications for marriage would have produced legal consequences in many different contexts, including 'housing and residential security of tenure, social security benefits, citizenship and immigration, taxation, pensions, inheritance, life insurance policies, criminal law (bigamy)'.[155] The House of Lords was not in a position to decide what the precise implications of a hypothetical invalidation of section 11(c) would have been in these manifold contexts. Lord Hope reiterated this concern, stating that 'problems of great complexity would be involved if recognition were to be given to same sex marriages'.[156] The message that the Court was seeking to send was clear—piecemeal reform of the complex legislative matrix was not viable.[157]

The collateral consequences that would have resulted had the Indian Supreme Court struck down section 377 of the IPC in *Naz Foundation* were slightly more complex. Oral hearings for the case concluded in the Supreme Court in March 2012. At that time, section 377 was also the criminal offence that was relied upon to prosecute those who were accused of child sexual assault and sexual assault of women (falling short of rape).[158] The Supreme Court was quite clearly conscious of the utility of section 377 in such cases. It cited several judgments[159]

---

[154] Although this statement was made in relation to the application of section 3 of the HRA, the same consequences would have followed a hypothetical invalidation of the statutory provision.

[155] *Bellinger* (n. 4), para 42.

[156] The same qualification applies: Lord Hope's statement refers to the problem with relying on section 3 of the HRA, but the same problems would remain if the statutory provision was, hypothetically speaking, struck down. *Bellinger* (n. 4) para 69.

[157] *Nicol* (n. 153).

[158] At the time, the offence of rape under section 375 required vaginal penetration. Non-consensual penetration of the anus, urethra, or mouth was punishable under section 377.

[159] *Khanu* v. *Emperor*, AIR 1925 Sind 286; *Lohana Devchand* v. *State*, AIR 1968 Guj 252; *State of Kerala* v. *Kundumkara Govindan*, 1969 Cri LJ 818; *Fazal Choudhury* v. *State of Bihar*, (1982) 3 SCC 9; *Kedar Nath* v. *State of Rajasthan*, 1985 (2) WLN 560; *Calvin Francis* v. *State of Orissa*, 1992 (2) Crimes 455; *State* v. *Bachmiya Musamiya*, 1998 (3) Guj LR 2456; *Bhikari Charan Sahu* v. *State*, 1992 Cri LJ 488.

reflecting prosecutions for such non-consensual conduct under section 377 and said:

> All the aforementioned cases refer to non consensual and markedly coercive situations and the keenness of the court in bringing justice to the victims who were either women or children cannot be discounted while analyzing the manner in which the section has been interpreted. We are apprehensive of whether the Court would rule similarly in a case of proved consensual intercourse between adults.[160]

Thus, the Court was under the apprehension that striking down section 377 would have implied jettisoning a statutory provision punishing sexual assault of women and children. This apprehension was echoed in a subsequent judgment of the Supreme Court, involving an appeal by the defendant against his conviction for sodomy and murder of a child:[161]

> We have no doubt in our mind that such types of crimes preceded by Pederasty are extremely brutal, grotesque, diabolical and revolting, which shock the moral fiber of the society, especially when the passive agent is a minor. Recently, this Court in [*Naz Foundation*] ... has also refused to strike down Section 377, even if such acts are indulged in by consenting individuals.... Indian society and also the International society abhor pederasty, an unnatural sex, i.e. carnal intercourse between a man and a minor boy or a girl. *When the victim is a minor, consent is not a defence, irrespective of the views expressed at certain quarters on consensual sex between adults.* (Emphasis added)

But the story gets more complicated than this. Not unusually, the Supreme Court actually delivered its judgment in December 2013, 21 months after the oral hearings in the case concluded.[162] Two noteworthy events occurred in the intervening period. First, the Union Parliament enacted the Protection of Children from Sexual Offences Act, 2012, which entered into force later that year. The act penalizes a wide range of sexual offences perpetrated against children, including those that would have previously been prosecuted under section 377. Second, following the horrific sexual assault of a young woman in Delhi

---

[160] *Naz Foundation* (n. 3), para 38.

[161] *Anil v. State of Maharashtra*, (2014) 4 SCC 69, paras 22, 29.

[162] Reserving judgment for extended periods of time after the conclusion of oral hearings is a regular practice at the Indian Supreme Court.

in December 2012,[163] the Union Parliament widened the definition of rape under section 375 of the IPC to encompass the kinds of sexual assault that were previously covered by section 377.[164] Remarkably, the Supreme Court took no notice of these two changes to the criminal law in its judgment.[165] Later, petitions seeking a review of the Supreme Court's judgment in *Naz Foundation* on the basis that it had ignored these legislative changes were summarily dismissed without reasons.[166]

As a matter of fact, therefore, the striking down of section 377 on the date that the *Naz Foundation* judgment was delivered would not have produced the collateral consequences that it would have on the date that the oral hearings concluded.[167] However, since this chapter focuses on the influence of specific constitutional remedies on judicial decision-making, what is crucial to sustain the argument made here is not the actual state of the law, but the *Court's perception of the state of the law*. After all, the Court's decision to uphold rather than strike down section 377 was based on its own understanding of the situation.

Taking a step back, in both *Naz Foundation* and *Bellinger*, the interpretive route at stage two was contemplated but eventually eschewed. This took the form of two rounds of litigation in *Naz Foundation*, in which the Delhi High Court read down section 377 but the Supreme Court (incorrectly) considered it impermissible to do so. In *Bellinger*,

---

[163] See T.K. Rajalakshmi, 'A Nation Outraged' *Frontline* (Chennai, 25 January 2013).

[164] Criminal Law (Amendment) Act, 2013. This was based on the recommendation of the report of a committee headed by Justice J.S. Verma. See Justice J.S. Verma, Justice Leila Seth, and Gopal Subramanium, *Report of the Committee on Amendments to Criminal Law* (23 January 2013), <http://www.prsindia.org/uploads/media/Justice%20verma%20committee/js%20verma%20committe%20report.pdf> accessed 24 September 2016.

[165] The Protection of Children from Sexual Offences Act, 2012 did not find mention in the Court's judgment. The Criminal Law (Amendment) Act, 2013 was taken cognizance of, but in a different context.

[166] *Naz Foundation* v. *Suresh Kumar Koushal*, MANU/SC/0080/2014.

[167] However, if section 377 had been struck down, then there would be no law effectively penalizing child sexual assault and sexual assault of women (falling short of rape) for those interim offences which took place before the amendments to the law entered into force. This collateral consequence is, of course, much narrower than that envisaged by the Supreme Court.

the section-3 route was considered and rejected by the House of Lords. The outcome of the two cases turned out to be the same as in the *Sharma* cases and *Thompson*: the British court issued a declaration of incompatibility, the Indian court masked its real rights reasoning and upheld the statute. A major reason for which the Indian Supreme Court chose to uphold section 377 is that striking down the provision would have, from the Court's perspective, produced undesirable collateral consequences and left a 'hiatus in the criminal law'.[168] In other words, the immediacy of the remedy had an asymmetric effect on the Indian Supreme Court's decision.[169]

In *Bellinger*, on the other hand, the House of Lords was aware that issuing a declaration of incompatibility would invite Parliament to scrutinize the incompatible statute. Parliament, unlike the Court, would be well placed to consider the collateral consequences that would be produced by changing the law. Thus, a comparison of *Naz Foundation* and *Bellinger* shows how the difference in the nature of the power to strike down and the declaration of incompatibility veered the Courts towards different conclusions after they decided that rights-compliant interpretation was not a realistic possibility. The Indian Supreme Court felt compelled to withhold its true rights reasoning, whereas the House of Lords brought its rights reasoning to bear.

If the Indian Supreme Court was empowered to make a formal declaration of incompatibility (carrying the same institutional rigour), it might have been tempted to do so in *Naz Foundation* so as to compel Parliament to deal effectively with the collateral consequences produced by making any changes to section 377. The Court's concluding comment that Parliament was free to amend or delete section 377 provides support for this proposition. Constitutionally speaking, this clarification was wholly unnecessary—to say that Parliament can

---

[168] These words are borrowed from the opinion of Ackermann J. of the Constitutional Court of South Africa in *National Coalition for Gay and Lesbian Equality* v. *Minister of Justice*, [1998] ZACC 15, para 71. Unlike in *Naz Foundation*, the South African Court struck down the common law offence of sodomy in its entirety on the basis that non-consensual sexual acts still remained adequately criminalized under other laws.

[169] See Justice Gerard Hogan, 'Declarations of Incompatability, Inapplicability and Invalidity: Rights, Remedies and the Aftermath' Lecture at the University of Oxford (1 February 2013).

amend a law which the Supreme Court has declared constitutionally valid is a platitude. What the Court was really seeking to do was to invite parliamentary attention to a situation that it did not consider it could suitably address.

It is worth clarifying that the role played by the power to strike down legislation in Indian courts' decisions to rethink the constitutionality of legislation and put aside their genuine rights reasoning is a matter of degree.[170] In *Sharma II*, the fact that the Court was left with no choice but to strike down the statutory provisions played a controlling role in the Indian Supreme Court's decision—the Court clearly had rights-based concerns about the RTIA and the manner in which it was functioning, but felt uncomfortable derailing the institutional machinery of the RTIA. In *Naz Foundation*, however, the power to strike down legislation seemed to play a significant, but not controlling, role in the Indian Supreme Court's ultimate decision. The Court's unsympathetic attitude towards the LGBT community—describing it as a 'miniscule' minority[171] with 'so-called rights'[172]—suggests that other ideological reasons may have also played a part in its decision to uphold the colonial-era provision criminalizing homosexuality.

### Emergency and Anti-terrorism Legislation: *Kartar Singh* and Belmarsh Prison Case

#### *The Kartar Singh Case*

The third pair of cases reflecting the refusal of Indian courts to articulate their genuine rights reasoning consists of the Indian Supreme Court's judgment in *Kartar Singh v. State of Punjab*[173] and the House

---

[170] Naturally, other factors also influence the decision-making process of courts when reviewing primary legislation. One of these, for example, is the nature and purpose of the statute: penal (*Ram Chandra Bhagat* v. *State of Jharkhand*, (2010) 13 SCC 870, para 16) and fiscal (*Krishi Utpadan Samiti* v. *Pilibhit Pantnagar Bheej Ltd*, (2004) 1 SCC 391) statutes tend to be construed strictly against the state.

[171] *Naz Foundation* (n. 3), para 43.

[172] *Naz Foundation* (n. 3), para 52.

[173] See n. 5.

of Lords' judgment in the Belmarsh Prison case.[174] In *Kartar Singh*, a five-judge bench of the Indian Supreme Court took up over 400 writ petitions, petitions by special leave and criminal appeals,[175] in which the constitutional validity of the Terrorist and Disruptive Activities (Prevention) Act, 1987 (TADA) and other anti-terrorism legislation[176] had been challenged. TADA, and its predecessor statute enacted in 1985,[177] were passed by the Union Parliament in the backdrop of military groups engaging in guerrilla-style conflict in many regions of India, including Punjab, Kashmir, Andhra Pradesh, and parts of the North East.[178] However, one of the immediate catalysts for TADA was the assassination of Prime Minister Indira Gandhi in 1984 by her Sikh bodyguards.[179]

In effect, TADA set up a parallel criminal justice process for the speedy trial of those engaging in terrorist activities. It provided for the establishment of special courts to deal with terrorist offences, reversed the burden of proof on defendants in certain cases, altered existing rules of evidence to render confessions to senior police officers admissible, and denied rights of appeal to state High Courts. TADA was not meant to be a permanent fixture in the criminal justice regime, and had a sunset clause of two years (although it was repeatedly extended by Parliament until it finally lapsed in 1995). As one Member of Parliament put it, this radical statute was necessitated by the 'extraordinary times'.[180] Another put the point even more robustly: 'Punjab is burning. The legend goes

---

[174] See n. 6.

[175] EPW Commentary, 'Black Law and White Lies: A Report on TADA' (1995) 30 Economic and Political Weekly 977, p. 979.

[176] The other statutes that were challenged were: Terrorist and Disruptive Activities (Prevention) Act, 1985; the Terrorist Affected Areas (Special Courts) Act, 1984; and the Code of Criminal Procedure (UP Amendment) Act, 1976.

[177] Terrorist and Disruptive Activities (Prevention) Act, 1985.

[178] Jayanth K. Krishnan, 'India's "Patriot Act": POTA and the Impact on Civil Liberties in the World's Largest Democracy' (2004) 22 Law and Inequality 265, p. 267.

[179] This was an act of retaliation for 'Operation Bluestar', on which see Robert L. Hardgrave and Stanley A. Kochanek, *India: Government and Politics in a Developing Nation* (Thomson 2008), p. 175.

[180] Statement of Jagan Nath Kaushal, cited by the Indian Supreme Court in *Kartar Singh* (n. 5), para 27.

that in the rivers of Punjab milk used to flow [*sic*] but they are now drenched with blood. There is hatred all over.'[181]

TADA was subjected to two lines of attack in the Supreme Court: first, that it was not within the confines of federal legislative power, and second, that many of its provisions violated fundamental rights under the Constitution. The Supreme Court rejected the first argument, on the basis that the statute did not deal with 'public order' or 'law and order' (state subjects), but was better classified as dealing with the 'defence of India', a subject reserved for federal legislation. But the Court found it more tricky to negotiate many aspects of the second argument. In a radical departure from the existing criminal justice regime, section 15 provided that confessions made to police officers not lower than the rank of superintendent would be admissible in the trial of offences under the statute. This provision was challenged on the basis that it violated the right to equality (Art. 14) and the right to life (Art. 21) under the Constitution.

Writing for the majority, Pandian, J. was conscious of the history of custodial torture in India, which underpinned the rule of general criminal law that confessions made to police officers were untrustworthy. He stated:[182]

> [W]ith the years of experience both at the Bar and on the Bench [we] have frequently dealt with cases of atrocity and brutality practiced by some overzealous police officers resorting to *inhuman, barbaric, archaic and drastic method of treating the suspects* in their anxiety to *collect evidence by hook or by crook* and wrenching a decision in their favour. We remorsefully like to state that on few occasions even custodial deaths caused during interrogation are brought to our notice. We are very much distressed and deeply concerned about the oppressive behavior and the most *degrading and despicable practice adopted by some of the police officers* even though no general and sweeping condemnation can be made. (Emphasis added)

One might have expected this sense of 'distress' at the 'despicable' practice of police officers to translate into the striking down of section 15. There was sufficient jurisprudential support for this conclusion,

---

[181] Statement of Kamal Chaudhary, cited by the Indian Supreme Court in *Kartar Singh* (n. 5), para 27.

[182] *Kartar Singh* (n. 5), para 251.

since the Court had, more than one-and-a-half decades earlier, held that the right to life under Art. 21 embodied the constitutional guarantee of substantive due process, meaning that any law circumscribing that right would need to be fair, just, and reasonable.[183] But in a curious leap of logic, the Court held that in spite of finding it dangerous, 'at the first impression', to allow confessions to be made admissible, it preferred not to strike down the statutory provision.[184] The reasons offered for this change of heart were the competence of Parliament to enact the statutory provision, the gravity of terrorism that was endangering the integrity of the nation, and the unwillingness of victims and the general public to come forward and give evidence.[185]

That the majority's rights-based discomfort with section 15 persisted is evident from its issuance of supplementary guidelines, with uncertain binding value,[186] about the recording of confessions. These included that confessions be recorded in the same language in which the person is examined, that the defendant be produced before a magistrate without unreasonable delay, that the police be required to respect the right to silence of the defendant, and that a committee be set up at the central and state levels to review the functioning of the statute.[187] These guidelines were often ignored, and secured little traction in practice.[188]

[183] *Maneka Gandhi* v. *Union of India*, AIR 1978 SC 597. See K. Balagopal, 'In Defence of India' (1994) 29 Economic and Political Weekly 2054. In *NCT of Delhi* v. *Navjot Sandhu*, AIR 2005 SC 3820 (Reddi J.), the Supreme Court, by way of obiter dictum, offered many grounds on which statutory provisions rendering confessions to police officers valid could be struck down for failing to comply with substantive due process. It also expressed 'formidable doubt' about the correctness of the decision in *Kartar Singh*.

[184] *Kartar Singh* (n. 5), para 253.

[185] *Kartar Singh* (n. 5), para 253.

[186] Pandian J. held that: 'The Central Government may take note of these guidelines and incorporate them by appropriate amendments in the Act and the Rules' (*Kartar Singh*(n. 5), para 263). Subsequent judgments of the Supreme Court doubted the binding force of these guidelines; see *Lal Singh* v. *State of Gujarat*, AIR 2001 SC 746, para 23; *S.N. Dube* v. *NB. Bhoir*, AIR 2000 SC 776, para 32.

[187] *Kartar Singh* (n. 5), para 263 (Pandian J.).

[188] EPW Commentary (n. 175), p. 978.

The majority's change of mind on section 15 was not simply a change of heart (or more fittingly, a change of rights reasoning). The decision—which effectively compromised a routine protection against torture[189]—was heavily influenced by the desire to avoid striking down a statutory provision that was conceived as an essential part of the national security apparatus, and which the government asserted as being crucial in dealing with challenges of the time. Ramaswamy J.'s dissent also indicates that remedial considerations were foremost in the minds of the judges. Like the majority, he acknowledged that it was 'obnoxious' to confer upon police officers the power to record confessions,[190] but took his reasoning to its logical conclusion by deciding that section 15 was unconstitutional. However, his judgment indicated that he would have suspended the striking down of section 15 for a year, so as to enable Parliament to make suitable amendments to the statute.[191]

The Court adopted a similar approach of putting aside its genuine rights reasoning vis-à-vis section 19 of TADA, which denied the right of appeal to state high courts (instead permitting an appeal as of right directly to the Supreme Court). The Central Government considered this as a crucial aspect of delivering the statute's promise of swift trials in cases of terrorism. This provision applied even in cases where a defendant, who was charged for committing offences under TADA and other criminal legislation, was acquitted for the TADA offences but convicted for offences under the ordinary criminal law.

The majority noted a number of problems with this statutory provision. It was a serious access to justice impediment, because it would effectively mean that defendants from remote parts of the country would be unable to file appeals against their conviction.[192] It also saw

---

[189] Jinee Lokaneeta, 'Extraordinary Laws and Torture in India in an Era of Globalization' in Alison Brysk (ed.), *The Politics of the Globalization of Law: Getting from Rights to Justice* (Routledge 2013), p. 206.

[190] *Kartar Singh* (n. 5), para 406. See also the dissent of Sahai J.: *Kartar Singh* (n. 5), paras 454, 455.

[191] *Kartar Singh* (n. 5), para 423. Possible explanations for the majority's preference to uphold section 15 rather than adopt the course chosen by Ramaswamy J. are discussed in the following section of this chapter.

[192] *Kartar Singh* (n. 5), para 295 (Pandian J.).

no logic in the operation of section 19 in cases where defendants were not convicted of offences under TADA. Pandian J. went as far as to say that the provision denied 'fair play and justice', was 'unreasonable', and compromised the objectives of the criminal justice system.[193]

Based on the Supreme Court's established substantive due process jurisprudence, this was enough of an indictment of section 19 for it to be struck down. But without explaining its decision any further, the Court pointed out that these 'practical difficulties' would not render the provision constitutionally invalid.[194] Similar to the judgments in *Naz Foundation* and *Sharma II*, it advised Parliament to take note of these difficulties and make suitable amendments to the law.[195] In his separate opinion, Sahai J. followed the reasoning of the Court, observing that Parliament needed to reconsider section 19 since it resulted in a denial of justice to the large segment of defendants who lacked the wherewithal to appeal to the Supreme Court.[196]

It is important to understand the Court's 'messaging' in its analysis of these two questions. It did not hold that although sections 15 and 19 violated fundamental rights, it would refuse to strike them down. This would have been clearly impermissible, given that the Court is obliged to strike down a statutory provision that violates rights (and which cannot be given a rights-compliant interpretation, as was the case with sections 15 and 19). The Court's holding, arrived at with 'apparent hesitation' (as the Supreme Court described it in a later case),[197] was that although sections 15 and 19 were deeply problematic, they were not inconsistent with fundamental rights and would not be struck down. Hence, when deciding the validity of sections 15 and 19, the Court was influenced by the nature of the remedy to mask its genuine rights reasoning with a form of rights reasoning that enabled it to uphold the provisions.

Overall, the Court read down some of the provisions of TADA, and upheld the constitutional validity of many others. The only statutory provision that was struck down was section 22 (which, in respect of

---

[193] *Kartar Singh* (n. 5), paras 294, 295 (Pandian J.).
[194] *Kartar Singh* (n. 5), para 297 (Pandian J.).
[195] *Kartar Singh* (n. 5), para 297 (Pandian J.).
[196] *Kartar Singh* (n. 5), para 457 (Sahai J.).
[197] *Navjot Sandhu* (n. 188) (Reddi J.).

some defendants, attached the same evidentiary value to identification through photographs as identification through test parades).[198]
This was peculiar, because none of the parties had addressed detailed
arguments in respect of section 22. The invalidation of section 22—a
provision which was by no means a central plank of the anti-terrorism
regime set up by TADA—turned out to be a fig leaf for the majority's
reluctance to strike down other provisions (such as sections 15 and
19) that posed far greater challenges to the protection of constitutional
rights.

### The Belmarsh Prison Case

Compare *Kartar Singh* with the Belmarsh Prison case, which is
amongst the most widely known judgments under the HRA. Several
foreign nationals filed appeals to the House of Lords against their
detention under Part 4 of the Anti-Terrorism, Crime and Security Act,
2001 (ATCSA). Part 4 was enacted in a similar national security context
as TADA. The government considered it a crucial response to the terrorist attacks in New York and Washington on 11 September 2001,
following which the UK, like many other western democracies, faced
terrorist threats on a large scale. This is evident from the following
statement made by the New Labour government's home secretary in
Parliament:[199]

> Let us recall for a moment not just what happened on 11 September, but
> what has happened since. Let us recall the interviews given and the video
> recordings made by bin Laden and the al-Qaeda group, which have spelt
> out their determination not simply to threaten once, but to threaten the
> civilian populations of the United States and those working with it. It is
> for that reason that we are proposing measures allowing us to take ratio-
> nal, reasonable and proportionate steps to deal with an internal threat
> and an external, organised terrorist group that could threaten at any time
> not just our population, but the populations of other friendly countries.

Part 4 enabled the home secretary to detain indefinitely, on reasonable suspicion and without charge or trial, foreign terrorist suspects
who could not be deported by virtue of the UK's obligations under

---

[198] See *Kartar Singh* v. (n. 5), paras 360, 361 (Pandian J.).

[199] HC Deb 19 November 2001, vol. 375, col. 22 (David Blunkett).

the Convention.[200] These detention provisions were intended to be temporary, and expressly derogated from the rights set out in Art. 5 of the Convention.[201]

One of the key questions before the House of Lords was whether the detention provisions unfairly discriminated between nationals and non-nationals. The government sought, and to some extent was granted, a high degree of judicial deference on whether there was an emergency threatening the life of the nation and what the proportionate steps for dealing with that emergency would be.[202] However, the judges considered the distinction between nationals and non-nationals plainly discriminatory.[203] Lord Bingham noted that the threat to national security did not emanate solely from foreign nationals, or for that matter, foreign nationals who could not be deported.[204] Lord Nicholls made a similar point, holding that although British citizens also posed a threat to national security, the government did not find it necessary to impose a draconian detention regime to curb that threat.[205] The majority therefore chose to declare section 23 of the ATCSA incompatible with the Convention.

The judges were careful to clarify that their declaration would not be binding on Parliament. Lord Bingham asserted that the declaration

---

[200] In *Chahal* v. *United Kingdom*, (1997) 23 EHRR 413, the Strasbourg Court held that the prohibition on torture under Art. 3 of the Convention included an absolute prohibition against deportation in cases where the proposed deportee faced a real risk of torture or inhuman or degrading treatment. The UK government regarded the inability to deport some foreign terrorist suspects as impeding anti-terrorism efforts, and Part 4 of the ATCSA was their response to that problem. See Aileen Kavanagh, 'Constitutionalism, Counterterrorism, and the Courts: Changes in the British Constitutional Landscape' (2011) 9 International Journal of Constitutional Law 172, p. 180.

[201] See Human Rights Act 1998 (Designated Derogation) Order, 2001.

[202] Belmarsh Prison case (n. 6), paras 29, 42 (Lord Bingham), para 79 (Lord Nicholls), para 116 (Lord Hope).

[203] Lord Hoffman went a step further by refusing to accept that terrorism posed a threat to the life of the nation, and thus warranted a derogation from the UK's obligations under the Convention; see Belmarsh Prison case (n. 6), paras 96, 97.

[204] Belmarsh Prison case (n. 6), para 32.

[205] Belmarsh Prison case (n. 6), para 77.

of incompatibility would not 'override the sovereign legislative authority of the Queen in Parliament', since the HRA provided that the only
immediate remedy (under section 10) lay with the relevant minister,
who was accountable to Parliament.[206] Lord Scott was at pains to make
the point even clearer, observing that the declaration would 'not in the
least' affect the validity of section 23 under domestic law, and that its
import was political rather than legal.[207] Baroness Hale also noted that
the declaration of incompatibility would not invalidate section 23 or
any executive action taken in pursuance of it.[208]

It is worthwhile analysing the precise purpose of these observations
from the Bench. They were not, as it may appear at first glance, merely
bland clarifications of the remedial scheme set up by the (relatively)
newly enacted HRA—15 declarations of incompatibility had already
been made before the Belmarsh Prison case, nine of which survived
appeal. The judges were making a more subtle point—that, at least
formally speaking, in the sensitive area of national security, the declaration of incompatibility enabled the courts to specify their provisional
understanding of rights subject to Parliament's putatively final and
authoritative understanding of rights.

### The Influence of the Remedy

The highest courts in India and the UK were both inclined to hold that
provisions of anti-terrorism legislation were inconsistent with human
rights. Similar legislation was at issue before both courts—temporary,
'problem-solving'[209] statutory measures that were intended to deal with
the exigencies of the time and established a parallel criminal justice
system for terrorism-related offences. Both Courts quickly acknowledged that a rights-compliant reading of the statutory provisions was
not possible. But the nature of the remedy available prompted different outcomes. At the cusp of stages two and three, the Indian Supreme

---

[206] Belmarsh Prison case (n. 6), para 42.

[207] Belmarsh Prison case (n. 6), para 142.

[208] Belmarsh Prison case (n. 6), para 220.

[209] See Ujjwal Kumar Singh, 'Mapping Anti-terror Legal Regimes in India' in
Victor V. Ramraj, Michael Hor, and Kent Roach (eds), *Global Anti-terrorism Law
and Policy* (Cambridge University Press 2009), p. 442.

Court refused to strike down provisions of the TADA, preferring to hold back its genuine understanding of the rights implications of the statute in order to avoid striking down its key provisions. The House of Lords, on the other hand, made a declaration of incompatibility, with each of the judges on the majority emphasizing that its declaration, unlike a power to strike down legislation, did not hamper Parliament's authority to decide whether to amend the law.

Some scholars attribute the contrasting outcomes in *Kartar Singh* and the Belmarsh Prison case to differences in standards of judicial review.[210] The Indian Supreme Court adopted the relatively light-touch standard of reasonableness review, requiring the government to justify that its legislation was within a range of reasonable alternatives, whereas the House of Lords applied a full-scale proportionality analysis, charging the government with justifying the precise balance struck by the legislature. But explaining away these decisions based on standards of review obscures the processes of rights reasoning that took place in both courts. The Indian Supreme Court's inclination to strike down sections 15 and 19 of TADA was based on the very same reasonableness standard of review that is mistakenly relied upon to justify the differences between the two cases. A genuine application of rights reasoning by the Court would have prompted the invalidation of sections 15 and 19, even on the reasonableness standard of review. The different outcomes of the two cases are, therefore, better explained by the nature of the remedies available to both courts.

Another point about these two cases is worth noting. One of the most common criticisms of the declaration of incompatibility is that it guarantees no remedy to individual litigants, in spite of an acknowledgement that their rights have, in the court's view, been violated. The detainees in the Belmarsh Prison case were not released for a long time, and immediately following their release, were subjected to 'control orders' under the Prevention of Terrorism Act, 2005.[211] But the remedial counterfactual in the *Kartar Singh* case was equally unsatisfactory,

<hr/>

[210] Kent Roach, 'Judicial Review of the State's Anti-terrorism Activities: The Post-9/11 Experience and Normative Justifications for Judicial Review' (2009) 3 Indian Journal of Constitutional Law 138.

[211] K.D. Ewing and Joo-Cheong Tham, 'The Continuing Futility of the Human Rights Act' [2008] PL 668, p. 670.

because the terrorist suspects secured no benefit from the Supreme Court's reluctant upholding of the provisions of TADA. However, unlike in Belmarsh Prison case, this was also accompanied by the court disguising its genuine understanding of rights in order to avoid invoking the power to strike down legislation.

## Remedies of Duty or Discretion?

It is important to bear in mind that the cases from the Indian Supreme Court do not convey the idea that the statutes in question were 'unconstitutional yet nonetheless' would 'be accepted by the court'.[212] Although decisions of that kind would harbour problems of their own,[213] they would not involve a failure by the Court to express its genuine rights reasoning (even if that reasoning does not produce an outcome that the litigant expects). In the *Sharma* cases, *Naz Foundation*, and *Kartar Singh*, the Indian Supreme Court felt compelled to uphold the statutory provisions before it as constitutionally valid. The message that the Court was seeking to send in each of these cases was close to this: although we have serious constitutional concerns about the statutory provision that is challenged in this case, we will uphold it—therefore, the question of exercising the power to strike down legislation does not arise. This is because the 'power' to strike down legislation actually transforms into a 'duty' to do so once the court has found legislation unconstitutional. Judges have frequently acknowledged that they are duty-bound to strike down legislation that violates, and cannot be read consistently with, constitutional rights.[214]

In contrast, the declaration of incompatibility under section 4 of the HRA has always been considered a discretionary remedy. The White Paper to the Human Rights Bill stated that the provision '*enables*

---

[212] Mark Tushnet, *Weak Courts, Strong Rights: Judicial Review and Social Welfare Rights in Comparative Constitutional Law* (Princeton University Press 2009), p. 38.

[213] Primarily, the fact that the Court would be denying a remedy to the parties in the case.

[214] *Devi Das* v. *State of Punjab*, AIR 1967 SC 1895, para 18; *Maharao Singhji* v. *Union of India*, AIR 1981 SC 234, para 50; *Delhi Transport Corporation* v. *DTC Mazdoor Congress*, AIR 1991 SC 101, para 249. For an exception, see *Malpe Vishwanath Acharya* v. *State of Maharashtra*, AIR 1998 SC 602, para 31.

a formal declaration to be made that its provisions are incompatible with the Convention' (emphasis added).[215] Section 4(2) makes it plain that even once a court is satisfied that a provision of primary legislation is inconsistent with Convention rights, it 'may' make a declaration of that incompatibility. Some scholars predicted that in practice, this discretion would transform into a duty.[216] These predictions have not materialized, since there have been cases following the enactment of the HRA in which judges have found incompatibilities but refused to make declarations of incompatibility.[217] Prominent among these is *Nicklinson*,[218] in which the Supreme Court was tasked with deciding whether the English law criminalizing assisted suicide[219] violated the right to privacy under Art. 8 of the Convention, and whether a code published by the Director of Public Prosecutions,[220] on the prosecution of those who assisted suicide, was lawful. Three of the judges (Lords Neuberger, Mance, and Wilson) acknowledged that even if the law, as it stood, was incompatible with Convention rights and could not be

---

[215] Home Office (n. 23), para 2.9.

[216] Lord Lester, 'The Art of the Possible: Interpreting Statutes under the Human Rights Act' (1998) 6 EHRLR 665, p. 672, arguing that 'the courts will in theory have a discretion as to whether to make a declaration of incompatibility. But in practice … they will surely regard themselves as under a duty to make a declaration. This is the only remedy they will be able to give for the breach of the victim's Convention rights'; David Bonner, Helen Fenwick, and Sonia Harris-Short, 'Judicial Approaches to the Human Rights Act' (2003) 52 ICLQ 549, p. 561.

[217] *R (Hooper)* v. *Secretary of State for Work and Pensions*, (2005) 1 WLR 1681 (Lord Hoffman); *R (Chester)* v. *Secretary of State for Justice*, [2014] AC 271; *R (Nicklinson)* v. *Ministry of Justice*, [2014] UKSC 38 (Lord Neuberger, Lord Mance, and Lord Wilson). The declaration of incompatibility is also discretionary in another sense: that it may not be made unless the circumstances show 'that the legislative provision in question has affected a Convention right of the applicant for the declaration in a manner that is incompatible with that right'; see *R (Animal Defenders International)* v. *Secretary of State for Culture*, (2008) 2 WLR 781, para 42 (Lord Scott).

[218] See n. 217.

[219] Suicide Act, 1961, section 2(1).

[220] Policy for Prosecutors in Respect of Cases of Encouraging or Assisting Suicide, 2010.

given a rights-compliant interpretation, no declaration of incompatibility would be issued. Lord Neuberger explained:[221]

> It would, of course, be unusual for a court to hold that a statutory provision, conventionally construed, infringed a Convention right and could not be construed compatibly with it, and yet to refuse to make a declaration under section 4 of the 1998 Act. However, there can be no doubt that there is such a power: section 4(2) states that if there is an incompatibility, the court 'may' make a declaration to that effect, and the power to grant declaratory relief is anyway inherently discretionary. The possibility of not granting a declaration of incompatibility to enable the legislature to consider the position is by no means a novel notion.

This remedial difference effectively means that for courts in the UK, rights reasoning need not necessarily align with the remedy chosen by the court. In other words, the court may well, on the basis of its genuine rights reasoning, find a provision of primary legislation inconsistent with a Convention right but choose not to make a declaration of incompatibility. Indian courts, on the other hand, do not have the liberty to decouple the right from the remedy in this way, resulting in a situation in which they are compelled to tuck away their genuine rights reasoning in cases in which there is no interpretive solution and where they wish to avoid exercising the power to strike down legislation.

## Remedial Discretion under the Indian Constitution

The cases from India demonstrate that the power to strike down often proves to be an 'unappealingly blunt instrument'[222] and can adversely affect courts' willingness to express their true understanding of rights. But one important factor that remains to be considered is the question of remedial discretion—whether the Indian Supreme Court could have modified the effects of the power to strike down legislation to avoid the collateral damage that would have ensued following the *Sharma* cases, *Naz Foundation*, and *Kartar Singh*, had the power been invoked in those cases. The notion of remedial discretion can be expressed in

---

[221] *Nicklinson* (n. 217), para 114.

[222] Eoin Carolan, 'The Relationship between Judicial Remedies and the Separation of Powers: Collaborative Constitutionalism and the Suspended Declaration of Invalidity' (2011) Irish Jurist 180, p. 184.

many different ways: the exercise of 'weak-form' powers by courts in a strong-form system,[223] the development of 'intermediate remedies',[224] or the use of collaborative techniques to prompt the legislature to play a role in the crafting of the remedy for the violation of rights.

As experience from constitutional courts around the world has shown, there are at least three kinds of intermediate remedies that courts use to soften the effects of a power to strike down or disapply primary legislation: prospective overruling, suspended striking down or declarations of invalidity, and de facto or informal declarations of incompatibility (made in the absence of specific textual authorization). Prospective overruling enables courts to limit their decisions that overrule established precedent to future situations, excluding its application to situations that relied on the overruled precedent.[225] Suspended declarations of invalidity, which are frequently employed by courts in Canada, enable courts to remand complex issues for legislative consideration.[226] They allow legislatures to adopt remedies that courts would not be able to adopt[227] and seek to minimize disruption to the statutory regime.[228]

Further, it is not inconceivable to think of courts in systems lacking an equivalent of section 4 of the HRA making informal or de facto declarations of incompatibility indicating that a provision of primary legislation is inconsistent with fundamental rights.[229] However, owing

[223] Mark Tushnet, 'Alternative Forms of Judicial Review' (2003) 101 Michigan Law Review 2781, p. 2793.

[224] Carolan (n. 222), pp. 184, 187.

[225] Wolfgang Friedmann, 'Limits of Judicial Lawmaking and Prospective Overruling' (1966) 29 MLR 593, p. 602.

[226] Sujit Choudhry and Kent Roach, 'Putting the Past Behind Us? Prospective Judicial and Legislative Constitutional Remedies' (2003) 21 SCLR 205, p. 248.

[227] Kent Roach, 'Principled Remedial Discretion under the Charter' (2004) 25 SCLR 101, p. 145.

[228] Choudhry and Roach (n. 226), p. 231.

[229] David Dyzenhaus, 'The Incoherence of Constitutional Positivism' in Grant Huscroft (ed.), *Expounding the Constitution: Essays in Constitutional Theory* (Cambridge University Press 2008) 144. In New Zealand, courts have recognized a power to make a declaration of inconsistency even though the Bill of Rights Act, 1990 contains no express provision resembling section 4 of the HRA. However, these declarations may be difficult to make routinely; see Claudia Geringer, 'On a Road to Nowhere: Implied Declarations of Inconsistency and the New Zealand Bill of Rights Act' (2009) 40 VUWLR 613.

to textual and institutional constraints, Indian courts are likely to remain hesitant to rely upon such devices that are commonly invoked by courts in some other jurisdictions. These constraints will now be considered.

## Textual Constraints

The constitutional text in India hampers, or at the least fails to facilitate successfully, the exercise of remedial discretion by courts reviewing primary legislation for compliance with rights. Article 13(2) provides that any law made in contravention of fundamental rights 'shall, to the extent of the contravention, be void'. Although this provision leaves room for judicial tools such as 'reading down' and severability at stage two of the analysis, it seems to provide little elbow room for courts to modify the effects of a declaration that a statutory provision is void and unconstitutional for violating fundamental rights. The Indian Constitution does not contain a provision resembling section 172(1)(b) of the South African Constitution, expressly permitting courts to 'limit the retrospective effect' of the power to strike down or suspend the effects of the power to strike down 'to allow the competent authority to correct the defect'.[230]

The Indian Constitution, however, contains a more broadly framed provision than section 172(1)(b). Article 142 empowers the Supreme Court to make any order 'as is necessary for doing complete justice in any cause or matter pending before it'.[231] The Court has described the expression 'complete justice' as being 'couched with elasticity to meet myriad situations'.[232] This provision could conceivably be interpreted to enable the Supreme Court to invoke the doctrine of prospective

---

[230] Section 102(2) of the Scotland Act, 1998 also contains a similar provision. However, it should be noted that Acts of Scottish Parliament are treated as subordinate legislation for the purposes of the HRA (HRA, section 21(1)). See also section 175(6)(b) of the Constitution of Zimbabwe, 2013.

[231] The Constitutions of Bangladesh (Art. 104) and Pakistan (Art. 187(1)) contain similar provisions.

[232] *Ashok Kumar Gupta* v. *State of UP*, (1997) 5 SCC 201. See also Ajit Sharma, 'Inherent Powers of the Supreme Court under the Constitution' (2006) Practical Lawyer (June) 12.

overruling or make suspended declarations of invalidity. At first glance, such an interpretation may even seem perfectly consistent with the Supreme Court's broader interpretive philosophy, given that it has, over the years, moved from a narrow, positivistic approach to a 'broad, purposive' approach in interpreting many constitutional provisions.[233]

However, the Supreme Court's jurisprudence is replete with cases in which the Court has interpreted constitutional provisions expansively to increase, rather than temper, the *general* exercise of judicial power.[234] Some of the most prominent cases in which courts have engaged in expansive interpretation of the Constitution provide evidence of this practice. The best place to start is with a case under Art. 142 itself. In 2002, the Supreme Court read its power to do 'complete justice' under Art. 142 as enabling it to reopen decided cases even after the constitutionally mandated procedure[235] for doing so had been exhausted.[236] The Court thus established a jurisdiction allowing it to deal with 'curative petitions', as the Court refers to them, without the specific authorization of the constitutional text.

---

[233] Bert Neuborne, 'The Supreme Court of India' (2003) 1 International Journal of Constitutional Law 476, pp. 479, 480. See also S.P. Sathe, 'India: From Positivism to Structuralism' in Jeffrey Goldsworthy (ed.), *Interpreting Constitutions: A Comparative Study* (Oxford University Press 2007), p. 215.

[234] See Chintan Chandrachud, 'Constitutional Interpretation' in Sujit Choudhry, Madhav Khosla, and Pratap Bhanu Mehta (eds), *The Oxford Handbook on the Indian Constitution* (Oxford University Press 2016), p. 73. As Schauer points out, constitutional interpretation necessarily involves questions concerning the allocation of power; see Frederick Schauer, 'The Occasions of Constitutional Interpretation' (1992) 72 Boston University Law Review 729, p. 734. Robert Leckey suggests that this claim is not necessarily accurate in the Canadian context, since judges there have issued suspended declarations of invalidity without textual authorization; see Robert Leckey, 'Suspended Declarations of Invalidity and the Rule of Law' (*UK Constitutional Law Association*, 12 March 2014) <https://ukconstitutionallaw.org/2014/03/12/robert-leckey-suspended-declarations-of-invalidity-and-and-the-rule-of-law/> accessed 24 September 2016.

[235] Constitution of India, Art. 137.

[236] *Rupa Ashok Hurra* v. *Ashok Hurra*, AIR 2002 SC 1771. A number of conditions were stipulated before cases would be reopened. For criticism of this judgment, see Arvind P. Datar, *Commentary on the Constitution of India* (2nd edn, LexisNexis Butterworths Wadhwa 2007), p. 928.

The most well-known example of expansive interpretation of constitutional provisions, *Kesavananda Bharati* v. *State of Kerala*,[237] also facilitated a radical increase in judicial power. In the context of a struggle for constitutional custodianship between the judiciary and Parliament, the Supreme Court held that Parliament's power to amend the Constitution under Art. 368 could not be invoked to alter, abrogate, or destroy the 'basic structure' or 'essential features' of the Constitution. It provided a non-exhaustive catalogue of 'essential features' of the Constitution, which has been incrementally developed in subsequent decisions.[238] The Supreme Court therefore developed a jurisdiction to review the validity of constitutional amendments on substantive grounds. From 1973 onwards, it assumed the paradoxical power to strike down constitutional amendments on the basis that they were unconstitutional.

A third example of expansive interpretation of the constitutional text to increase judicial power comes from the interpretation of Art. 21 of the Indian Constitution, which provides that '[n]o person shall be deprived of his life or personal liberty except according to procedure established by law'. The early case law interpreted this provision quite narrowly, refusing to infuse it with substantive due process guarantees.[239] In later cases,[240] however, the Indian Supreme Court read this provision to include a substantive component. The Court thus extended its scope of judicial review under Art. 21 to include substantive, in addition to procedural, elements.[241] Within this jurisprudential context, it

---

[237] AIR 1973 SC 1461 ('Basic Structure case'). For commentary on the case, see Granville Austin, *Working a Democratic Constitution: A History of the Indian Experience* (Oxford University Press 2003); Sudhir Krishnaswamy, *Democracy and Constitutionalism in India* (Oxford University Press 2010); T.R. Andhyarujina, *The Kesavananda Bharati Case* (Universal Law Publishing 2011).

[238] See *Minerva Mills* v. *Union of India*, AIR 1980 SC 1789; *L. Chandra Kumar* v. *Union of India*, AIR 1997 SC 1125; *Special Reference No 1 of 2002*, AIR 2003 SC 87.

[239] *A.K. Gopalan* v. *State of Madras*, AIR 1950 SC 27.

[240] *Satwant Singh* v. *Union of India*, AIR 1967 SC 1836; *R.C. Cooper* v. *Union of India*, AIR 1970 SC 564; *Maneka Gandhi* (n. 183).

[241] For further commentary, see S.P. Sathe, 'Judicial Activism: The Indian Experience' (2001) 6 Washington University Journal of Law and Policy 29; Neuborne (n. 233); Manoj Mate, 'The Origins of Due Process in India: The Role of Borrowing in Personal Liberty and Preventive Detention Cases' (2010) 28 Berkley Journal of International Law 216; Abhinav Chandrachud, *Due Process of*

is unlikely that the Indian Supreme Court would be willing to limit its general judicial powers by circumscribing the effects, or diluting the binding force, of its own decisions (even though, on the analysis in this book, limiting judicial power in this way would probably also increase judicial power specific to the case by enabling judges to strike down a statute which they would have otherwise upheld).

The Indian Supreme Court has, however, invoked the doctrine of prospective overruling relying upon Art. 142 and other constitutional provisions.[242] Two objections against the analysis in this book may stem from this observation. First, could the Indian Supreme Court not have invoked this doctrine in the *Sharma* cases, *Naz Foundation*, and *Kartar Singh* rather than having brushed aside its genuine rights reasoning, stepping back to stage one to uphold the validity of the statutes challenged? Second, does the invocation of this doctrine under the powers conferred by Art. 142 not contradict the argument that judges have relied upon expansive interpretation of constitutional provisions only to increase judicial power? Both these attractive arguments are misconceived.

On the first issue, invoking the doctrine of prospective overruling in *Naz Foundation*, the *Sharma* cases, and *Kartar Singh* would not have solved the Indian Supreme Court's concerns with the invocation of the power to strike down legislation. The Court's concerns in these cases were not restricted to the impact of the decision on past conduct. In the *Sharma* cases and *Kartar Singh*, the Court would have been perturbed by the impact of a strike down on the functioning of the RTIA and TADA, respectively. In *Naz Foundation*, the Court was (albeit misguidedly) concerned about the collateral consequences *following* a decision that section 377 of the IPC was unconstitutional and invalid.

The response to the second question is that although the doctrine of prospective overruling limits the impact of the judicial decision in question, the case that imported[243] the doctrine into India involved a

---

*Law* (Eastern Book Company 2011); Zia Mody, *Ten Judgments That Changed India* (Penguin Books 2013), Chapter 2.

[242] Constitution of India, Arts 32, 141.

[243] Several cases from the US (*Great Northern Railway* v. *Sunburst Oil & Refining Co*, (1932) 287 US 358; *Chicot County Drainage District* v. *Baxter State Bank*, (1940) 308 US 371; *Griffin* v. *Illinois*, (1956) 351 US 12; *Linkletter* v. *Walker*, (1965) 381 US 618) were cited in support of the doctrine of prospective overruling.

dramatic expansion of general judicial powers. In *Golak Nath* v. *State of Punjab*,[244] the Indian Supreme Court held that Parliament had no power to amend the fundamental rights set out in Chapter III of the Constitution, overturning existing precedent[245] holding that Parliament was permitted to amend any provision of the Constitution. Hence, for the first time, the Court effectively assumed the power to strike down all amendments to Part III of the Constitution.[246] Within this context, the majority in *Golak Nath* invoked the doctrine of prospective over-ruling to avoid the complexities that would have resulted from previous amendments to Part III being called into question. Therefore, the narrative of expansive construction of constitutional provisions has remained confined to cases in which the Indian Supreme Court has augmented its general powers, most often by broadening the scope of judicial review.

## Institutional Constraints

In addition to the textual constraints noted above, the Indian Supreme Court's scope to employ devices that temper the exercise of the power to strike down legislation is also constrained by institutional factors. Even in cases where the Court has sought to prompt legislative change through some form of 'advice-giving',[247] Parliament has either failed to respond, or taken an agonizing amount of time to respond, to the Court's advice. In *Vishaka* v. *State of Rajasthan*,[248] a public interest litigation case, the Court issued a list of guidelines for the prevention of sexual harassment of women in the workplace. The Indian Supreme Court recognized that the primary responsibility of ensuring the safety

---

[244]   AIR 1967 SC 1643.

[245]   *Shankari Prasad* v. *Union of India*, [1952] 1 SCR 89; *Sajjan Singh* v. *State of Rajasthan*, AIR 1965 SC 845.

[246]   This power was short-lived, since the judgment in *Golak Nath* (n. 244) was overruled by the Indian Supreme Court in the Basic Structure case (n. 237).

[247]   According to Neal Kumar Katyal, '[a]dvicegiving occurs when judges recommend, but do not mandate, a particular course of action based on a rule or principle in a judicial case or controversy'; see Neal Kumar Katyal, 'Judges as Advicegivers' (1998) 50 Stanford Law Review 1709, p. 1710.

[248]   AIR 1997 SC 3011.

of women lay with the legislature and the executive, and stated that its guidelines would remain in force only until Parliament enacted suitable legislation to plug the existing legislative vacuum.[249] These seemingly stop-gap (and in hindsight, poorly implemented[250]) guidelines remained in force for over 16 years, until Parliament finally enacted legislation[251] on the subject.

Another example is *State of MP* v. *Shyam Sunder Trivedi*,[252] where the Indian Supreme Court lamented the frequency of the torture and murder of suspected criminals in police custody, and urged the government and Parliament to consider implementing a Law Commission recommendation[253] to transfer the evidential burden of proof on to the defendant police officer once it was established that bodily injury was caused to a person in police custody. In spite of reminders from the Bench,[254] this recommendation has not been implemented.

Unlike the declaration of incompatibility in the UK, informal 'nudges' to the legislature in India lack institutional grounding. A declaration of incompatibility is not just a freewheeling judicial assertion that primary legislation is inconsistent with Convention rights— it forms part of an institutional network set up under the HRA. The Strasbourg Court comprises an important part of this institutional network: a finding from the Court that the UK law is incompatible with Convention rights (which is very likely if a declaration of incompatibility has been made by a domestic court) renders the UK in breach of its international law obligations. The JCHR closely monitors responses

---

[249] *Vishaka* (n. 248), paras 3, 16.

[250] Failure to implement the guidelines was widespread; see Daphne Barak-Erez and Jayna Kothari, 'When Sexual Harassment Law Goes East: Feminism, Legal Transplantation, and Social Change' (2011) 47 Stanford Journal of International Law 177, p. 185. The Supreme Court itself failed to implement the guidelines for many years within its own administrative machinery.

[251] Sexual Harassment of Women at Workplace (Prevention, Prohibition and Redressal) Act, 2013.

[252] (1995) 4 SCC 262, para 17.

[253] Law Commission of India, *One Hundred and Thirteenth Report on Injuries in Police Custody* (Law Commission, 1985), para 5.2.

[254] *D.K. Basu* v. *State of West Bengal*, AIR 1997 SC 610, para 28; *The Court on its own Motion* v. *State of Punjab*, (2011) 1 ILR (P&H) 307.

to declarations of incompatibility made by domestic courts and adverse decisions against the UK by the Strasbourg Court.[255]

As Sathanapally argues, the JCHR engages in 'sustained, critical correspondence' with government departments over their responses to declarations of incompatibility.[256] Declarations of incompatibility, along with JCHR reports tracking responses to such declarations, receive generous press coverage.[257] This institutional grounding of the declaration of incompatibility ensures that first, there is clarity about the matter in respect of which a declaration of incompatibility has been made, and second, there are effective monitoring and accountability mechanisms to track the government's responses to declarations of incompatibility. The role of the JCHR and the Strasbourg Court in adding institutional bite to the declaration of incompatibility is considered at length in Chapter 5.

In contrast, the Indian Supreme Court's informal advice to change the law lacks the institutional bite given to the declaration of incompatibility by the Strasbourg Court and the JCHR. There is neither any comparable international mechanism in India, nor any monitoring body that systematically holds the government accountable for compliance with informal recommendations of the Indian Supreme Court. Courts are institutionally unequipped to monitor the government or Parliament's responses to judgments that find primary legislation to be inconsistent with human rights.[258]

Structural factors also impact upon the efficacy of the Court's recommendations. The Court speaks too much and in too many voices. The total number of cases it decides annually is close to 700 times that of

---

[255] Janet L. Hiebert, 'Parliament and the Human Rights Act: Can the JCHR Help Facilitate a Culture of Rights?' (2006) 4 International Journal of Constitutional Law 1, p. 21; Aileen Kavanagh, 'The Joint Committee on Human Rights: A Hybrid Breed of Constitutional Watchdog' in Murray Hunt, Hayley Hooper, Paul Yowell (eds), *Parliaments and Human Rights: Redressing the Democratic Deficit* (Bloomsbury 2015).

[256] Aruna Sathanapally, *Beyond Remedies: Open Remedies in Human Rights Adjudication* (Oxford University Press 2012), p. 161.

[257] However, declarations of incompatibility (and matters arising under the HRA more generally) do not necessarily receive favourable press coverage. There are sections of the media that are discernibly anti-HRA.

[258] Kavanagh (n. 255).

the UK Supreme Court.[259] Decision-making in the court is diffuse—the 31-member Court usually sits in benches of two or three judges.[260] This makes it challenging for academia, mainstream media, and civil society to keep up with informal judicial recommendations to change the law and hold governments to account for their responses to such recommendations.[261] These structural features accentuate the 'legislative lag'[262] that is inevitable following most exercises of judicial review. All these factors suggest that the Court could not have been confident of a prompt (or indeed, any) legislative response if it chose to make suspended declarations of invalidity (or to suspend the effects of the power to strike down) in cases like *Naz Foundation*, the *Sharma* cases, and *Kartar Singh*. Further, the Indian Supreme Court is also likely to remain conscious of the fact that since advice to the legislature is not binding, it may be disregarded,[263] directly undermining the authority and legitimacy of its 'advisory' role.

The arguments that have been made thus far might come across as slightly surprising to close observers of the Indian Supreme Court's human rights' jurisprudence. It has sometimes been christened as the world's most powerful court,[264] ahead even of the court that generates the most academic commentary—the US Supreme Court. Scholars such as Fredman,[265] Shripati,[266] and Kothari,[267] have lauded the court's

---

[259] See 'Introduction'.

[260] Nick Robinson, 'Structure Matters: The Impact of Court Structure on the Indian and US Supreme Courts' (2013) 61 American Journal of Comparative Law 173. Robinson describes the Court as 'polyvocal'.

[261] See Khaitan (n. 134).

[262] Brianne J. Gorod, 'The Collateral Consequences of Ex Post Judicial Review' (2013) 88 Washington Law Review 903, p. 921.

[263] Katyal (n. 247), p. 1721.

[264] Sathe (n. 233), p. 265.

[265] Sandra Fredman, *Human Rights Transformed: Positive Rights and Positive Duties* (Oxford University Press 2008), Chapter 5.

[266] Vijayashri Sripati, 'Toward Fifty Years of Constitutionalism and Fundamental Rights in India: Looking Back to See Ahead' (1998) 14 American University International Law Review 413, p. 453.

[267] Jayna Kothari, 'Social Rights and the Indian Constitution' (2004) 2 Law, Social Justice & Global Development Journal <https://docs.escr-net.org/usr_doc/kothari_article2.doc> accessed 24 September 2016.

ability to expand its range of constitutional remedies to effectively protect socio-economic rights. These remedies include the quite remarkable writ of 'continuing mandamus', enabling the Court to supervise the implementation of its orders.[268] The Court has signalled a willingness to hold government officials that fail to comply with its orders in contempt of court.[269]

However, in spite of the Indian Supreme Court's relative success in adapting its range of remedies to secure executive compliance with socio-economic rights, primary legislation that is inconsistent with fundamental rights is of an entirely different order. It is inconceivable for the Supreme Court to direct Parliament, by way of a mandatory order, to introduce fresh legislation or amend existing legislation to secure compliance with human rights.[270] The only alternative for the Court is to urge the government and Parliament, through soft admonition, censure, or advice, to change the law to secure a more satisfactory outcome from a human rights perspective. Such admonition does not

---

[268] Fredman (n. 265), p. 128; Manoj Mate, 'Two Paths to Judicial Power: The Basic Structure Doctrine and Public Interest Litigation in Comparative Perspective' (2010) 12 San Diego Journal of International Law 175, p. 196. As Endicott notes, the Indian Supreme Court's 'remedial orders can be as creative as its constitutional interpretations'; see Timothy Endicott, 'Arbitrariness' (2014) 27 Canadian Journal of Law and Jurisprudence 49.

[269] However, the extent to which the Indian Supreme Court actually uses the power of contempt to secure implementation of its orders in socio-economic rights cases is disputed. See Fredman (n. 265), p. 128 (arguing that that the Court 'is not loath to use' its contempt power even against high-ranking officials) and Nick Robinson, 'Expanding Judiciaries: India and the Rise of the Good Governance Court' (2009) 8 Washington University Global Studies Law Review 1, p. 55 (arguing that the Court 'almost never' actually holds government officials in contempt). It may be that the threat of using its contempt power constitutes a sufficient sanction to secure compliance with the Court's orders, even if the threat rarely materializes in the form of contempt proceedings.

[270] However, in an unprecedented judgment, the Court 'directed the government' to enact a law governing 'hawkers' and street vendors within nine months of its judgment in Gainda Ram v. MCD, (2010) 10 SCC 715. Parliament eventually enacted legislation—Street Vendors (Protection of Livelihood and Regulation of Street Vending) Act, 2014—on the subject, approximately 32 months after the 'time limit' set by the Court had expired.

carry contempt sanctions and Parliament's cognizance of it cannot be supervised. Thus, the Indian Supreme Court's considerable remedial discretion in many socio-economic rights cases does not carry over to cases where primary legislation is found inconsistent with human rights.

Overall, these constraints indicate that the Indian Supreme Court would be reluctant to exercise remedial discretion in contexts like the *Sharma* cases, *Naz Foundation*, and *Kartar Singh*. As noted above, the Court's exercise of remedial discretion is constrained by constitutional text. Institutional factors suggest that even if the Court were to exercise remedial discretion in such cases, it would be unlikely to precipitate a change (or at the least, a reasonably swift change) in the law. The Court would remain conscious of the fact that Parliament and the government's failure to take heed of informal declarations of incompatibility could impact upon its institutional legitimacy. In cases where Parliament ignores informal declarations of incompatibility, the affected class of citizens would remain in the same position as they would have been had there been no such declaration.

\*\*\*

The nature and consequences of the power (or more fittingly, duty) to strike down legislation influences the behaviour of Indian courts in the process of reviewing legislation for compliance with constitutional rights.[271] Cases in which a declaration of incompatibility is made in the UK and which, formally speaking, are expected to correspond with the

---

[271] In a paper submitted to the UK Commission on a Bill of Rights, Faulks and Fisher argue that '[e]xperience in jurisdictions where domestic Courts have a "strike down" power suggests that a Supreme Court is more reluctant to exercise the power where it has immediate effect, than where a declaration of incompatibility is issued and the matter is referred back to a democratically elected Parliament'; see Lord Faulkes QC and Jonathan Fisher QC, 'Unfinished Business' in *A UK Bill of Rights? The Choice Before Us* (vol. 1, Commission on a Bill of Rights, 2012), p. 190. Curiously however, they cite no evidence in support of this assertion. For criticism, see Mark Elliott, 'A Damp Squib in the Long Grass: The Report of the Commission on a Bill of Rights' (2013) 2 EHRLR 137, p. 146.

exercise of the power to strike down legislation in India, produce asymmetrical results in practice. Confronted with the prospect of stifling legislation that has a strong and relatively recent democratic mandate, causing serious collateral damage to the legislative matrix, or jettisoning legislation that is an important part of the national security apparatus, Indian courts have reluctantly reconsidered the validity of a statute under challenge. This produces a disguised form of rights reasoning that replaces the Court's genuine understanding of rights with an understanding that enables it to avoid striking down legislation. In similar situations, courts in the UK have expressed their genuine understanding of rights by making a declaration of incompatibility, leaving it to Parliament and the government to address the inconsistency with Convention rights. This dynamic offers an alternative account for the superiority of the new model of judicial review over the old model— one that concerns the inability of courts to express their genuine rights reasoning under the old model, rather than the ability of legislatures to do so under the new model.

The Indian Supreme Court may be unwilling to issue informal declarations of incompatibility, suspended declarations of invalidity, or invoke other intermediate remedies by virtue of textual constraints. More importantly, however, institutional constraints suggest that even if it were to do so, the Indian Parliament and government are unlikely to respond in the manner that the Court would hope. This is in contrast with the declaration of incompatibility in the UK, which is given institutional purchase by the JCHR (which holds the government to account for responses to declarations of incompatibility) and the Strasbourg Court (which transforms matters of domestic parliamentary discretion into international obligations). The institutional purchase of declarations of incompatibility under the HRA, compared to that accompanying intermediate remedies falling short of the power to strike down legislation in India, is analysed in detail in Chapter 5.

# 5 Collateral Institutions to Judicial Review

Chapter 4 explained the positive claim of this book: that the UK's model of rights protection is superior to that in India on account of the nature of the remedy available in the UK (the declaration of incompatibility), which enables British courts to express their genuine rights reasoning in cases in which Indian courts, although armed with the power to strike down legislation, find it difficult to do so. But constitutional remedies do not function in isolation, and to consider their effects without examining the institutions that exist around them is to miss an important part of the picture.

This chapter will therefore consider the institutional apparatus accompanying the declaration of incompatibility in the UK on the one hand, and informal recommendations to change the law (or intermediate remedies falling short of the power to strike down legislation) in India on the other. Although the declaration of incompatibility may look like a freestanding advisory remedy at first glance, it is given significant institutional purchase by the JCHR and the European Court of Human Rights in Strasbourg (Strasbourg Court). The work of these institutions will be compared with India's National Human Rights Commission in New Delhi (NHRC), which finds it difficult to influence legislative activity.

Before proceeding, a brief point of clarification is in order. A formalist would perhaps be perturbed by comparisons between institutions that are quite differently composed, and that exercise varied powers and functions. It, therefore, bears justifying why a joint parliamentary committee, a supranational court, and an independent human rights monitoring body are collectively considered. As explained in the Introduction, this book prefers function over form and adopts a moderate version of functionalism. It is within the mandate of the JCHR, the Strasbourg Court, and the NHRC to follow up on declarations of incompatibility or judicial recommendations to amend the law and these institutions, to one extent or another, comply with this mandate. These three 'collateral institutions',[1] therefore, can fairly be described as functional equivalents worthy of comparison for the purposes of this study.

Nevertheless, this does not imply that the differences between them can be overlooked. In fact, as the chapter progresses, it becomes clear that differences in respect of (a) whether monitoring declarations of incompatibility or judicial recommendations to amend the law is a primary or peripheral function of the institution; (b) the overall scope of the institution's functions; and (c) the resources at the disposal of the institution have a major bearing on the manner in which they are able to perform these functions in practice.

## The United Kingdom

### The Joint Committee on Human Rights

This section will consider the role of the JCHR, with particular focus on its function of holding the government to account in securing responses to declarations of incompatibility.

### Composition and Functioning of the Joint Committee on Human Rights

When the HRA was being debated in Parliament, the JCHR was considered one of its most important institutional accompaniments. The white paper issued by the government referred to the need to establish 'a new Parliamentary Committee with functions relating to human rights', which could conduct inquiries into a range of human rights issues relating to the European Convention for the Protection

---

[1] These institutions are 'collateral' to the institutions that form the primary focus of this book: courts and legislatures.

of Human Rights and Fundamental Freedoms, 1950 (Convention) and publish reports to assist the government and Parliament in deciding what action to take.[2] The proposal was for the committee to be another of the select committees of both Houses of Parliament. Yet, a parliamentary committee with a scrutiny function relating to human rights was unprecedented in Britain,[3] where orthodoxy suggested that rights could be sufficiently protected by Parliament as a collective body.

As it happened, the JCHR was formed shortly after the HRA came into force, with its first meeting scheduled for 2001. Its terms of reference were remarkably wide:

(i)   matters relating to human rights in the United Kingdom (but excluding consideration of individual cases)

(ii)  proposals for remedial orders, draft remedial orders and remedial orders made under the Human Rights Act 1998

(iii) in respect of draft remedial orders and remedial orders, whether the special attention of the House should be drawn to them on any of the grounds specified in HC Standing Order No. 151 (Statutory Instruments (Joint Committee)).

The JCHR has 12 members—six from the House of Commons and six from the House of Lords—as well as a specialist legal advisor.[4] The constitution of the JCHR from both Houses of Parliament ensures that it is not dominated by a single party, and rises above party political considerations.[5] Like other select committees, it operates with a high degree of consensus,[6] and is widely perceived as an independent, impartial body.

---

[2] Home Office, *Rights Brought Home: The Human Rights Bill* (Cmd 3782, 1997), paras 3.6, 3.7.

[3] Robert Blackburn, 'A Human Rights Committee for the U.K. Parliament: The Options' (1998) 5 EHRLR 534.

[4] The two legal advisors to the JCHR thus far have been David Feldman (a public law scholar) and Murray Hunt (a barrister).

[5] Janet L. Hiebert, 'Parliament and the Human Rights Act: Can the JCHR Help Facilitate a Culture of Rights?' (2006) 4 International Journal of Constitutional Law 1, p. 16.

[6] Aileen Kavanagh, 'The Joint Committee on Human Rights: A Hybrid Breed of Constitutional Watchdog' in Murray Hunt, Hayley Hooper, and Paul Yowell (eds), *Parliaments and Human Rights: Redressing the Democratic Deficit* (Bloomsbury 2015), p. 115.

Although the JCHR was not entirely satisfied with the 'unhelpfulness'[7] of its vague terms of reference, it was quick to construe them broadly. The JCHR was clear that its primary work involved pre-legislative scrutiny of bills. In fact, in its first few years, it aspired to provide a comprehensive scrutiny service for all bills. In addition, the JCHR conducted thematic inquiries and monitored government responses to adverse Strasbourg Court judgments and (domestic) declarations of incompatibility. As Hiebert and Kelly note, its activities ranged from the 'proactive' (holding governments accountable for decisions that potentially infringed upon rights) to the 'reactive' (revisiting legislation following a domestic or international finding that it was inconsistent with rights).[8] These activities are not entirely distinct, and can converge—for instance, when the JCHR examines a bill that seeks to address a declaration of incompatibility, it effectively wears its 'proactive' and 'reactive' hats at the same time.[9] We also know what the JCHR considers as being beyond its remit—public education about human rights or the promotion of a culture of human rights in society (distinct from the promotion of a culture of human rights in government).[10] The JCHR typically meets at least once a week when Parliament is in session, and requests written responses not only from those in government, but also from interested parties such as legal practitioners, NGOs, etc.[11]

---

[7] A term used by the JCHR in one of its reports. It articulated that its terms of reference failed to provide any insight into what it actually does; see Joint Committee on Human Rights, *The Work of the Committee in the 2001–2005 Parliament* (Nineteenth Report of Session 2004–05, HL 112, HC 552), p. 9.

[8] Janet L. Hiebert and James B. Kelly, *Parliamentary Bills of Rights: The Experiences of New Zealand and the United Kingdom* (Cambridge University Press 2015), p. 7.

[9] An example of this is when the JCHR considered the Gender Recognition Bill, 2004, which sought to address the declaration of incompatibility made by the House of Lords in *Bellinger* v. *Bellinger*, [2003] 2 AC 467: [2003] UKHL 21 and the adverse judgment by the Strasbourg Court in *Goodwin* v. *UK*, [2002] IRLR 664.

[10] According to the JCHR, these are matters that are best left to a human rights commission; see Joint Committee on Human Rights, *The Case for a Human Rights Commission* (Sixth Report of Session 2002–03, HL 67-I, HC 489-I), pp. 33–4.

[11] Michael C. Tolley, 'Parliamentary Scrutiny of Rights in the United Kingdom: Assessing the Work of the Joint Committee on Human Rights' (2009) 44 Australian Journal of Political Science 41, p. 45.

Scholars agree that it is hard to measure objectively the performance of the JCHR, since the influence of parliamentary committees tends to be subtle and silently exercised.[12] Although the JCHR's success in persuading Parliament to carry out amendments to legislation has been limited, it has performed a valuable role in fostering a culture of human rights in government.[13] JCHR reports are also cited by MPs during parliamentary debates from time to time.[14]

### The JCHR's Role in Monitoring Responses to Declarations of Incompatibility

Most people focus their attention on the pre-legislative role of the JCHR—getting the government to think about the human rights implications of its proposed legislation.[15] However, the JCHR also plays the important post-legislative role of monitoring and scrutinizing the government's responses to declarations of incompatibility and adverse judgments from Strasbourg.

In the early years of the JCHR's existence, it was thought that the main role of the JCHR in relation to declarations of incompatibility would be to supervise executive remedial orders under section 10 of the HRA. This was also clearly reflected in the JCHR's terms of reference. However, it soon became clear that remedial orders would only be exceptionally used to address declarations of incompatibility—the more typical response being to fall back upon primary legislation. Only three remedial orders have been made for the 20 declarations of incompatibility that have attained finality thus far.[16] Indeed, in the first decade of the HRA's existence, only one remedial order[17] was issued in respect of a declaration of incompatibility.

[12] Kavanagh (n. 6), p. 131.

[13] Hiebert (n. 5). See also David Feldman, 'Can and Should Parliament Protect Human Rights?' (2004) 10 European Public Law 635, p. 651.

[14] See, for example, HL Deb 11 April 2002, vol. 633, col. 602 (Lord Filkin); HL Deb 11 April 2002, vol. 633, col. 604 (Lord Clement-Jones); HL Deb 5 July 2012, vol. 738, col. 885 (Lord Lester).

[15] This is understandable, since pre-legislative scrutiny comprises a majority of the JCHR's work.

[16] See Appendix B.

[17] Mental Health Act 1983 (Remedial) Order, 2001.

When it became clear that primary legislation would be the usual port of call for governments responding to declarations of incompatibility, the JCHR widened its net to supervise and monitor all of the government's responses to declarations of incompatibility, whatever form they took. In fact, had the JCHR restricted itself to supervising remedial orders, a major lacuna would have emerged, since its scrutiny role is triggered only when a bill is introduced—a matter that is entirely within the prerogative of the government. As we shall see, the JCHR's monitoring of all government's responses to declarations of incompatibility not only allows it to consider the substantive merits of legislation proposed by the government, but also enables it to ask the government when and how unremedied declarations of incompatibility will be addressed.

In its early reports, the JCHR issued guidance to government departments on how to respond to declarations of incompatibility.[18] It was recommended that ministers inform the JCHR about a declaration of incompatibility as soon as it had been made, and no later than 14 days after the judgment—a fair expectation since declarations of incompatibility cannot be made without notice to the Crown.[19] Minsters were asked to provide a full text of the declaration and a copy of the judgment to the JCHR. It was similarly recommended that the minister provide details of any appeal to the JCHR. The JCHR also suggested a timetable for compliance with final declarations of incompatibility, including that final decisions about how to remedy incompatibilities be taken no later than six months after the date of the judgment.

Although the government accepted these recommendations in 'spirit' and 'principle', it refused to commit itself to the strict timetable set out by the JCHR, noting that it may not always be possible to adhere to these limits in practice.[20] It agreed to amend the 'Guide to Whitehall Departments' (issued by the erstwhile Department of Constitutional Affairs) to include the JCHR's recommendations, but failed to do so for many years thereafter.[21]

---

[18] Joint Committee on Human Rights, *Making of Remedial Orders* (Seventh Report of Session 2001–02, HL 58, HC 473).

[19] HRA, section 5.

[20] Joint Committee on Human Rights (n. 7), Appendix 2 (Letter from Yvette Cooper, member of Parliament (MP)).

[21] This promise remained unfulfilled for five years; see Joint Committee on Human Rights, *Monitoring the Government's Response to Court Judgments Finding*

It is a mistake to argue, as some have, that in its early years, the JCHR did not 'attempt to monitor and report on' the government's responses to declarations of incompatibility[22] or that there was no 'follow-up duty' in relation to such declarations.[23] The JCHR's recommendations and the government's acceptance of them, even if in principle, rebuts these claims. Government departments had also informally agreed to keep the JCHR informed about responses to declarations of incompatibility.[24] Lord Lester, one of the early members of the JCHR, said that the Committee had 'entered into a constructive dialogue with the Government in relation to the operation of judicial declarations of incompatibility under section 4, and remedial orders under section 10 of the HRA'.[25]

As a matter of fact, the JCHR began monitoring the government's compliance with declarations of incompatibility soon after it started functioning. This was generally done informally, by sending letters to ministers of relevant departments.[26] The JCHR's correspondence in relation to *R (M)* v. *Secretary of State for Health*[27] (in which the Administrative Court declared provisions of the Mental Health Act, 1983 incompatible with Convention rights because they did not permit patients to seek a review of who would be appointed as their 'nearest relative') demonstrates this. The government had accepted the declaration of

---

*Breaches of Human Rights* (Sixteenth Report of Session 2006–07, HL 128, HC 728), p. 41. The responsibilities of the Department of Constitutional Affairs were assumed by the Ministry of Justice in May 2007.

[22] Tolley (n. 11), p. 49.

[23] Aruna Sathanapally, *Beyond Disagreement: Open Remedies in Human Rights Adjudication* (Oxford University Press 2012), p. 140.

[24] Joint Committee on Human Rights, *The Committee's Future Working Practices* (Twenty-Third Report of Session 2005–06, HL 239, HC 1575), Appendix 1 (Klug Report), para 10.10.

[25] Anthony Lester QC, 'Parliamentary Scrutiny of Legislation under the Human Rights Act 1998' (2002) 33 Victoria University of Wellington Law Review 1, p. 21.

[26] Much of this correspondence seems to be unpublished, since the JCHR did not maintain a policy of publishing correspondence in relation to declarations of incompatibility at the time. This changed after reforms to the working practices of the JCHR.

[27] [2003] EWHC 1094 (Admin).

incompatibility in this case and initially planned to address it through a remedial order. Later, the remedial order route was abandoned in favour of introducing fresh primary legislation. These developments were closely tracked by the JCHR, which continuously sought to hold the government to account for delays in addressing the declaration. This is borne out by the following extract from a letter written by the chairperson of the JCHR to the minister of state in the department of health:[28]

> Your letter of 18 March proposed to introduce a remedial order by way of the urgent procedure. Copies of our correspondence on this matter are enclosed. My Committee welcomed the decision to introduce a remedial order by way of the urgent procedure, in part because of the risk that progress by way of the non-urgent procedure might compromise the right to liberty of individuals other than the applicant in the case, over a period of several months. We are therefore particularly concerned that, some nine months later, the remedial order has not as yet been introduced.

As it turned out, barring *Smith* v. *Scott*,[29] the prisoner voting rights case, this was the longest time a government had taken to address a declaration of incompatibility.[30] However, the JCHR continued to chase the government through regular correspondence until the remedial legislation came into being, condemning the delay as 'highly regrettable'.[31] It later said that it wished to be much more closely informed of the proposed timetable for remedying an incompatibility and of the government's precise reasons for not pursuing a remedial order (particularly, one would assume, when it had initially planned to do so).[32] The JCHR's correspondence with ministers sought to make it clear that declarations of incompatibility could not be left to 'accumulate with impunity' and that Parliament was keeping a close eye on the conduct of the government.[33]

[28] Joint Committee on Human Rights (n. 7), Appendix 9.

[29] [2007] CSIH 9. For further discussion of this case and the developments surrounding it, see the following section in this chapter.

[30] It took over 66 months for the declaration of incompatibility to be remedied by the Mental Health Act, 2007. A graph reflecting the government's response times to declarations of incompatibility is set out in Chapter 3 and in the following section of this chapter.

[31] Joint Committee on Human Rights (n. 7), p. 78.

[32] Joint Committee on Human Rights (n. 21), p. 44.

[33] Joint Committee on Human Rights (n. 7), p. 41.

The JCHR also established an expectation that government departments would in fact positively address declarations of incompatibility. In relation to *Bellinger*[34] (which declared the law on recognition of gender reassignment for the purposes of marriage to be incompatible with Convention rights), it said that although the declaration of incompatibility would 'not oblige the Government to introduce remedial legislation as a matter of national law', the government had 'very properly decided that it ought to act'.[35] The point was made even more robustly in a subsequent report, in which it was said that the HRA 'preserves Parliament's ability to disagree with domestic courts on questions of compatibility, and, if it agrees that there is an incompatibility, to decide how it should be remedied. However, this role is subject always to the final decision of the ECtHR on compatibility, with which the UK must ultimately comply or withdraw from membership of the Council of Europe'.[36]

In 2006, following a report by its specialist advisor, Professor Francesca Klug, the JCHR brought about changes to its working practices. The Klug Report recognized that although the JCHR was monitoring responses to declarations of incompatibility through informal arrangements with government departments, this needed to be institutionalized in order to enable Parliament to hold the government to account effectively and retain a central role in the implementation of the HRA.[37] The JCHR had not, in the past, systematically scrutinized declarations of incompatibility when they were made, nor recommended to Parliament whether and how the government should respond to them.[38] The government had not always been forthcoming in providing information to the JCHR, and the fact that the JCHR's correspondence with minsters was unpublished allowed this to escape public notice.[39]

---

[34] See n. 9.

[35] Joint Committee on Human Rights, *Draft Gender Recognition Bill* (Nineteenth Report of Session 2002–03, HL 188-I, HC 1276-I), p. 10.

[36] Joint Committee on Human Rights (n. 21), p. 12.

[37] Joint Committee on Human Rights (n. 24), Appendix 1, para 13.12, noting that if Parliament does not monitor declarations of incompatibility, then '"parliamentary sovereignty" remains "executive sovereignty" in all but name'.

[38] Francesca Klug and Helen Wildbore, 'Breaking New Ground: The Joint Committee on Human Rights and the Role of Parliament in Human Rights Compliance' (2007) 3 EHRLR 231, p. 246.

[39] Joint Committee on Human Rights (n. 7), p. 42.

Accordingly, the JCHR resolved to assume a more proactive role in relation to declarations of incompatibility, both in terms of pressing the government to take action and recommending what action should be taken to address the declaration appropriately.[40] In terms of the JCHR's resource allocation, this was made possible by shifting away from the comprehensive pre-legislative scrutiny service for all bills to focusing on bills that raised significant human rights issues. Under the new sifting and scrutiny system, the legal advisor to the JCHR would review all government bills, private bills, and draft bills, and report only on those that raised significant human rights issues.[41] The JCHR also began publishing correspondence with ministers on declarations of incompatibility, increasing public awareness and raising the stakes for a government seeking to delay compliance with such declarations. It also resolved to publish annual reports on the implementation of declarations of incompatibility and adverse judgments from Strasbourg. These transparency-promoting measures made it increasingly difficult for governments to avoid declarations of incompatibility by stealth.

Soon thereafter, the JCHR issued a comprehensive guidance note on how government departments were expected to respond to declarations of incompatibility.[42] This note reiterated some of the existing JCHR recommendations to government departments (for instance, that final decisions about how to remedy incompatibilities should be made no later than six months after the date of the judgment). The note also said that the JCHR would consider the possibility of legislative response even before a declaration of incompatibility became final, if it believed that the chances of success in appeal were slim. It made two other important points—first, that the JCHR expected remedial action to 'demonstrate a commitment to full implementation rather than

[40] Joint Committee on Human Rights (n. 24), p. 21.

[41] According to Murray Hunt, this would increase the 'practical impact' of the Committee's legislative scrutiny work; see Murray Hunt, 'The Joint Committee on Human Rights' in Alexander Horne, Gavin Drewry, Dawn Oliver (eds), *Parliament and the Law* (Hart 2013), p. 223.

[42] Joint Committee on Human Rights, *Enhancing Parliament's Role in Relation to Human Rights Judgments* (Fifteenth Report of Session 2009–10, HL 85, HC 455), Annex: Guidance for Departments on Responding to Court Judgments on Human Rights.

minimal compliance',[43] and second, that its monitoring of a declaration of incompatibility would cease only when the remedial measure was not only enacted, but also in force.[44]

The second point is particularly significant because it would stifle the possible governmental strategy of having remedial legislation enacted in Parliament to appease the JCHR, but allowing the incompatibility to persist by delaying the enforcement of the legislation. In many cases, there have been considerable delays between the enactment of remedial legislation and its entry into force. Figure 5.1 shows those declarations of incompatibility where there was a time lag between the enactment of remedial legislation and its entry into force. As it makes clear, it took over 15 months for the remedial legislation (the Mental Health Act, 2007) that addressed the declaration of incompatibility in $M$[45] to enter into force. The corresponding figure for the Gender Recognition Act, 2004 (addressing the declaration of incompatibility in *Bellinger*[46]) was about nine months, and the Protection of Freedoms Act, 2012 (addressing the declaration of incompatibility in R *(Royal College of Nursing* v. *SSHD*[47]) was about four months.

Initially, the responsibility for responding to declarations of incompatibility was not centralized in any single department of government.[48] Rather, the department relevant to the declaration of incompatibility that was made would be expected to inform the JCHR about the declaration and correspond with it on its proposed remedial measures. On account of variances amongst government departments on the quality and level of engagement with the JCHR,[49] the Committee sought

---

[43] Joint Committee on Human Rights (n. 42), p. 73.

[44] All this guidance is being gradually mainstreamed by government departments; see Kavanagh (n. 6), p. 139.

[45] See n. 27.

[46] See n. 9.

[47] [2011] PTSR 1193.

[48] Sathanapally (n. 23), p. 135.

[49] See Joint Committee on Human Rights (n. 21), pp. 51–2:

Unfortunately, during the course of our work during this session the engagement of responsible Government Departments has not generally been very rigorous or systematic, but rather more ad-hoc. Information is often provided only when chased by us. When responses have been provided to our

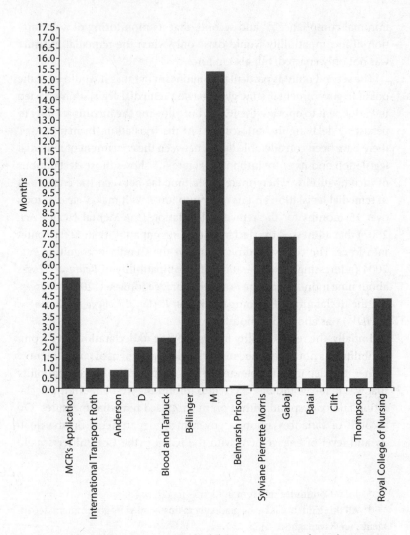

**Figure 5.1**   Delay between Enactment and Entry into Force of Legislation

questions, they have varied greatly in their quality. In a significant number of
cases we have had to ask for further information and a better explanation of
the Government's views.

to persuade the Human Rights Division in the Ministry of Justice to assume a central coordinating role as regards responses to declarations of incompatibility and adverse judgments from Strasbourg.[50] Formally, the government responded cautiously, rejecting this recommendation with a caveat that it would consider how the Ministry of Justice might work effectively with other government departments.[51] However, in practice, the Human Rights Division of the Ministry of Justice has gradually assumed the role envisaged for it by the JCHR.

The Ministry of Justice now produces approximately annual[52] reports highlighting declarations of incompatibility and adverse Strasbourg Court judgments, along with government responses. It records every declaration of incompatibility made, whether an appeal from the declaration is pending, whether the declaration has been overturned or upheld, and what action the government proposes to take in relation to the declaration. The database produced by the Ministry of Justice has quickly become the authoritative compendium of declarations of incompatibility in the UK.[53] Although the JCHR has lamented the infrequent updating of the database,[54] it does provide a publicly accessible

[50] Joint Committee on Human Rights (n. 21), p. 52.

[51] Joint Committee on Human Rights (n. 42), p. 50.

[52] Over the last six years, the reports have been published in January 2009, July 2010, September 2011, September 2012, October 2013, and December 2014.

[53] However, the database is known to contain some errors; see Chintan Chandrachud, 'Reconfiguring the Discourse on Political Responses to Declarations of Incompatibility' (2014) PL 624, p. 625.

[54] The JCHR has sought to press the Ministry of Justice to update and review the database on a quarterly basis. The JCHR also noted that the database was not easily accessible on the website of the Ministry of Justice. See Joint Committee on Human Rights, *Monitoring the Government's Response to Human Rights Judgments: Annual Report 2008* (Thirty-First Report of Session 2007–08, HL 173, HC 1078), p. 35. The JCHR itself had committed to writing to the Ministry of Justice and the lead department in relation to a declaration of incompatibility within three months of the final judgment having been handed down with recommendations; see Joint Committee on Human Rights (n. 21), p. 53. In general, however, the JCHR has appreciated the publication of the annual reports by the Ministry of Justice, which it claims to have been of 'considerable assistance' to it; see Joint Committee on Human Rights, *Human Rights Judgments* (Seventh Report of Session 2014–15, HL 130, HC 1088), p. 23.

report card, of sorts, of the government's compliance with declarations of incompatibility. Thus, the annual reports shed valuable light on the government's compliance record. The Human Rights Division of the Ministry of Justice corresponds with relevant government departments about declarations of incompatibility and asks questions such as: 'What are you doing? How far have you got? What is the next stage? Anything we can do to help?'[55] Such correspondence keeps the issue raised by the declaration of incompatibility alive and puts pressure on the relevant government department to address the incompatibility.

The JCHR embraced its revised role in relation to declarations of incompatibility by continuing to correspond with ministers and hold the government to account on the timing and merits of its response. In *R (Sylviane Pierrette Morris) v. Westminster City Council and First Secretary of State (No 3)*[56] and *R (Gabaj) v. First Secretary of State*,[57] section 185(4) of the Housing Act, 1996 was declared incompatible with Art. 14 of the Convention on the basis that it required a dependent of a British citizen to be disregarded when determining whether the citizen had a priority need for accommodation, when that dependent was subject to immigration control. The government took a very long time to address the incompatibility and to bring remedial legislation into effect. The JCHR wrote to the Minster for Housing, seeking his proposed response to the declaration. The minister's reply was as follows:[58]

> I am writing to advise you that the Government has given this matter careful consideration but the Secretary of State has not yet come to a decision whether to repeal or amend section 185(4). This matter raises some important policy issues and consequently further consideration and consultation with other Government departments will be necessary before a final decision can be made. However, I should like to assure the Committee that the Government intends to remedy the incompatibility as quickly as possible.

While the government continued to ponder over how to address the incompatibility, the JCHR expressed concern about the fact that

---

[55] Joint Committee on Human Rights (n. 42), p. 50.
[56] [2006] 1 WLR 505.
[57] Administrative Court, 28 March 2006.
[58] Joint Committee on Human Rights (n. 24), Appendix 4.

the government had not analysed the impact of the continuation of the incompatible provision on individual rights.[59] It then recommended that the government swiftly provide 'a detailed draft of their proposed remedy, together with the detailed reasons for their view'.[60] The government proposed to remove the discrimination in the social housing regime that was declared incompatible with the Convention, but retained elements of discrimination in the new regime, which was a cause of concern to the JCHR. The JCHR corresponded extensively with the government, seeking a fuller explanation of its views, and made it clear that it was of the opinion that the proposed regime would also be incompatible with Convention rights.[61]

Similar iterative correspondence followed the Court of Appeal's declaration of incompatibility in *R (Baiai)* v. *SSHD*.[62] In that case, the Court was considering the compatibility of the government's 'Certificate of Approval' scheme for marriages involving a person subject to immigration with the Convention. The Court in effect made two declarations of incompatibility—one based on the right to marry without discrimination, and a broader declaration based on nationality discrimination. The government accepted the first declaration, but appealed to the House of Lords against the second.

While the appeal was pending, the JCHR engaged in detailed correspondence with the relevant minister, asking, in particular, why the discriminatory elements of the scheme had not been removed.[63] The minister pointed out that a revised scheme would only be introduced following a final decision by the House of Lords. The JCHR continued to press the government for detailed a justification of its conduct, highlighting that:[64]

---

[59] Joint Committee on Human Rights (n. 21), p. 45.

[60] Joint Committee on Human Rights (n. 21), p. 47.

[61] Joint Committee on Human Rights, *Monitoring the Government's Response to Human Rights Judgments* (n. 54), p. 39. The new statutory regime has not (yet) been declared incompatible with Convention rights.

[62] [2008] QB 143.

[63] Joint Committee on Human Rights, *Monitoring the Government's Response to Human Rights Judgments* (n. 54), p. 40.

[64] Joint Committee on Human Rights, *Monitoring the Government's Response to Human Rights Judgments* (n. 54), p. 41.

In cases like this, where the Government accepts part of a statutory scheme is incompatible with the Convention, but proposes to appeal against a wider declaration of incompatibility, a choice must be made about the timing of any reform. This choice must clearly strike a balance between the cost, administrative inconvenience and parliamentary time involved in removing the incompatibility and the detriment suffered by those who are affected by the ongoing application of the incompatible provisions. In our view this balance can only be struck on a case-by-case basis.

The government later notified the JCHR of its plan to address the incompatibility through a remedial order, but failed to provide it with details about the substance of, and timetable for, the order, for a significant period of time. The JCHR made a damning statement against the government in its next report, demonstrating that delays would not enable declarations of incompatibility to fall under the radar:[65]

> We are concerned that it is now almost a year since we asked for further information on this case. The relevant declaration of incompatibility is over three years old and yet we still have no clear proposals to scrutinise or any timetable for action.... In the light of the earlier prolonged delay in this case, further procrastination is unacceptable. We call on the Government to publish its draft Order and its timetable for reform as soon as possible.

The JCHR's practice and procedure of corresponding with government ministers over declarations of incompatibility became increasingly entrenched. In accordance with its guidance, in some cases, the JCHR's correspondence began even when declarations of incompatibility were awaiting appeal in higher courts. In *R (Black)* v. *Secretary of State for Justice*,[66] the Court of Appeal declared section 35(1) of the Criminal Justice Act, 1991 incompatible with Art. 5(4) of the Convention, since it left the decision of parole of long-term determinate sentence prisoners to the Secretary of State. The chairperson of the JCHR promptly sent a letter[67] to the Secretary of State for Justice within weeks of the

---

[65] Joint Committee on Human Rights (n. 42), p. 47. The incompatibility was later remedied by the Asylum and Immigration (Treatment of Claimants, etc.) Act 2004 (Remedial) Order, 2011.

[66] [2008] 3 WLR 845.

[67] The following is an extract from the letter:

I would be grateful if you would tell us: (a) whether there is currently any appeal pending against this decision; (b) if not, whether the Government

Court of Appeal judgment, even though it was ultimately to be reversed by the House of Lords.[68]

The JCHR has not taken kindly to government apathy in notifying it about responses to declarations of incompatibility. For instance, the government sought to remedy one declaration of incompatibility[69] through secondary legislation, about which it did not inform the JCHR. A strong reprimand from the JCHR was to follow:[70]

> We are ... concerned by the fact that the secondary legislation designed to respond to this declaration of incompatibility was not drawn to our attention by the Government. We recommend that in future the Government *always* draws such instruments to the attention of this Committee, to ensure that Parliament receives the advice of its expert human rights committee about whether the instrument remedies the incompatibility identified by the courts.

Thus, the JCHR ensures that the government cannot allow declarations of incompatibility to slide off the political agenda. Through frequent correspondence and reports, it presses the government to notify it of the form, timing, and substance of its proposed response. Much has been written about the JCHR's modest record in actually persuading the government to carry substantive amendments to proposed legislation.[71] But one thing is clear—the JCHR places continued pressure on government departments showing passive resistance to declarations of incompatibility.[72] This ensures that the government cannot simply tide over declarations of incompatibility and lean on

---

intends to amend Section 35 to remedy this incompatibility (and if not, why not); (c) whether the Government plans to remove this incompatibility by way of a remedial order (and if not, why not).

See Joint Committee on Human Rights, *Monitoring the Government's Response to Human Rights Judgments* (n. 54), pp. 90–1.

[68] *R (Black) v. Secretary of State for Justice*, [2009] UKHL 1.

[69] *R (T) v. Chief Constable of Greater Manchester*, [2013] EWCA Civ 25.

[70] Joint Committee on Human Rights, *Human Rights Judgments* (n. 54), p. 18.

[71] K.D. Ewing and Joo-Cheong Tham, 'The Continuing Futility of the Human Rights Act' [2008] PL 668, p. 693; Tolley (n. 11), p. 49.

[72] Sathanapally (n. 23), p. 140.

the burden of inertia that such declarations place on those seeking a change in the law.

The JCHR has taken many transparency-promoting measures, including publishing all its correspondence with government departments, releasing an annual report on government responses to declarations of incompatibility, and pressing the Ministry of Justice to publish an annual database of declarations of incompatibility. All this makes it fairly simple for human rights activists, pressure groups, and the society at large to track government responses to declarations of incompatibility.[73] Through constant correspondence, follow-up, reminders, and, to use its own language, 'chasing',[74] of ministers, the JCHR has effectively imposed a principle of legality-type requirement[75] on the government. The government cannot simply retain legislation that has been declared incompatible with Convention rights on the books without manifesting an unequivocal intention of doing so. The theoretical option of complete 'ignorance' of declarations of incompatibility, which many of the commentators on the HRA have alluded to,[76] has remained just that—purely theoretical.

In many cases, even when the government has been haphazard in notifying the JCHR about declarations of incompatibility, the JCHR has continued to take its role of monitoring government responses

[73] As Kavanagh notes, '[T]he power of publicity is an extremely important form of influence which the JCHR brings to bear'; see Kavanagh (n. 6), p. 135.

[74] Joint Committee on Human Rights (n. 21), p. 51.

[75] The classic statement of the principle of legality comes from Lord Hoffman in *R* v. *SSHD, Ex p Simms* [2000] 2 AC 115, p. 131: 'Parliament must squarely confront what it is doing and accept the political cost. Fundamental rights cannot be overridden by general or ambiguous words. This is because there is too great a risk that the full implications of their unqualified meaning may have passed unnoticed in the democratic process.'

[76] See Jessica Simor, 'Publication Review: Non-derogable Rights and States of Emergency' (1998) 3 EHRLR 360, p. 364; Jonathan Cooper and Adrian Marshall-Williams (eds), *Legislating for Human Rights: The Parliamentary Debates on the Human Rights Bill* (Hart 2000), p. 156; Bernadette Harkin, 'Section 3(1) of the Human Rights Act and the Rule of Law' (2008) 14 UCL Jurisprudence Review 21, p. 31; Fergal F. Davis and David Mead, 'Declarations of Incompatibility, Dialogue and the Criminal Law' (2014) 43 Common Law World Review 62, p. 81.

seriously. Of course, we should be mindful of the context in which the JCHR operates vis-à-vis declarations of incompatibility. Thus far, there have been less than two declarations of incompatibility a year,[77] making its task of identifying these declarations and monitoring government responses relatively uncomplicated. How its effectiveness in doing so might change with a relative increase in the number of declarations of incompatibility is difficult to predict. JCHR recommendations are clearly not binding on Parliament or the government. Nevertheless, in the current state of play, the JCHR makes it almost impossible for any government to ignore declarations of incompatibility in the hope that they will fade from the public consciousness.

## The Strasbourg Court

As noted in the Introduction, the Strasbourg Court is a supranational court established under the Convention. It decides applications made by individuals, groups, NGOs, or member states, claiming that a member state has violated the rights set out in the Convention or its protocols. The Court only considers applications after all domestic remedies have been exhausted.[78] It may award 'just satisfaction' to applicants.[79] Its judgments are binding on member states that are party to the judgment, and the Committee of Ministers of the Council of Europe (CoE) supervises their execution.[80]

The Strasbourg Court also rallies institutional weight behind the declaration of incompatibility. This happens in two ways. First, British courts give significant traction to Strasbourg Court decisions when deciding cases, including challenges to primary legislation, under the HRA. Second, the Strasbourg Court grants a margin of appreciation to decisions taken by national authorities in member states, including courts. Practice has shown that the mere possibility of an adverse ruling against the government in Strasbourg has often been sufficient to

[77] Section 3 of the HRA has (by far) been the more frequently invoked remedy between sections 3 and 4. See Christopher Crawford, 'Dialogue and Rights-Compatible Interpretations under section 3 of the Human Rights Act 1998' (2014) 25 KLJ 34.

[78] Convention, Art. 35(1).

[79] Convention, Art. 41.

[80] Convention, Art. 46.

compel a change in the law following a declaration of incompatibility. These matters will now be considered in turn.

## Section 2(1) of the HRA: —Taking Strasbourg Court Decisions into Account

> If you come and listen to a human rights case being argued in the [UK] Supreme Court, you will be struck by the amount of time counsel spend referring to and discussing the Strasbourg case law. They treat it as if it were the case law of our domestic courts.[81]

Baroness Hale's extrajudicial observations provide a striking glimpse into the role that Strasbourg case law plays in domestic adjudication under the HRA. The existing constitutional arrangements in the UK give Strasbourg Court case law a level of importance that is highly unusual in the domestic context. Section 2(1) of the HRA states that when deciding cases in respect of Convention rights, courts 'must take into account' decisions of the Strasbourg Court. The first thing to note about this section is that it does not, as some people have argued,[82] give Strasbourg judgments merely persuasive authority in domestic courts. Nor are Strasbourg Court decisions binding in domestic courts.[83] Rather, they are a 'mandatory relevant consideration'[84] that courts are obliged to consider when deciding matters concerning Convention rights. Further, section 2(1) is not restricted only to Strasbourg Court judgments to which the UK is a party.

From the early case law under the HRA, courts developed what came to be known as the 'mirror principle' in their approach to Strasbourg

---

[81] Baroness Hale, 'Argentoratum Locutum: Is Strasbourg or the Supreme Court Supreme?' (2012) 12 Human Rights Law Review 65, p. 68.

[82] Sathanapally (n. 23), p. 116.

[83] Sir Phillip Sales, 'Strasbourg Jurisprudence and the Human Rights Act: A Response to Lord Irvine' [2012] PL 253, p. 255; Lord Irvine, 'A British Interpretation of Convention Rights' Lecture at the UCL Judicial Institute (London, 14 December 2011) <https://www.ucl.ac.uk/laws/judicial-institute/files/British_Interpretation_of_Convention_Rights_-_Irvine.pdf> accessed 24 September 2016; Conor Gearty, 'On Fantasy Island: British Politics, English Judges and the European Convention on Human Rights' (2015) 1 EHRLR 1, p. 7.

[84] Sales (n. 83), p. 257.

jurisprudence. This principle, which was first articulated in *R (Alconbury Developments)* v. *Secretary of State*,[85] requires domestic courts to follow 'clear and constant' jurisprudence of the Strasbourg Court. However, if the Strasbourg Court arrived at a conclusion that was fundamentally at odds with a principle of the British Constitution, courts would not need to follow it.[86] The most famous exposition of the mirror principle was to come from Lord Bingham soon after it was expounded, in his judgment in *R (Ullah)* v. *Special Adjudicator*: 'The duty of national courts is to keep pace with the Strasbourg jurisprudence as it evolves over time: no more, but certainly no less.'[87] The justification for this principle was that since the Convention was an international agreement, the meaning of Convention rights needed to be uniform across all 47 member states. Therefore, the Strasbourg Court should be considered the authoritative interpreter of the Convention.[88]

In another case, Lord Brown suggested a modification to Lord Bingham's test so that it would read: 'no less, but certainly no more'.[89] He argued that as a practical matter, British courts would be well served to commit errors of under-enforcement rather than errors of over-enforcement of Convention rights. This was because in cases involving the former, aggrieved parties could take their case to Strasbourg, whereas in cases involving the latter, the government would have no choice but to allow the error to stand. Practice developed to the effect that judgments of the Grand Chamber of the Strasbourg Court, consisting of 17 judges, would be treated as more authoritative than other judgments.[90]

It was made clear from the start that Strasbourg Court judgments would not necessarily be presumptively final. To begin with, only 'clear and constant' jurisprudence would be followed. Further, even clear and

---

[85] [2003] 2 AC 295, para 26 (Lord Slynn).

[86] *Alconbury Developments* (n. 85), para 76 (Lord Hoffman).

[87] [2004] UKHL 26, para 20.

[88] This rationale has critics. Baroness Hale, for instance, notes that 'anything we decide here [in the UK] is not likely to have any effect in other member states. They probably pay about as much attention to how we interpret the Convention rights as we pay to how they do, which is hardly any attention at all'; see Hale (n. 81), p. 71.

[89] *R (Al-Skeini)* v. *Secretary of State for Defence*, [2008] 1 AC 153, para 106.

[90] Alan Paterson, *Final Judgment: The Last Law Lords and the Supreme Court* (Hart 2013), p. 225.

constant jurisprudence that was at odds with some fundamental principle of the Constitution or misunderstood some aspect of the domestic
law would not be followed.[91] There were many variations of this second
exception, including that decisions which 'misunderstood',[92] were 'mis-
informed about',[93] or were based on an 'imperfect understanding'[94] of,
domestic law or procedure, would not be followed.

Nevertheless, the ground covered by the mirror principle encapsu-
lates many cases in which domestic judges feel compelled to follow
Strasbourg jurisprudence with which they have serious or principled
disagreement. This is best reflected in the House of Lords' judgment in
*SSHD v. AF (No 3)*,[95] on the compliance of closed material procedures,
an essential part of the government's anti-terrorism framework, with
the right to a fair trial. Just before that judgment, a Grand Chamber of
the Strasbourg Court decided a case[96] that had a decisive impact on the
Lords' decision. Lord Carswell made the point subtly, noting that even
though 'not all may be persuaded' by the Strasbourg Court's decision,
they were obliged to apply it.[97] Lord Hoffman, on the other hand, said
that he would follow the Strasbourg Court judgment 'with very considerable regret', even though he believed that the decision 'was wrong'
and destroyed a 'significant part of this country's defences against terrorism'.[98] The most famous opinion in the case was Lord Rodger's, who
said: 'Even though we are dealing with rights under a United Kingdom
statute, in reality, we have no choice: *Argentoratum locutum, iudicium fini-
tum*—Strasbourg has spoken, the case is closed' (italics added).[99] This
case shows that even when British domestic courts genuinely disagree
with clear and constant Strasbourg jurisprudence, they have no choice
but to follow it. Derogation from the Strasbourg case law enters the
picture only when Strasbourg has committed some more fundamental

---

[91] Lord Irvine describes this as an 'exceptionality' qualification; see Irvine
(n. 83).

[92] *R v. Lyons*, [2002] UKHL 447, para 46.

[93] *Lyons* (n. 92), para 46.

[94] *Doherty v. Birmingham City Council*, [2009] AC 367, para 88.

[95] [2009] UKHL 28.

[96] *A v. United Kingdom*, (2009) 49 EHRR 29.

[97] *AF (No 3)* (n. 95), para 108.

[98] *AF (No 3)* (n. 95), para 70.

[99] *AF (No 3)* (n. 95), para 98.

error, such as misunderstanding an aspect of domestic law. The Supreme Court recognized this in a subsequent case, where it was held that disagreement with Strasbourg is not an option where its jurisprudence is clear and authoritative, and it has expressed a coherent view.[100]

The duty to take Strasbourg jurisprudence into account, coupled with courts' interpretation of that duty, has significant implications for the declaration of incompatibility. A British judgment making a declaration of incompatibility based on a clear and constant line of Strasbourg jurisprudence is likely to find favour in Strasbourg. This also establishes an incentive for British courts to follow Strasbourg jurisprudence, since doing so would strengthen the normative force of the declaration of incompatibility itself. As McGoldrick says, '[T]he "political imperative" to pass remedial legislation would clearly be weaker, if a UK court or tribunal has interpreted the Convention rights beyond Strasbourg case law.'[101] Litigants that see a declaration of incompatibility remain unaddressed can take their case to Strasbourg with the expectation of a judgment against the government.[102]

More recently, however, there have been a number of cases in which the Supreme Court has showed an appetite to disagree with Strasbourg, and engaged in 'dialogue' with it over the scope and effect of Convention rights. This has prompted some commentators to argue that British courts are moving away from the mirror principle, and no longer feel obliged to follow Strasbourg jurisprudence in the same way as they did before.[103] But these cases are easily reconcilable with the early cases expounding upon the mirror principle, because they involve Strasbourg Court jurisprudence which, in the Supreme Court's view, has misunderstood aspects of domestic law.

For instance, the issue before the Supreme Court in *Horncastle*[104] was whether a criminal conviction based solely or to a decisive degree on

[100]  *R v. Horncastle*, [2010] 2 AC 373, para 119 (Lord Brown).

[101]  Dominic McGoldrick, 'The United Kingdom's Human Rights Act 1998 in Theory and Practice' (2001) 50 (4) International and Comparative Law Quarterly 901, 924.

[102]  Aileen Kavanagh, *Constitutional Review under the UK Human Rights Act* (CUP 2009) 284. See also Nicholas Bratza, 'The Relationship between the UK Courts and Strasbourg' (2011) EHRLR 505, 511.

[103]  Paterson (n. 90), p. 231; Gearty (n. 83), p. 7.

[104]  See n. 100.

the statement of a witness whom the defendant has had no chance of cross-examining would necessarily infringe upon the right to a fair trial under Art. 6 of the Convention. Strasbourg Court jurisprudence suggested that it would, but the Supreme Court refused to follow Strasbourg. Lord Phillips set out the position succinctly:[105]

> The requirement to 'take into account' the Strasbourg jurisprudence will normally result in the domestic court applying principles that are clearly established by the Strasbourg court. There will, however, be rare occasions where the domestic court has concerns as to whether a decision of the Strasbourg court sufficiently appreciates or accommodates particular aspects of our domestic process. In such circumstances it is open to the domestic court to decline to follow the Strasbourg decision, giving reasons for adopting this course. This is likely to give the Strasbourg court the opportunity to reconsider the particular aspect of the decision that is in issue, so that there takes place what may prove to be a valuable dialogue between the domestic court and the Strasbourg court. This is such a case.

Taking into consideration the Supreme Court's judgment, a Grand Chamber of the Strasbourg Court later modified its position.[106]

In another case,[107] the Supreme Court acknowledged once again that it would not be bound to follow each and every decision of the Strasbourg Court. However, where there was a clear and constant line of decisions whose effect was 'not inconsistent with some fundamental substantive or procedural aspect' of the law, and 'whose reasoning does not appear to overlook or misunderstand some argument or point of principle', the Strasbourg jurisprudence would be followed.[108] The Supreme Court said that the Strasbourg Court did not commit any of

---

[105] *Horncastle* (n. 100), para 11 (Lord Phillips).

[106] *Al-Khawaja and Tahery* v. *United Kingdom*, [2012] 54 EHRR 23. Judges have disagreed on what the culmination of the process of dialogue will be if the Strasbourg Court continues to disagree with British courts. In evidence to a parliamentary committee, Lord Phillips said that the Strasbourg Court would have the last word in such cases, whereas Lord Judge disagreed; see Evidence Session No. 5, Evidence to the House of Lords Constitution Committee (19 October 2011) <http://www.parliament.uk/documents/lords-committees/constitution/JAP/JAPCompiledevidence28032012.pdf> accessed 24 September 2016.

[107] *Manchester City Council* v. *Pinnock*, [2011] 2 AC 104.

[108] *Manchester City Council* (n. 107), para 48.

these errors in its jurisprudence, and therefore followed it. Another striking aspect of the case was that the Strasbourg Court's judgment had disagreed with two previous decisions of the majority on the House of Lords,[109] confirming the minority view. Dissenting opinions significantly raise the stakes in such situations, because they would compel the Supreme Court wishing to depart from Strasbourg jurisprudence to not only posit that Strasbourg fundamentally misunderstood the domestic position, but also that their brethren in dissent did.

There have been mixed views from the bench about whether British courts can leap ahead of Strasbourg by giving more generous interpretations to Convention rights than the Strasbourg Court. The majority in *Ambrose v. Harris*[110] observed that Strasbourg should be closely followed, since it was not within domestic courts' role to expand Convention rights. This confirms the continuing likelihood of declarations of incompatibility being 'affirmed'[111] in Strasbourg. However, in a powerful dissent, Lord Kerr deprecated what he described as '*Ullah*-type reticence' by the judges, noting that it was not open to the domestic judges to refuse to determine the application of a Convention right simply because Strasbourg had not spoken.[112] Similarly, in another case, Lord Brown observed that it would be 'absurd' to await an authoritative decision from Strasbourg before a domestic court could arrive at a finding that Convention rights had been violated.[113]

However, even the opinions enabling British courts to move ahead of Strasbourg jurisprudence point towards an expected affirmation of the domestic court judgment in Strasbourg, implying that the institutional purchase of the declaration of incompatibility remains powerful. Lord Kerr, for example, referred to anticipating Strasbourg's decision on an issue, as part of engaging in a process of dialogue with that Court.[114] Lord Brown said that even though a domestic

---

[109] *Harrow London Borough Council v. Qazi*, [2004] 1 AC 983; *Kay v. Lambeth London Borough Council*, [2006] 2 AC 465.

[110] [2011] 1 WLR 2435.

[111] This is a slight misnomer, since a Strasbourg Court decision is not an appeal from a domestic decision in a technical legal sense.

[112] *Ambrose* (n. 110), para 126.

[113] *Rabone v. Pennine Care NHS Trust*, [2012] UKSC 2, para 112. See also *BBC v. Sugar*, [2012] UKSC 4, para 59 (Lord Wilson).

[114] *Ambrose* (n. 110), paras 126, 130.

decision can expand Convention rights, it must 'flow naturally from existing Strasbourg case law' and could not expand the scope of the Convention beyond what was 'reasonably envisaged' by the Strasbourg Court.[115] The example he provided is instructive for the purposes of this chapter:[116]

> Suppose, for example, that the domestic court was inclined to give a Convention right an altogether greater reach than Strasbourg showed any likelihood of giving it, but that, so interpreted, the right would plainly conflict with domestic legislation. Is it seriously to be suggested that, pursuant to section 4 of the Human Rights Act 1998, the court could and should make a declaration of incompatibility? ... I cannot suppose that Parliament so intended or, indeed that such an approach would lead to satisfactory results.

On similar lines, Lord Wilson said in another case that the Supreme Court could leap ahead of Strasbourg, as long as it did not act 'extravagantly'.[117] These observations make it plain that the judges—including those who posit that domestic courts can leap ahead of Strasbourg—have remained highly conscious of the approval of their decisions (including declarations of incompatibility) in Strasbourg.

## The Margin of Appreciation

The second reason for which the declaration of incompatibility is likely to find favour in Strasbourg is the Strasbourg Court's application of the 'margin of appreciation' doctrine. It is worth noting at the outset that even though the Strasbourg Court is not an appellate court in the strict sense, it does not consider applications de novo. As with most international courts,[118] it only considers matters after all domestic remedies have been exhausted.[119] This means that the Strasbourg Court usually has the benefit of a domestic court ruling in its case materials.

---

[115] *Rabone* (n. 113), paras 112, 113.

[116] *Rabone* (n. 113), para 114.

[117] *BBC* (n. 113), para 59.

[118] Natsu Taylor Saito, 'Justice Held Hostage: U.S. Disregard for International Law in the World War II Internment of Japanese Peruvians: A Case Study' (1998) 40 Boston College Law Review 275, p. 326.

[119] Convention, Art. 35(1).

It conceives of its role as reviewing, rather than replacing, the decision of the domestic court.[120]

The margin of appreciation doctrine enables the Strasbourg Court to perform this reviewing function. According to the doctrine, the Court grants national authorities a margin of appreciation when reviewing their decisions. The doctrine found no explicit mention in the original text of the Convention.[121] But Protocol 15, which will enter into force when the states parties have signed and ratified it, will incorporate the doctrine into the preamble to the Convention.[122] The width of the margin of appreciation varies according to the circumstances of the case and the Convention rights engaged.[123]

The doctrine has a subsidiarity-based rationale, acknowledging that national authorities are better placed to delineate the scope and content of Convention rights in the first instance. As the Strasbourg Court famously put it in *Handyside*: 'By reason of their direct and continuous contact with the vital forces of their countries, State authorities are in principle in a better position than the international judge to give an opinion on the exact content of [the rights in question].'[124] This rationale was reiterated in the Brighton Declaration at the High Level Conference on the Future of the European Court of Human Rights,

---

[120] *Handyside* v. *United Kingdom*, (1979-80) 1 EHRR 737, para 50; *Wingrove* v. *United Kingdom*, (1997) 24 EHRR 1, para 53; *Von Hannover* v. *Germany (No 2)*, (2012) 55 EHRR 15, para 125.

[121] Michael R. Hutchinson, 'The Margin of Appreciation Doctrine in the European Court of Human Rights' (1999) 48 International and Comparative Law Quarterly 638, p. 639.

[122] According to Article 1 of Protocol 15, amending the Convention on the Protection of Human Rights and Fundamental Freedoms (2013):

> At the end of the preamble to the Convention, a new recital shall be added, which shall read as follows: 'Affirming that the High Contracting Parties, in accordance with the principle of subsidiarity, have the primary responsibility to secure the rights and freedoms defined in this Convention and the Protocols thereto, and that in doing so they enjoy a margin of appreciation, subject to the supervisory jurisdiction of the European Court of Human Rights established by this Convention.'

[123] Hutchinson (n. 121), p. 640; Dean Spielmann, 'Whither the Margin of Appreciation?' (2014) 67 CLP 49, p. 54.

[124] *Handyside* (n. 120), para 48.

where it was stated that the margin of appreciation 'reflects that the Convention system is subsidiary to the safeguarding of human rights at national level and that national authorities are in principle better placed than an international court to evaluate local needs and conditions'.[125]

The margin of appreciation has significant implications for the declaration of incompatibility. Since the margin includes domestic judicial decisions,[126] declarations of incompatibility fall within its ambit. Thus, a domestic judicial ruling that primary legislation is incompatible with Convention rights increases the likelihood that Strasbourg will also find that Convention rights have been violated. This is not a matter on which scholars universally agree. Some have argued that the margin of appreciation doctrine instead decreases the likelihood of success for litigants who go to Strasbourg armed with a declaration of incompatibility[127]—however, they fail to acknowledge that the margin of appreciation includes not only political decisions, but also domestic judicial decisions declaring legislation incompatible with Convention rights. The Strasbourg Court has gone so far as to say that in many contexts, it would reach a conclusion contrary to the national court only if the latter's decision was 'manifestly unreasonable'[128] or 'cannot reasonably be justified'.[129]

Others have argued that the Strasbourg Court will not inevitably reach the same conclusion as a domestic court because domestic courts

---

[125] Council of Europe, 'Brighton Declaration' (*High Level Conference on the Future of the European Court of Human Rights*, 2012), <http://www.echr.coe.int/Documents/2012_Brighton_FinalDeclaration_ENG.pdf> accessed 26 February 2015.

[126] *Handyside* (n. 120), para 48; *A* (n. 96), paras 154, 174.

[127] Rabinder Singh, 'The Place of the Human Rights Act in a Democratic Society' in Jeffrey Jowell and Jonathan Cooper (eds), *Understanding Human Rights Principles* (Hart 2001), p. 200; Mark Elliott, 'Parliamentary Sovereignty and the New Constitutional Order: Legislative Freedom, Political Reality and Convention' (2002) 22 LS 340, p. 349 (however, he does accept that in such situations, the rationale for application of the margin of appreciation doctrine is 'somewhat undermined'); Francesca Klug, 'Judicial Deference under the Human Rights Act 1998' (2003) 2 EHRLR 125, p. 132.

[128] *A* (n. 96), para 174.

[129] *Wingrove* (n. 120), para 33 (Judge Bernhardt). See also Paul Mahoney, 'The Relationship Between the Strasbourg Court and the National Courts' (2014) 130 LQR 568, p. 572.

focus on the particular legislative provision, whereas the Strasbourg Court focuses on the violation of Convention rights in specific circumstances.[130] However, it is highly unlikely that a declaration of incompatibility will be made at the domestic level in a situation where litigants' Convention rights are not violated. The House of Lords has noted that barring in exceptional circumstances, it will refuse to make a declaration of incompatibility in the abstract, without the actual violation of victims' Convention rights having been established.[131]

Declarations of incompatibility thus occupy an unusual position. Even though they are often treated as a finding against the government, since they provide no automatic legal redress, litigants armed with a declaration may take their case to Strasbourg. This results in a situation in which the margin of appreciation benefits not only Convention-violating conduct,[132] but also Convention-protecting conduct.[133]

On some occasions,[134] British courts have undertaken the task of predicting whether a particular matter would be within the state's margin of appreciation. Such analysis puts the cart before the horse—the margin of appreciation granted by Strasbourg will include the very judgment that has predicted what the width of the margin is likely to be. So even if British domestic courts make a declaration of incompatibility on a matter that they predict to be within the margin of appreciation, their judgment is likely to be affirmed in Strasbourg, since, through their own judgment, they would have effectively altered how the margin is viewed.[135] As Lord Hoffman put it, 'The margin of appreciation is there for division between the three branches of government.... There is

---

[130] Alison Young, 'Making Rights Real: The Human Rights Act in its First Decade (Review)' (2009) 68 Cambridge Law Journal 473, pp. 474–5.

[131] R (Rusbridger) v. Attorney General, [2004] 1 AC 357, paras 56, 57.

[132] This is what Tushnet has argued; see Mark Tushnet, Weak Courts, Strong Rights: Judicial Review and Social Welfare Rights in Comparative Constitutional Law (Princeton University Press 2009), p. 142.

[133] It could also prompt the government to contest the domestic court's decision in Strasbourg; see A (n. 96), para 157.

[134] R (Countryside Alliance) v. Attorney General, (2008) 1 AC 719; R (Nicklinson) v. Ministry of Justice, (2014) 3 WLR 200.

[135] This may foster reluctance to make declarations of incompatibility in such situations (on which, see Chapter 3).

no principle by which it is automatically appropriated by the legislative branch.'[136]

## The Practice: The Threat of Going to Strasbourg

Having said all this, the practice has remained somewhat disconnected from the theory of litigants taking their case to Strasbourg following a declaration of incompatibility. In many cases, the Strasbourg Court has strengthened the declaration of incompatibility through a judgment before, rather than after, the declaration was made. Here, an application to Strasbourg was not required following a declaration of incompatibility, since a change of law was forthcoming. The House of Lords' decision in *R (Anderson)* v. *SSHD* [137] (making a declaration of incompatibility against the law which enabled the Home Secretary to decide the tariff period for prisoners sentenced for life), for example, was based on the Strasbourg Court's judgment in *Stafford* v. *United Kingdom*.[138] Following the decision, the Home Secretary had been advised that a possible application to Strasbourg would almost certainly result in a judgment against the government.[139] Parliament soon enacted primary legislation[140] removing the incompatibility.

However, there have been cases in which litigants, armed with a declaration of incompatibility, have actually threatened to take their case to Strasbourg. The force of that threat, combined with other factors, has placed enough pressure on the government to change the law. Of course, establishing causation for the government or Parliament's choices is always a tricky exercise, and it is difficult to know the precise extent of the role played by the litigant's threat in the government's decision. Nevertheless, let us consider a few examples.

In *Blood and Tarbuck* v. *Secretary of State for Health*,[141] Ms Diane Blood sought a declaration that provisions of the Human Fertilisation and

---

[136] *In re G (Adoption: Unmarried Couple)*, (2009) 1 AC 173, para 37.

[137] (2003) 1 AC 837.

[138] (2002) 35 EHRR 1121.

[139] Vikram Dodd and Clare Dyer, 'His Life in Whose Hands? Sarah Payne Killer Ordered to Serve 50 Years' *The Guardian* (London, 25 November 2002).

[140] Criminal Justice Act, 2003, section 303(b)(i).

[141] Administrative Court, 28 February 2003 (unreported).

Embryology Act, 1990 were incompatible with the Convention in that they specified that when a child was conceived with the sperm of a deceased man, he would not be treated as the father of the child. At this early stage, she threatened to take her case to the Strasbourg Court in the event that the law was not amended. The government's initial reaction was to contest the case in the domestic court 'tooth and nail', and urge Ms Blood not to take the case to Strasbourg.[142] However, the government ultimately relented and consented to the issuance of a declaration of incompatibility in the domestic proceedings. Soon after the Administrative Court made a declaration of incompatibility, Ms Blood suggested that she would be prepared to bring a 'further challenge' to Strasbourg if the government did not act promptly.[143] About six months later, the law was retrospectively amended to enable men to be treated as the father of a child in such circumstances, subject to certain conditions.[144] Parliamentary debates make it clear that the threat of proceedings in Strasbourg, in which the government would 'inevitably face condemnation', formed a major impetus behind the declaration.[145]

The threat to go to Strasbourg following a declaration of incompatibility was still clearer in *Bellinger*,[146] in which the House of Lords declared a statutory provision[147] (that failed to recognize the marriage of a post-operative male to female transsexual to a man) incompatible with Convention rights. Mrs Bellinger repeatedly warned that she would take her case to Strasbourg. She did so in an interview shortly after the Lords' decision, in the following words:[148]

> I am extremely saddened today knowing that I have gone all the way through the British legal system and it has failed me [Mrs Bellinger was

---

[142] HL Deb 4 July 2003, vol. 650, col. 1156 (Lord Lester).

[143] Joshua Rozenberg, 'Diane Blood Wins Fight over Husband's Name' *The Telegraph* (London, 1 March 2003).

[144] Human Fertilisation and Embryology (Deceased Fathers) Act, 2003.

[145] HL Deb (n. 142).

[146] See n. 9.

[147] Matrimonial Causes Act 1973, section 11(c).

[148] BBC News, 'Transsexual Marriage Not Legal' (*BBC News*, 10 April 2003), <http://news.bbc.co.uk/1/hi/england/lincolnshire/2934919.stm> accessed 5 March 2015.

seeking a remedy under section 3 rather than section 4 of the HRA]. Now I fear I am left with no choice other than to seek redress in the European courts, a possibility my legal team will now look into.

As Parliament continued to retain the incompatible law on the books, Mrs Bellinger later went ahead and filed an application in the Strasbourg Court.[149] However, the Strasbourg Court was not called upon to make a decision, since the application was withdrawn after the law was changed[150] in order to address the incompatibility.

These cases provide evidence of the fact that the Strasbourg Court's 'bark' (or the threat of a litigant going to the Strasbourg Court armed with a declaration of incompatibility), combined with other factors, has been sufficient to prompt the government to change the law following a declaration of incompatibility. In most cases, its 'bite' has not been required. Can it be said that the government may find it worthwhile to call the bluff of a litigant armed with a declaration of incompatibility, by taking no steps to address the incompatibility?

There has only been a single occasion on which the Strasbourg Court has arrived at a judgment on the application of a litigant armed with a domestic declaration of incompatibility. That was *A* v. *SSHD*,[151] involving a challenge to the Anti-Terrorism, Crime and Security Act, 2001 (ATCSA), which allowed the indefinite detention without trial of foreign terrorist suspects. The litigants threatened to go to Strasbourg in the event that the government did not address the incompatibility promptly:[152] a threat that soon materialized into an application. Even after it was filed, the withdrawal of the case was used as a bargaining chip for the government to take immediate action.[153] The Strasbourg

---

[149] *Bellinger* v. *UK*, App No 43113/04; Brice Dickson, *Human Rights and the United Kingdom Supreme Court* (Oxford University Press 2013), p. 277.

[150] By the Gender Recognition Act, 2004.

[151] (2005) 2 AC 68 ('Belmarsh Prison case').

[152] BBC News, 'Terror Detainees Win Lords appeal' (*BBC News*, 16 December 2004), <http://news.bbc.co.uk/1/hi/uk/4100481.stm> accessed 5 March 2015.

[153] BBC News, 'Terror Detainees Turn to Europe' (*BBC News*, 7 February 2005) <http://news.bbc.co.uk/1/hi/uk/4243061.stm> accessed 5 March 2015: 'A Liberty spokesperson added that the papers submitted to the European Court of Human Rights in Strasbourg will be withdrawn if the government revokes its derogation and deals with the detainees appropriately.'

Court confirmed the conclusions of the House of Lords, both on the question of whether there was an emergency threatening the life of the nation, and whether the state measures complied with the requirements of the Convention.[154] Under its margin of appreciation doctrine, the Strasbourg Court accorded a high degree of institutional respect to the judgment of the House of Lords, observing that it would displace the conclusions of the House only if satisfied that it 'had misinterpreted or misapplied Art. 15 or the Court's jurisprudence under that article or reached a conclusion which was manifestly unreasonable'.[155] This was in spite of the Strasbourg Court's normal line of reasoning that derogating measures are usually strictly required, and hence legitimate, under Art. 15 of the Convention.[156] Thus, this case suggests that the proverbial 'bite' (or a decision of the Strasbourg Court) is likely to prove as difficult for the government as the 'bark' (or the threat of filing an application in Strasbourg).

Having said that, it is now worth addressing the elephant in the room—*Smith*,[157] the prisoner voting rights case. As I noted in Chapter 2, the declaration of incompatibility made in that case is the only one that has not (yet) been addressed by primary legislation or through a remedial executive order. As is often the case, the first judgment highlighting that domestic legislation imposing a blanket ban on the voting rights of prisoners was inconsistent with Convention rights came from the Strasbourg Court,[158] following which a British domestic court made a declaration of incompatibility. In a subsequent case, the Court of Appeal[159] and Supreme Court[160] refused to make further declarations of incompatibility on the same issue, since the previous declaration

---

[154] *A* (n. 96).

[155] *A* (n. 96), para 174.

[156] Mark Elliott, 'United Kingdom: The "War on Terror," U.K.-style: The Detention and Deportation of Suspected Terrorists' (2010) 8 International Journal of Constitutional Law 131.

[157] See n. 29.

[158] *Hirst v. UK (No 2)*, [2005] ECHR 681. See also *Greens and MT v. UK*, [2010] ECHR 1826; *Scoppola v. Italy (No 3)*, [2012] ECHR 868. The Divisional Court had initially refused to make a declaration of incompatibility: *Hirst v. Attorney General*, (2001) EWHC Admin 239.

[159] *R (Chester) v. Secretary of State for Justice*, (2011) 1 WLR 1436.

[160] *R (Chester) v. Secretary of State for Justice*, [2014] AC 271.

was already on the table. Why has the pressure exerted by Strasbourg not yet prompted an amendment to the law in this case?

The answer emanates from multiple factors that have conspired together to found a stalemate. The ban on prisoner voting rights has been inaccurately portrayed as a fundamental and longstanding facet of British law, with which a *foreign* court was attempting to interfere. As one Conservative MP remarked in the House of Commons, 'It is the settled view of the British people, through their elected representatives in the British Parliament, that prisoners should not have the right to vote, and it has been that way since 1870.'[161] However, as Murray demonstrates, restrictions on franchise historically 'rested on very limited legal authority' and were subject to several exceptions by the middle of the twentieth century.[162] This is a point which, although not lost on the judges,[163] has been drowned out in the political discourse. In turn, this idea has also channelled a wave of Euroscepticism and suspicion about the interference of the Strasbourg Court in domestic policymaking. Oddly enough, even MPs from the two largest parties who otherwise take pro-civil libertarian positions have staunchly defended the ban on prisoner voting rights.[164]

The judgments from Strasbourg have also attracted considerable ire from politicians because they touch upon what is widely considered a sacrosanct aspect of the British constitutional project: parliamentary sovereignty and the legislative process. This is because in making its decision, the Strasbourg Court had taken into account that the Westminster Parliament had not substantively debated the ban on prisoner voting rights in the context of contemporary penal policy and current human rights standards.[165]

Finally, the narrative underlying the issues, or the faces of the prisoner voting rights movement, have not helped in reshaping the public consciousness. The original claim in the Strasbourg Court was brought by John Hirst, described by one scholar as an 'an axe-wielding killer

---

[161]  HC Deb 10 February 2011, vol. 523, no. 116, col. 536 (Phillip Hollobone).

[162]  C.R.G. Murray, 'A Perfect Storm: Parliament and Prisoner Disenfranchisement' (2012) 66 Parliamentary Affairs 1, p. 3.

[163]  *Chester* (n. 160), para 126 (Lord Sumption).

[164]  Murray (n. 162), p. 22.

[165]  *Hirst* (n. 158), para 79.

celebrating his win with champagne as he pours YouTube abuse on the authorities'.[166] The domestic case in the Supreme Court seeking a further declaration of incompatibility involved two claims by prisoners serving life sentences for murder, prompting one of the judges hearing the case to observe that she had 'no sympathy at all' for either of them.[167]

# India

It is now worth examining the institutional apparatus accompanying intermediate remedies in India. Since India is neither party to the Convention nor a signatory to the Optional Protocols allowing individual petitions to international human rights monitoring bodies,[168] it has no Strasbourg Court equivalent. But following up on judicial recommendations of changes to the law is within the mandate of the NHRC, to whose functioning this chapter will now turn.

## The National Human Rights Commission

### Composition and Functions of the National Human Rights Commission

The NHRC is a statutory commission established under the Protection of Human Rights Act, 1993 (PHRA).[169] It was established in the political

---

[166]   Gearty (n. 83), p. 4.

[167]   *Chester* (n. 160), para 99 (Baroness Hale).

[168]   Sunil Bhave, 'Deterring Dowry Deaths in India: Applying Tort Law to Reverse the Economic Incentives that Fuel the Dowry Market' (2007) 40 Suffolk University Law Review 291, p. 307. On the viability of India signing these optional protocols, see Meghana Shah, 'Rights under Fire: The Inadequacy of International Human Rights Instruments in Combating Dowry Murder in India' (2003) 19 Connecticut Journal of International Law 209, p. 223.

[169]   The NHRC was originally established under the Protection of Human Rights Ordinance, 1993, which was replaced by the PHRA. The PHRA also empowered state governments to establish human rights commissions at the state level. For analysis of the functioning of State Human Rights Commissions, see Harsh Dobhal and Mathew Jacob, *Rugged Road to Justice: A Social Audit of State Human Rights Commissions in India* (Vol. 1, Human Rights Law Network 2012).

context of widespread reports of custodial violence and atrocities per-petrated by police officials—an issue that attracted condemnation from several NGOs, including Amnesty International and Asia Watch.[170] The Prime Minister Narasimha Rao–led Congress government feared an international backlash, leading to repercussions in the nation's rela-tionship with financial institutions.[171]

Implicit in the statement of objects and reasons in the PHRA was the need for establishing an institutional structure to protect human rights—one that would foster greater accountability and transparency in the administration of government.[172] The PHRA prescribed that the NHRC would consist of: (a) a former Chief Justice of the Indian Supreme Court, who would be its chairperson; (b) a current or former judge of the Indian Supreme Court; (c) a current or former Chief Justice of a High Court; and (d) two members who had 'knowledge of, or practical experience in, matters relating to human rights' (in practice, these are usually bureaucrats).[173] Appointments to the NHRC were to be made by the President of India on the recommendation of a com-mittee consisting of members of the government and the opposition. Owing to its judge-heavy composition, the NHRC is considered a highly respected and independent commission.[174]

---

[170] Arun Ray, *National Human Rights Commission of India: Formation, Functioning and Future Prospects* (2nd edn, Khama 2004), p. 85.

[171] Vijayashri Sripati, 'India's National Human Rights Commission: A Shackled Commission?' (2000) 18 Boston University International Law Journal 1, p. 9.

[172] National Human Rights Commission, *Annual Report (2001–2002)* <http://nhrc.nic.in/documents/AR01-02ENG.pdf> accessed 24 September 2016, para 2.4.

[173] PHRA, section 3. In addition, the chairpersons of the National Commis-sion for Minorities, the National Commission for the Scheduled Tribes, and the National Commission for Women would be ex-officio members of the Commission.

[174] Sripati (n. 171), p. 11; Virendra Dayal, 'Evolution of the National Human Rights Commission, 1993-2002: A Decennial Review' (2002) 1 Journal of the National Human Rights Commission 40, p. 42. Although, on occasion, the government and opposition have sparred over the appointment of some of its members; see 'BJP Opposes NIA Chief's Appointment as NHRC member' *The Indian Express* (New Delhi, 30 March 2013); 'BJP opposes Cyriac Joseph's

The NHRC is entrusted with performing a large range of statutory functions,[175] including inquiring into individual complaints of human rights violations (and making recommendations for redress to the government), intervening in human rights proceedings that are pending before courts, visiting jails to examine the living conditions of inmates, studying international human rights treaties and making recommendations for their effective implementation, spreading human rights literacy, and encouraging the efforts of NGOs.[176] From its inception, therefore, the NHRC was set up with a broad mandate that included many functions—such as public education on human rights issues— that were specifically excluded from the JCHR's mandate.

The function that is relevant for the purposes of this chapter is set out in section 12(d) of the PHRA, which enables the NHRC to 'review the safeguards provided by or under the Constitution or any law for the time being in force for the protection of human rights and recommend measures for their effective implementation'. Read broadly, this function empowers the NHRC to follow up and pursue judicial recommendations of changes to the law on human rights grounds. The NHRC's functions suggest that it follows two trajectories: the first, a fast-track trajectory for redressing immediate wrongs; the second, a slow-track trajectory seeking to ingrain a culture of human rights protection in India.[177]

Given its wide remit, the NHRC now has a dedicated staff of over 300 people at its office in New Delhi.[178] It is advised by a number of thematic expert groups, such as the groups on mental health, disability, legal issues, NGOs, right to food, refugees, and emergency medical

---

appointment to NHRC' *The Times of India* (New Delhi, 17 May 2013). There has also been some criticism on the under-representation of communities on the Commission; see Kuldip Nayar, 'Why No Representation to Women?' *The Hindu* (Chennai, 15 December 1998).

[175] Dayal (n. 174), p. 41.

[176] PHRA, section 12.

[177] National Human Rights Commission, *Annual Report (1994–1995)* <http://nhrc.nic.in/ar94_95.htm> accessed 24 September 2016, para 2.2.

[178] Justice Rajendra Babu, 'Lecture at the Foundation Day Function of National Human Rights Commission' (New Delhi, 12 October 2007) <http://nhrc.nic.in/speeches.htm#12th October, 2007> accessed 24 September 2016.

care. The NHRC sets high standards of transparency and accessibility for itself: its decisions are made public, its proceedings are conducted in the open, complaints can be made to it in the complainant's language of choice, and complainants do not need to pay fees to access the Commission.[179] It publishes reports annually, which, according to the PHRA, need to be presented in Parliament by the central government along with a 'memorandum of action taken or proposed to be taken' on the recommendations of the NHRC.[180]

Within its vast range of functions, it is quite clear that the NHRC's focus has been on addressing individual complaints of human rights violations. Although it has no power to make binding orders in such cases, it provides recommendations to the government on how to address individual complaints. On the whole, it has been quite successful in reducing the burden on the courts.[181] Its caseload has grown exponentially since inception. In its first year, the NHRC received 496 complaints. In 1999, the figure stood at over 54,000.[182] In 2014, it received over 90,000 complaints in a single year.[183] A large part of the NHRC's annual report is dedicated to describing an illustrative set of complaints it received in the year, with the objective of showing the 'variety and scope' of human rights issues being dealt with by it as well as the wide geographical footprint of the NHRC.[184]

## Implementation of Directions to the Executive

The NHRC has also had modest success in prodding the executive to implement guidelines or directions laid down by the courts to ensure

---

[179] National Human Rights Commission, *Annual Report (1998–1999)* <http://nhrc.nic.in/ar98_99.htm> accessed 24 September 2016, para 2.4.

[180] PHRA, section 20(2).

[181] Buhm-Suk Baek, 'RHRIs, NHRIs and Human Rights NGOs' (2012) Florida Journal of International Law 235, pp. 256–7.

[182] National Human Rights Commission (n. 179), para 16.1.

[183] Justice K.G. Balakrishnan, 'Lecture on Human Rights Day, 2014' (New Delhi, 10 December 2014) <http://nhrc.nic.in/Documents/Speech_By_Chairperson_NHRC_On_HumanRightsDay2014.pdf> accessed 24 September 2016.

[184] National Human Rights Commission, *Annual Report (1993–1994)* <http://nhrc.nic.in/ar93_94.htm> accessed 24 September 2016, para 5.6.

that legislation is enforced in a manner that is sensitive to human rights concerns. Conscious of the problem of a large number of prisoners being kept in prison while awaiting trial, the Supreme Court, in *Common Cause* v. *Union of India*,[185] issued several directions for the release on bail of such prisoners.[186] The NHRC welcomed the judgment on the basis that it would bring about much-needed reduction in prison population,[187] and vigorously pursued the implementation of the court's directions. Members of the NHRC engaged with prison and legal aid authorities to chalk out how the directions should be implemented.[188] Prison authorities were also asked to send monthly reports to the NHRC, in order to enable it to assess the impact of the judgment.[189] In *Joginder Kumar* v. *State of Uttar Pradesh*,[190] the Supreme Court directed police authorities to allow people who were arrested to inform a relative or friend of their arrest. In order to encourage them to comply with the Court's judgment, the NHRC circulated copies of it to Directors General of Police in all states.[191] Thereafter, the Home Ministry of the Government of India also advised states to follow the Supreme Court's directions.[192]

In its well-known judgment in *D.K. Basu* v. *State of West Bengal*,[193] the Supreme Court issued comprehensive guidelines on arrest and detention procedures.[194] In spite of highlighting this judgment in its

---

[185] AIR 1996 SC 1619.

[186] These directions included, for example, the release on bail of prisoners (a) who were charged with offences subject to a maximum of three years in prison; (b) who had already spent six months in prison; and (c) where the trial was pending for more than a year.

[187] National Human Rights Commission, *Annual Report (1995–1996)* <http://nhrc.nic.in/ar95_96.htm> accessed 24 September 2016, para 3.34.

[188] National Human Rights Commission, *Annual Report (1997–1998)* <http://nhrc.nic.in/ar97_98.htm> accessed 24 September 2016, para 3.35.

[189] National Human Rights Commission, *Annual Report (1996–1997)* <http://nhrc.nic.in/ar96_97.htm> accessed 24 September 2016, para 3.51.

[190] AIR 1994 SC 1349.

[191] National Human Rights Commission (n. 187), para 3.20.

[192] National Human Rights Commission (n. 189), para 12.

[193] AIR 1997 SC 610.

[194] These guidelines included: (a) that police personnel carrying out the arrest should bear clear identification; (b) that police officers should prepare a

annual report,[195] the central government did not consider how it would address the judgment in its 'memorandum of action taken'. Taking serious note of this lapse, the NHRC reported that the government would need to comply with the Court's guidelines, and that a failure to do so would attach contempt sanctions[196]—an important point which, as noted in Chapter 4, distinguishes guidelines to the executive from recommendations to the legislature.

Having said that, the NHRC has not always found it easy to secure the cooperation of the executive. Governments have sometimes delayed complying with, or sidestepped, its recommendations. Notice what the NHRC said in its annual report for 2007–8:[197]

> [T]he Commission is constrained to point out ... [that] State Governments/ Union Territory Administrations and Ministries/Departments of the Central Government have delayed—if not effectively undone—the work of the Commission by their inaction towards its inquiries, notices and recommendations. It is disheartening to note that several cases before the Commission have not been resolved because the office of the concerned State Government/Union Territory Administration has not filed its reply or not complied with the Commission's orders in a case or submitted an action taken report.

### Prompting Amendments to Legislation

The NHRC has had less success in prompting legislative change on the few occasions that it has attempted to do so. Let us consider a few examples. The alarming number of prisoner deaths in police custody

---

memo of arrest, which should be attested by at least one witness; and (c) that the person arrested must be made aware of this right to have someone informed of his arrest or detention.

[195] National Human Rights Commission (n. 189), para 3.36.

[196] National Human Rights Commission (n. 188), para 3.12: 'It is of utmost importance that serious attention be paid by the Central as well as State Governments to the instructions of the Supreme Court in the second case, not least because it has stipulated that failure to carry out the instructions would attract penalties for commitment of contempt of the orders of the Court.'

[197] National Human Rights Commission, *Annual Report (2007–2008)* <http://nhrc.nic.in/Documents/AR/NHRC-AR-ENG07-08.pdf> accessed 24 September 2016, para 1.10.

has remained an important issue on the NHRC's agenda. In a case of custodial death, the Supreme Court recommended that the law be amended to place an evidential burden of proof on the police in such cases.[198] Soon thereafter, the Law Commission of India took the issue raised by the Supreme Court forward by suggesting that the government introduce a new section (114B) into the Indian Evidence Act, 1872 to reverse the burden of proof in cases of bodily injury or death of a prisoner in police custody.[199] The next step in the process was for the Supreme Court, reinforced by the Law Commission's recommendation, to suggest again that the government give 'serious thought' to reversing the burden of proof.[200] The NHRC's support for the recommendation was made unequivocal in its annual report for 1995–6: '[I]t is not enough for the Commission to react to custodial deaths or violence after they have occurred. It is far better to prevent such acts before they occur. The Commission is of the view that a recommendation of the Indian Law Commission ... should be acted upon.'[201] The NHRC then began lobbying the government to change the law based on the Supreme Court and Law Commission's recommendations. But these attempts were in vain. In spite of strongly urging the government to change the law on multiple occasions,[202] the recommendation was not implemented.[203] In response to a question on the floor of the Lok

---

[198]   *State of Uttar Pradesh* v. *Ram Sagar Yadav*, AIR 1985 SC 416, para 20.

[199]   Law Commission of India, *One Hundred and Thirteenth Report on Injuries in Police Custody* (Law Commission of India 1985).

[200]   *State of Madhya Pradesh* v. *Shyam Sunder Trivedi*, (1995) 4 SCC 262, para 17: 'The [Law Commission] recommendation, however, we notice with concern, appears to have gone un-noticed and the crime of custodial torture etc. flourishes unabated ... we hope that the Government and Legislature would give serious thought to the recommendation.'

[201]   National Human Rights Commission (n. 187), para 3.19.

[202]   National Human Rights Commission (n. 179), paras 3.19, 3.20; National Human Rights Commission, *Annual Report (2000–2001)* <http://nhrc. nic.in/ar00_01.htm> accessed 24 September 2016, para 16.25. The Supreme Court also continued to urge Parliament to change the law: *D.K. Basu* v. *State of West Bengal*, AIR 1997 SC 610, para 28; *The Court on its own motion* v. *State of Punjab*, (2011) 1 ILR (P&H) 307, para 8.

[203]   The Law Commission also reiterated its recommendation in a subsequent report; see Law Commission of India, *One Hundred and Fifty Second Report on Custodial Crimes* (Law Commission of India 1994), para 11.3.

Sabha in 2008,[204] the minister concerned said that the law would not be amended (on the flawed argument that in a subsequent report,[205] the Law Commission had not recommended the amendment).[206]

Another NHRC recommendation that was intended to deter unlawful violence committed by police authorities fell on deaf ears. Section 197 of the Code of Criminal Procedure, 1973 requires the prior sanction of the government for the criminal prosecution of public servants in relation to acts done in the course of their duties.[207] The NHRC suggested that section 197 be amended so as to obviate the necessity of governmental sanction for the prosecution of a police officer where a prima facie case of the commission of a custodial offence was established.[208] In spite of reminders from the NHRC,[209] this recommendation went unheeded. Once again, in response to a question on the floor of the Rajya Sabha, the Union Home Minister made it clear that section 197 would not be amended, with a succinct answer: 'No, Sir!'[210]

Why has the NHRC struggled to prompt changes to primary legislation? Evidence suggests that the Commission does not get the kind of parliamentary attention that it expects. By way of practice, the NHRC's annual reports are not published until they are tabled in Parliament— giving the government of the day an effective mechanism of postponing the release of the report (the contents of which are likely to be

---

[204] Lok Sabha, Unstarred Question No. 2717 (18 March 2008) (Answer by Radhika V. Selvi, Minister of State in the Minstry of Home Affairs); Asian Centre for Human Rights, *Torture in India* (Asian Centre for Human Rights 2010), p. 3.

[205] Law Commission of India, *One Hundred and Fifty Fourth Report on the Code of Criminal Procedure 1973* (Law Commission of India 1996).

[206] This argument was plainly wrong because the Law Commission's subsequent report only dealt with amendments to the Code of Criminal Procedure, 1973, not the Indian Evidence Act, 1872.

[207] On the interpretation of section 197, see Centre for Law and Policy Research, 'Legal Accountability of the Police in India' *(Centre for Law and Policy Research)* <http://clpr.org.in/wp-content/uploads/2014/02/140214-Police-Accountability-website.pdf> accessed 16 March 2015.

[208] National Human Rights Commission (n. 187), para 3.19.

[209] National Human Rights Commission (n. 179), para 3.19.

[210] Rajya Sabha, Unstarred Question No. 4644 (29 July 1998) (Answer by L.K. Advani, Minister of Home Affairs); Rakesh Bhatnagar, 'Need to Amend Statutes Governing the Police Force' *The Times of India* (New Delhi, 10 August 1998).

politically embarrassing).[211] Delays in the tabling of the NHRC's annual report on the floor of the house have become so commonplace that the opening paragraphs of most reports contain a statement of regret that Parliament did not consider the previous report on time. Here is an example extracted from the NHRC's annual report for 2004–5:[212]

The annual reports of the Commission serve as an [sic] essential sources of information on the human rights situation in the country. The Commission, therefore, expresses its deep concern over the delay in placing the annual report before the Parliament. The delay in tabling the report leads to further delay in getting a [sic] feedback about the action taken by the Government, and denies timely and comprehensive information on the work and concerns of the Commission, to the Members of Parliament and an opportunity to discuss its contents at the earliest and most appropriate time.

There are more general difficulties associated with influencing the parliamentary agenda. Prodding Parliament to change the law to address human rights concerns is a complicated process. The plenary bottlenecks in Parliament in recent years have placed a premium on parliamentary time.[213] Even though they can be made politically accountable, individual MPs cannot be held to account legally through contempt sanctions for failing to conform with judicial recommendations of changes to the law that have received the NHRC's stamp of endorsement.

[211] Josh Gammon, 'A Meek, Weak NHRC' (2007) 6 Combat Law 72, p. 75.

[212] National Human Rights Commission, *Annual Report (2004–2005)* <http://nhrc.nic.in/Documents/AR/AR04-05ENG.pdf> accessed 24 September 2016, para 1.4. See also National Human Rights Commission (n. 188), paras 1.3, 1.4; National Human Rights Commission (n. 179), paras 1.2, 1.3; National Human Rights Commission, *Annual Report (1999–2000)* <http://nhrc.nic.in/ar99_00.htm> accessed 24 September 2016, para 1.2; National Human Rights Commission (n. 202), para 1.2; National Human Rights Commission (n. 172), para 1.3; National Human Rights Commission, *Annual Report (2003–2004)* <http://nhrc.nic.in/Documents/AR/AR03-04ENG.pdf> accessed 24 September 2016, para 1.4; National Human Rights Commission, *Annual Report (2006–2007)* <http://nhrc.nic.in/Documents/AR/Annual%20Report%2006-07.pdf> accessed 24 September 2016, paras 1.2, 1.4.

[213] Tarunabh Khaitan, 'The Real Price of Parliamentary Obstruction' (2013) 642 Seminar 37.

It also seems that the NHRC does not invest heavily in legislative review[214] and following up on judicial recommendations to change the law, focusing more on its 'fast-track' function of redressing individual grievances.[215] From this perspective, the NHRC and the JCHR have moved in opposite directions. Interestingly, monitoring compliance with declarations of incompatibility or judicial recommendations to change the law began as peripheral functions for both bodies—in contrast with the Strasbourg Court, for which it was a more direct (even if not explicit) function. The JCHR's terms of reference did not explicitly refer to declarations of incompatibility, just as the PHRA did not refer to monitoring compliance with judicial recommendations to change the law. At its inception, the JCHR's primary role involved legislative review, whereas the NHRC focused on addressing individual complaints. However, following the Klug Report, the JCHR cut back on its comprehensive scrutiny service for all bills and invested greater resources in monitoring declarations of incompatibility. On the other hand, the NHRC faced a docket explosion—prompting increased resource allocation in favour of the 'fast-track' trajectory to the detriment of the 'slow track' trajectory.

We should also be mindful of the fact that there is no formal or informal requirement for the government to notify the NHRC when courts recommend changes to the law based on human rights considerations. This could mean that in some cases, the NHRC is either unaware that courts have made such a recommendation, or finds out about the recommendation after the issue has lost momentum. This can be contrasted with the JCHR, which has secured an in-principle commitment from the government to notify it of declarations of incompatibility as soon as possible, and in any case within 14 days after it is made.[216] This difference becomes all the more significant when there is no easily

---

[214] Sripati (n. 171), p. 26.

[215] Here, the reference is to post-enactment review. The NHRC has engaged in pre-enactment review from time to time; see National Human Rights Commission (n. 202).

[216] It is worth noting that under section 5(1) of the HRA, the government is entitled to notice when the court is considering whether to make a declaration of incompatibility. No such corresponding obligation exists on the Indian courts when they are considering making recommendations for legislative change. Hence, it is possible (albeit unlikely) that the government concerned may not itself know that such recommendations have been made.

accessible database of judicial recommendations to change the law (in India), as there is with declarations of incompatibility (in the UK).

The composition of the NHRC, which consists of retired judges and bureaucrats, is yet another factor. Its relatively apolitical posture is both a strength and a weakness: a strength, because it adds credibility to its role in dealing with individual complaints of human rights violations; a weakness, because none of its members are MPs or directly connected to the government or the opposition, making it difficult to galvanize political support for amending the law. Again, this stands in stark contrast with the JCHR, which is a committee of the Westminster Parliament. Although largely independent, its members are able to rally their political weight in order to compel the government at least to engage with the JCHR's recommendations.

We should be mindful of the fact that the NHRC's functions are even broader than that of the JCHR. The JCHR does not consider individual cases, which means that its focus is largely on the 'slow-track' trajectory. On the other hand, consideration of individual cases forms a salient part of the NHRC's functioning. The NHRC seeks to promote education about human rights not only in government (as the JCHR does), but also across society in general—a role that it fulfils by hosting seminars, workshops, and training programmes. It will be recalled that the JCHR's abandonment of its comprehensive pre-legislative scrutiny service for all bills unlocked some of its resources, enabling it to more effectively scrutinize responses to declarations of incompatibility. Similar sacrifices may be required for the NHRC to play a more effective role in influencing Parliament.[217]

The NHRC has had one major success story vis-à-vis legislative change. It persuaded Parliament not to renew the Terrorist and Disruptive Activities (Prevention) Act, 1987 (TADA),[218] a statute that

---

[217] McKinsey & Co was commissioned to report on the working practices of the NHRC. Submitted in 1997, the report suggested that the large volume of complaints received by the NHRC was impeding its ability to fulfil its other functions under the PHRA; see Asia Pacific Human Rights Network, 'National Human Rights Commission of India: Time to Stand Up and Speak Out' <http://www.asiapacificforum.net/about/annual-meetings/8th-nepal-2004/downloads/ngo-statements/ngo_india.pdf> accessed 16 March 2015.

[218] Sripati describes the NHRC as the 'decisive force' behind the non-renewal of TADA; see Sripati (n. 171), p. 25.

was widely considered harsh and draconian in its effects.[219] TADA had a sunset clause,[220] and with the question of renewal approaching, the Chairperson of the NHRC wrote a letter to all MPs strongly condemning the statute and recommending against its renewal. The strongly worded letter described the statute as incompatible with India's 'cultural traditions, legal history and treaty obligations' and stated that the NHRC would find it difficult to fulfil its mandate unless the law was repealed.[221] Even following the repeal of TADA, the NHRC monitored the position of those who had been arrested when the law was in force.[222]

It will be recalled from Chapter 4 that in *Kartar Singh* v. *State of Punjab*,[223] the Supreme Court upheld TADA in spite of expressing serious rights-based misgivings about some of its provisions. As was argued earlier in the book, the Court was reluctant to strike down a statute that formed an essential part of the national security apparatus. The most interesting part of the episode involving its non-renewal was that the NHRC managed to pressurize Parliament not to renew the law *in spite of*—rather than because of—the Supreme Court's judgment. In fact, part of its overall strategy was to produce a dossier in preparation for a petition asking the Court to review the judgment.[224] The NHRC found that even though the Supreme Court attempted to water down some of the provisions of TADA, these attempts were insufficient as the law 'yielded scope for gross abuse'.[225] The NHRC also observed that the Court did not adequately weigh the inherent defects in, and draconian procedure established by, the statute.[226]

---

[219] Susan Abraham, 'To Sir Rowlatt with Love' *The Hindu* (Chennai, 18 August 1999); Anil Kalhan, Gerald P. Conroy, Mamta Kaushal, Sam Scott Miller, and Jed S. Rakoff, 'Colonial Continuities: Human Rights, Terrorism, and Security Laws in India' (2006) 20 Columbia Journal of Asian Law 93, p. 145.

[220] For details, see V. Vijayakumar, 'Legal and Institutional Responses to Terrorism in India' in Victor V. Ramraj, Michael Hor, and Kent Roach (eds), *Global Anti-Terrorism Law and Policy* (2nd edition, Cambridge University Press 2012), p. 353.

[221] National Human Rights Commission (n. 177), para 4.5.

[222] National Human Rights Commission (n. 187), para 4.2.

[223] (1994) 3 SCC 569.

[224] National Human Rights Commission (n. 177), para 4.5.

[225] National Human Rights Commission (n. 177), Annexure 1.

[226] National Human Rights Commission (n. 177), Annexure 1.

Overall, it can be said that the NHRC does not manage to prompt legislative change based on judicial recommendations. This need not necessarily be seen as a failing of the NHRC—rather, the annual reports of the NHRC suggest that, in contrast with the JCHR, it does not conceive of this as being one of its primary institutional responsibilities. On the occasions on which the NHRC has attempted to precipitate legislative change, the outcomes have not been as it might have hoped. Unlike the domestic courts, the Strasbourg Court and the JCHR in the UK, the NHRC and the Indian courts have not been able to work in tandem to prompt amendments to legislation that raises rights-based concerns. The NHRC recently described itself in the following words: '[A]n institution that was unknown sixteen years ago is now very much part of life of the nation, and increasingly, of consequence to the quality of its governance.'[227] This may well be true, but not as regards the NHRC's influence on primary legislation.

\*\*\*

This chapter has examined the collateral institutions accompanying the declaration of incompatibility on the one hand, and on the other, intermediate remedies falling short of the power to strike down legislation in India. The declaration of incompatibility's institutional apparatus includes the JCHR and Strasbourg Court. These institutions strengthen the declaration of incompatibility, and affect the manner in which the new model of judicial review operates, in different ways. The JCHR presses the government to engage with declarations of incompatibility, ensuring that silence is not a realistic option on the table. The Strasbourg Court usually compels the Westminster Parliament to change the law following a declaration of incompatibility,[228] lest an aggrieved litigant armed with a declaration takes her case beyond British shores. Perhaps in the context of its vast range of functions, the NHRC has been quite

---

[227] National Human Rights Commission, *Annual Report (2008–2009)* <http://nhrc.nic.in/Documents/AR/Final%20Annual%20Report-2008-2009%20in%20English.pdf> accessed 24 September 2016, para 1.7.

[228] See HC Deb 23 February 2004, vol. 418, col. 64 (Tim Boswell): 'I suspect that, left to themselves, the Government might have been content to let the issue lie, but the European judgment has compelled them to act.'

successful. However, it has struggled on both these counts. The Indian Parliament has been able to ignore the NHRC's recommendations that intermediate remedies be given effect through amendments to the law. In substantive terms, it has found it difficult to influence the Indian Parliament to amend the law based on human rights concerns.

# Conclusion

Perhaps it is best to begin by reiterating the question that this book sought to answer: which model of judicial review, between those of India (the old model) and the UK (the new model), enables both legislatures and courts to assert their genuine understanding of rights more freely? This question was divided into two sub-questions:

1. Which legislatures can assert their genuine understanding of rights more freely?
2. Which courts can assert their genuine understanding of rights more freely?

The explanation emanating from a large part of the existing scholarship—that the Westminster Parliament would be able to assert its genuine understanding of rights by rejecting declarations of incompatibility more easily than a legislature seeking to reject exercises of the power to strike down legislation—was debunked in Chapters 2 and 3.

The decisional space and remedial space for responding to judgments striking down legislation and declarations of incompatibility in India and the UK respectively is remarkably similar. Political practice has shown that openly rejecting judgments striking down legislation or declarations of incompatibility is a difficult option that demands considerable political traction and requires the government in power to overcome significant hurdles. These include the pressure of public opinion and the possibility of an adverse ruling from the Strasbourg Court in the UK, and the assent of parliamentary supermajorities in India. Thus, the most common political response in both jurisdictions is to comply with the court's judgment, by giving effect to a declaration of incompatibility through legislation or a remedial order (in the UK), or allowing the judgment striking down legislation to stand (in India). Some scholars conceived of the superiority of the Human Rights Act, 1998 (HRA) as enabling Parliament to respond to judicial decisions more swiftly than in jurisdictions in which courts had the power to strike down legislation. However, this prediction has failed to materialize, and evidence suggests that the Indian Parliament responds slightly quicker to judgments striking down legislation than the British Parliament to declarations of incompatibility.

However, as explained in Chapters 4 and 5, the superiority of the UK's model of rights protection lies elsewhere—in the ability of British courts to express their genuine understanding of rights by making declarations of incompatibility in situations in which Indian courts are reluctant to do so, on account of the remedies available to them. Indian courts have demonstrated reluctance to exercise the power to strike down legislation when to do so would involve blackballing recent legislation with a strong democratic mandate, produce serious collateral consequences for other legislation, or stifle emergency national security legislation. Since the 'power' to strike down legislation actually transforms into a duty when legislation is found unconstitutional, this has also prompted Indian courts not to find rights-violating legislation unconstitutional in the first place. British courts have made declarations of incompatibility in analogous situations, in the knowledge that under section 4 of the HRA, the right is decoupled from the remedy, if only formally.

The fact that the declaration of incompatibility is a discretionary, as opposed to a mandatory, remedy has a far more significant impact on the question of 'balanced constitutionalism' than we might have initially imagined. Under the HRA, when judges are uncomfortable issuing a declaration, they can avoid doing so without compromising on their rights reasoning. In contrast, judges under the Indian Constitution confront the more difficult choice of either articulating their genuine rights reasoning and reluctantly striking down legislation, or masking their genuine rights reasoning and upholding it. The obvious solution may be to transform the power to strike down legislation into a discretionary remedy. But of course, this tends to undermine the rationale for the power (or judicial supremacy) itself, which operates on the fiction that courts are duty-bound to police the boundaries of the Constitution.

Thus, if we think back to the tables set out in Chapter 1, the appropriate explanation for the superiority of the UK's model of rights protection comes from the following table, which shows that the UK wins on sub-question 2, and there is no winner on sub-question 1. Therefore, the UK wins on the general question.

|                | UK | India |
|----------------|----|-------|
| Sub-question 1 | –  | –     |
| Sub-question 2 | ✓  | ✗     |

New models of judicial review risk facing what has been identified earlier in the book as the internal stability problem in the way in which they operate in practice. In other words, they either slide in the direction of parliamentary sovereignty or judicial supremacy, depending on how declarations of incompatibility play out in the political arena. Thus far, the declaration of incompatibility has not fallen fully on one side or another, although the practice of positively addressing declarations of incompatibility suggests that it has moved towards the judicial supremacy end of the spectrum. That the outright rejection of declarations of incompatibility remains possible (albeit difficult) reflects that the HRA has not fallen squarely on the side of judicial supremacy. Interestingly, the same can be said of the Indian scenario. Although constitutional design suggests that it is a case of full-scale judicial supremacy, the possibility of rejecting judgments striking down legislation indicates that it is not as far down on the judicial supremacy side of the spectrum as one might imagine at first glance. Statements made by MPs in both jurisdictions feed into this analysis. Whereas British MPs often describe the declaration of incompatibility in terms resembling a power to strike down legislation, Indian MPs have emphasized upon Parliament's power to revise judicial approaches to constitutional rights.

The external stability problem—or the fact that new models of judicial review are embodied in un-entrenched statutes that may be repealed by transient majorities—has played out much more visibly in the case of the HRA. The Conservative Party has consistently promised to repeal the HRA over the years. When it entered into coalition government with the Liberal Democratic Party (which takes a pro-HRA view) in 2010, the compromise between both sides was to establish a Commission that would examine whether to replace the HRA with a home-grown bill of rights, while building upon the UK's obligations under the Convention.[1] The majority of the Commission's members concluded that there was a strong argument in favour of a domestic bill of rights that would replace the HRA.[2] The Conservative Party similarly included the repeal of the HRA in its manifesto for the general elections of 2015,[3] in which it secured a narrow majority in the House of Commons.[4]

The future of the HRA hangs in the balance, and is contingent on the political appetite of the Conservative government. The effects of the repeal of the HRA (and its replacement with a British bill of rights) will depend on the precise terms of that bill of rights—a matter that has remained nebulous in political discourse.[5] But beyond the binary options of repealing or retaining the HRA lie a range of possibilities, including amending one or more of its provisions. Each of these possibilities could have a bearing upon the protection of rights through the balanced allocation of powers between the legislature and courts in the UK. For instance, the amendment or repeal of section 2(1), which requires British courts to 'take into account' decisions of the Strasbourg Court, may indirectly limit the normative force of declarations of incompatibility. This is because if domestic judicial decisions were no longer based on Strasbourg Court jurisprudence, the likelihood

---

[1] Francesca Klug and Amy Williams, 'The Choice Before Us? The Report of the Commission on a Bill of Rights' [2013] PL 460.

[2] Commission on a Bill of Rights, *A UK Bill of Rights? The Choice Before Us* (Commission on a Bill of Rights, 2012), para 12.7.

[3] Conservative Party, 'The Conservative Party Manifesto' (2015) <https://www.conservatives.com/manifesto> accessed 24 September 2016, pp. 60, 73.

[4] The Conservative Party secured a 12-seat majority in the House of Commons. It does not have a majority in the House of Lords. Therefore, it is fallacious to assume that any reform proposals can easily be pushed through the Houses of Parliament.

[5] Joshua Rozenberg, 'Why Human Rights Reform Could Trip Up Michael Gove' *The Guardian* (London, 11 May 2015) <https://www.theguardian.com/commentisfree/2015/may/11/human-rights-reform-michael-gove-justice-secretary> accessed 24 September 2016: 'The Conservatives were elected on a manifesto commitment to "scrap the Human Rights Act and curtail the role of the European court of human rights". But there was little detail on how that might be achieved.'

of them being 'affirmed' in Strasbourg could reduce. However, on the flipside, repealing section 2(1) does not guarantee that British courts will stop citing Strasbourg Court judgments as persuasive authority. In fact, expecting such a radical shift may be unrealistic—which could well mean that the *status quo ante* (of the Strasbourg Court affirming declarations of incompatibility of British courts) will remain in place in the near future, unless and until change takes place organically.

There are some indications that the Conservative government may seek to limit British courts' interpretive powers by introducing amendments to section 3 of the HRA.[6] Toning down the language of section 3 may result in a corresponding increase in the number of declarations of incompatibility. This could impact upon the culture of compliance (or at any rate, the pace of compliance) with such declarations. Given the small number of declarations of incompatibility made thus far, it will be interesting to see how the institutional systems in place—particularly the JCHR—will cope with a rise in the number of declarations. However, it is also possible that if the catchment area of section 3 were reduced, British courts would respond by refusing to make declarations of incompatibility in many cases that would previously have been dealt with under section 3, in order to control the number of declarations of incompatibility and preserve their authoritative value.

Thus, at least in the way that it has played out under the HRA, external instability is the price that the new model pays for ensuring a more balanced allocation of powers between the legislature and courts than models of judicial supremacy. Given this fact, one might expect courts to be strategic or restrained when making declarations of incompatibility to avoid existential crises of the kind that the HRA currently faces. To some extent, British courts have responded strategically to threats to repeal the HRA. As explained in Chapter 2, they have taken expected political reactions into account when deciding whether or not to make declarations of incompatibility. They have also offered, as a form of 'carrot dangling', suggestions about how declarations of incompatibility may be complied with by Parliament without significantly compromising its legislative policy.

[6] Conservative Party, 'Protecting Human Rights in the UK' (October 2014) <https://www.conservatives.com/~/media/files/downloadable%20files/human_rights.pdf> accessed 24 September 2016, p. 4.

However, it is fairly clear from the political discourse that the ire against the HRA stems primarily from European influences on decision-making under the HRA, rather than from the decisions of British courts per se. This is well demonstrated through the following statement made by a peer in the House of Lords, who was commenting on the difference between the judgment in *R (Thompson)* v. *Secretary of State*[7] (in which the UK Supreme Court declared unreviewable notification requirements under the Sexual Offences Act, 2003 to be incompatible with Convention rights) and the judgments from Strasbourg on the prisoner voting rights issue:[8]

> I have already said that every court *in this land* found in the same way as the UK Supreme Court with regard to the sex offenders register. On prisoner voting rights, *every UK court* that [initially] heard the claim that prisoners should have the right to vote rejected it. The only court that has found in favour of prisoners being given the right to vote is the European Court of Human Rights. There is a distinct difference and *we are responding to the UK Supreme Court* at this time.' (Emphasis added).

As Chapter 5 demonstrated, British courts have responded by outlining the limits of the 'mirror principle' under section 2(1). There has also been a resurgence in British courts' reliance on common law principles in recent cases under the HRA.[9] This has had a twofold effect: first, suggesting that Convention rights are not uniquely European (thereby strengthening their legitimacy in the domestic context) and second, indicating that the courts are establishing a safety valve in the event that the HRA is repealed.

The Indian context offers a good counterpoint. Judicial review under the Indian Constitution is now deeply entrenched, both legally and as a political fact. But history also warns us against being carried away by the effects of formal entrenchment. Judicial review under the Indian Constitution came under severe pressure during the Indira Gandhi-led Congress government of the 1970s. Through the judgment in *Kesavananda Bharati* v. *State of Kerala*,[10] and other decisions that are well

---

[7] [2011] 1 AC 331.

[8] HL Deb 5 July 2012, vol. 738, col. 887 (Baroness Stowell of Beeston).

[9] Roger Masterman and Se-Shauna Wheatle, 'A Common Law Resurgence in Rights Protection?' (2015) 1 EHRLR 57.

[10] AIR 1973 SC 1461 ('Basic Structure case').

documented elsewhere,[11] the Indian Supreme Court managed to salvage judicial review through that phase. This shows us that along with formal entrenchment, the entrenchment of bills of rights in practice depends upon political developments.

In both jurisdictions, the external stability problem has been linked to the identity and custodianship of the Constitution/bill of rights. In the early decades following the Indian Constitution's enactment, the Congress government considered itself as having a special claim over the Constitution's meaning—a spill over of the Congress party–dominated independence movement. These notions have withered away with the increase in the legitimacy of the Supreme Court in particular, and the Constitution more generally. In the UK, the Conservative Party often pejoratively describes the HRA as 'Labour's HRA',[12] suggesting similarly that custodianship of the statute has not yet traversed across party political lines. It may be that if the HRA survives these early challenges, it will gradually come to acquire legitimacy and cross-party political support. Nevertheless, it is hard to put out of one's mind the fact that the HRA can be amended or repealed with the assent of just 326 of the 650 members of the House of Commons, whereas amending the provisions of the Indian Constitution requires the assent of 363 of 545 members of the Lok Sabha.[13]

The next point to be made is that constitutional design is not determinative of how Constitutions or bills of rights will operate in practice.[14] At the time the HRA was enacted, scholars expected declarations

[11] Granville Austin, *Working a Democratic Constitution: A History of the Indian Experience* (Oxford University Press 2003).

[12] See, for example, Conservative Party (n. 3), p. 73: 'We will scrap Labour's Human Rights Act and introduce a British Bill of Rights which will restore common sense to the application of human rights in the UK'; Owen Bowcott, 'Cameron's Pledge to Scrap Human Rights Act Angers Civil Rights Groups' *The Guardian* (London, 1 October 2014) <https://www.theguardian.com/politics/2014/oct/01/cameron-pledge-scrap-human-rights-act-civil-rights-groups> accessed 24 September 2016: quoting Prime Minister David Cameron as having said, 'And as for Labour's Human Rights Act? We will scrap it, once and for all.'

[13] Assuming that both legislatures are at full strength and that there are no abstentions.

[14] Aruna Sathanapally, *Beyond Disagreement: Open Remedies in Human Rights Adjudication* (Oxford University Press 2012), pp. 223–4; Adrienne

of incompatibility to be non-binding exhortations that the Westminster Parliament could reject if it wished to do so. Similarly, Indian courts might have been expected to have the 'last word' on rights questions, given that they were invested with the power to strike down rights-offending legislation. Practice has defied expectations, and has shown that much depends on the politics of judicial review in both jurisdictions.

In India, the single-party dominance of the Congress made it easier to respond to judgments striking down legislation until the 1980s. Constitutional practice may also change, as was the case after the 1980s, when the rise of coalition governments and the simultaneous increase in the legitimacy of the courts rendered it difficult to respond to judgments striking down legislation. In the UK, the public pressure following a declaration of incompatibility as well as the looming spectre of the Strasbourg Court has made open defiance of declarations of incompatibility a genuinely difficult choice to exercise. The point about constitutional design also has a converse implication—as explained earlier with reference to possible amendments to sections 2 and 3 of the HRA, changes in constitutional design may not necessarily produce changes in constitutional practice that one may hope for or expect.

Overall, the position in both jurisdictions seems to be that mere disagreement with a declaration of incompatibility or a judgment striking down legislation is not enough to enable outright rejection by the legislature. A level of serious disagreement that is sufficient to mobilize considerable political support is closer to what is warranted. This is demonstrated by the Indian Parliament's responses to judgments striking down land reform legislation until the 1970s, given that it was a major political plank of the government of the day. The prisoner voting rights issue could turn out to be the analogous example from the UK—although it is easy to think of other, more obvious cases of when outright rejection is likely.[15]

However, we should also be cautious about describing the declaration of incompatibility as a de facto power to strike down legislation. To the extent that declarations of incompatibility are positively addressed

---

Stone, 'Constitutional Orthodoxy in the United Kingdom and Australia: The Deepening Divide' (2014) 38 Melbourne University Law Review 836.

[15] Sathanapally, for example, says that had the bans on political advertising or fox hunting been declared incompatible, open disagreement is likely to have followed; see Sathanapally (n. 14), p. 224.

in almost all cases, they seem to resemble a power to strike down legislation in their effects. But we cannot escape the fact that declarations of incompatibility have no immediate impact on legal rights, leaving a (sometimes considerable) time lag between the recognition of the right and the award of the remedy. This difference matters. As the experience from India shows, remedies do not necessarily work in a linear way. Courts are strategic actors, and the availability—or absence—of a certain remedy may influence their decisions. Linked to this is the fact that it is probably unreliable to place models of judicial review (like Canada's) that give courts a power to strike down legislation and the legislature a 'notwithstanding' clause in the same category as the HRA.[16] These models allocate burdens of inertia differently, and require the legislature to put its institutional weight behind the rejection of judgments striking down legislation.

Finally, this book suggests that the strength of constitutional remedies rides heavily upon the institutional apparatus accompanying it. Studying only the nature of the remedy and the amendment rule in a constitutional system provides for an under-inclusive analysis. This is best demonstrated by the work done by the JCHR and the Strasbourg Court vis-à-vis declarations of incompatibility in the UK. As explained in Chapter 5, the JCHR ensures that ignoring such declarations is not a realistic option, whereas the Strasbourg Court ensures that compliance is the norm. Intermediate remedies in India falling short of the power to strike down legislation do not have a comparable institutional apparatus, making it difficult for courts to invoke them (and indeed, leaning courts towards upholding rights-violating statutes on occasion). The NHRC has not enjoyed the same success as the JCHR and the Strasbourg Court in prompting Parliament to take notice of judicial recommendations, and amend legislation that is inconsistent with rights. This also suggests that merely transplanting the formal remedy (the declaration of incompatibility) into India may not change the way in which judicial review functions in practice, or ensure a more balanced allocation of decision-making about rights between courts and the legislature. We must be conscious that the remedy, without the corresponding institutional apparatus and the political culture underlying it, could have an altogether different currency.

[16] Sujit Choudhry, 'The Commonwealth Constitutional Model or Models?' (2013) 11 International Journal of Constitutional Law 1094.

# Appendix A: Political Responses to Judgments Striking Down Legislation in India

| No. | Case | Details | |
|-----|------|---------|---|
| 1. | *Motilal* v. *State of Uttar Pradesh*[1] | The Allahabad High Court made some observations about the constitutional impermissibility of nationalization of industry. This spurred a 'clarificatory addition'[2] to Art. 19(6) of the Constitution, making it clear that a legislative scheme of nationalization will not affect the freedom of trade under Art. 19(1)(g).[3] | |
| 2. | *Romesh Thapar* v. *State of Madras*[4] | The Supreme Court struck down section 9(1A) of the Madras Maintenance of Public Order Act, 1949 on the basis that it violated Art. 19(1)(a) of the Constitution. | |
| 3. | *Brij Bhushan* v. *State of Delhi*[5] | The Supreme Court struck down section 7(1)(c) of the East Punjab Public Safety Act, 1949 on the basis that it violated Art. 19(1)(a) of the Constitution. | |

[1] AIR 1951 All 257.

[2] Statement of Objects and Reasons, the Constitution (First Amendment) Act, 1951.

[3] Arvind P. Datar, *Commentary on the Constitution of India* (2nd edn, LexisNexis Butterworths Wadhwa 2007), p. 2298.

[4] AIR 1950 SC 124.

[5] AIR 1950 SC 129.

| Mode of Response | Prospective/ Retrospective | Response Time — between Decision and Enactment of Response (in Months) | Party in Government at the Time of Enactment of Response |
|---|---|---|---|
| Fundamental rights amendment—the Constitution (First Amendment) Act, 1951. | Retrospective | 13.2 | Indian National Congress (Interim Government) |
| Fundamental rights amendment—the Constitution (First Amendment) Act, 1951. | Retrospective | 12.7 | Indian National Congress (Interim Government) |
| Fundamental rights amendment—the Constitution (First Amendment) Act, 1951. | Retrospective | 12.7 | Indian National Congress (Interim Government) |

| No. | Case | Details | |
|-----|------|---------|---|
| 4. | *Amar Nath Bali v. State*[6] | The High Court of Punjab struck down section 4(1)(h) of the Indian Press (Emergency Powers) Act, 1931 on the basis that it violated Art. 19(1)(a) of the Constitution. | |
| 5. | *Shaila Bala Devi v. Chief Secretary*[7] | The High Court of Patna struck down section 4(1)(a) of the Indian Press (Emergency Powers) Act, 1931 on the basis that it violated Art. 19(1)(a) of the Constitution. | |
| 6. | *Srinivasa v. State of Madras*[8] | The High Court of Madras struck down section 4(1)(d) of the Indian Press (Emergency Powers) Act, 1931 on the basis that it violated Art. 19(1)(a) of the Constitution. | |
| 7. | *Tara Singh v. State*[9] | The High Court of Punjab struck down section 153A of the Indian Penal Code, 1860 (IPC) on the basis that it violated the freedom of speech and expression under Art. 19(1)(a) of the Constitution. | |
| 8. | *Kameshwar Singh v. State of Bihar*[10] | The High Court of Patna struck down the Bihar Land Reforms Act, 1950 for violating the right to equality under Art. 14. | |

[6] AIR 1951 P&H 18.
[7] AIR 1951 Pat 12.
[8] AIR 1951 Mad 70.
[9] AIR 1951 P&H 27.
[10] AIR 1951 Pat 91.

| Mode of Response | Prospective/ Retrospective | Response Time — between Decision and Enactment of Response (in Months) | Party in Government at the Time of Enactment of Response |
|---|---|---|---|
| Fundamental rights amendment—the Constitution (First Amendment) Act, 1951. | Retrospective | 9.1 | Indian National Congress (Interim Government) |
| Fundamental rights amendment—the Constitution (First Amendment) Act, 1951. | Retrospective | 8.1 | Indian National Congress (Interim Government) |
| Fundamental rights amendment—the Constitution (First Amendment) Act, 1951. | Retrospective | 7.5 | Indian National Congress (Interim Government) |
| Fundamental rights amendment—the Constitution (First Amendment) Act, 1951. | Retrospective | 6.6 | Indian National Congress (Interim Government) |
| Ninth Schedule amendment—the Constitution (First Amendment) Act, 1951. | Retrospective | 3.2 | Indian National Congress (Interim Government) |

| No. | Case | Details | |
|-----|------|---------|---|
| 9. | *State of West Bengal* v. *Bella Banerjee*[11] | The Supreme Court struck down a portion of proviso (b) to section 8 of the West Bengal Land Development and Planning Act, 1948 for violating the right to compensation on compulsory acquisition of private property by the state under Art. 31(2) of the Constitution. | |
| 10. | *Kunhikoman* v. *State of Kerala*[12] | The Supreme Court struck down the Kerala Agrarian Relations Act, 1961 in relation to its application to certain kinds of land, as it violated the right to equality under Art. 14 of the Constitution and did not fall within the protective garb of Art. 31A. | |
| 11. | *Sukapuram* v. *State of Kerala*[13] | The Kerala High Court struck down the Kerala Agrarian Relations Act, 1961 on the basis that it violated Arts 14, 19, and 31 of the Constitution and did not fall within the protection of Art. 31A. | |
| 12. | *R.C. Cooper* v. *Union of India*[14] | The Supreme Court struck down the Banking Companies (Acquisition and Transfer of Undertakings) Act, 1969, as it breached Art. 31 of the Constitution. | |

[11] AIR 1954 SC 170.
[12] AIR 1962 SC 273.
[13] AIR 1963 Ker 101.
[14] AIR 1970 SC 564.

| Mode of Response | Prospective/ Retrospective | Response Time — between Decision and Enactment of Response (in Months) | Party in Government at the Time of Enactment of Response |
|---|---|---|---|
| Fundamental rights amendment and Ninth Schedule amendment—the Constitution (Fourth Amendment) Act, 1955. | Retrospective | 16.5 | Indian National Congress |
| Fundamental rights amendment—the Constitution (Seventeenth Amendment) Act, 1964. | Retrospective | 30.5 | Indian National Congress |
| Fundamental rights amendment—the Constitution (Seventeenth Amendment) Act, 1964. | Retrospective | 19.5 | Indian National Congress |
| Fundamental rights amendment—the Constitution (Twenty-fifth Amendment) Act, 1971. | Retrospective | 26.3 | Indian National Congress |

| No. | Case | Details | |
|-----|------|---------|---|
| 13. | *Balmadies Plantations v. State of Tamil Nadu*[15] | The Supreme Court struck down one aspect of the Gudalur Janmam Estate (Abolition and Conversion into Ryotwari) Act, 1969 as it violated Arts 14, 19, and 31 of the Constitution and did not fall within the protection of Art. 31A. | |
| 14. | *Kunjukutty Sahib v. State of Kerala*[16] | The Supreme Court upheld a judgment of the Kerala High Court[17] striking down provisions of the Kerala Land Reforms Act, 1964, as amended in 1969 and 1971. | |
| 15. | *Malankara Rubber v. State of Kerala*[18] | The Supreme Court struck down provisions of the Kerala Land Reforms Act, 1964, as amended in 1969 and 1971, on the ground that they violated Art. 14 of the Constitution. | |
| 16. | *Paschimbanga v. State of West Bengal*[19] | The Calcutta High Court struck down section 2(c) of the West Bengal Land Holding Revenue Act, 1979. | |

[15] AIR 1972 SC 2240.
[16] AIR 1972 SC 2097.
[17] *Narayanan Nair v. State of Kerala*, AIR 1971 Ker 98.
[18] AIR 1972 SC 2027.
[19] MANU/WB/0564/1986.

| Mode of Response | Prospective/ Retrospective | Response Time — between Decision and Enactment of Response (in Months) | Party in Government at the Time of Enactment of Response |
|---|---|---|---|
| Ninth Schedule amendment—the Constitution (Thirty-fourth Amendment) Act, 1974. | Retrospective | 28.6 | Indian National Congress |
| Ninth Schedule amendment—the Constitution (Twenty-ninth Amendment) Act, 1972. | Retrospective | 1.4 | Indian National Congress |
| Ninth Schedule amendment—the Constitution (Twenty-ninth Amendment) Act, 1972. | Retrospective | 1.4 | Indian National Congress |
| Ninth Schedule amendment—the Constitution (Sixty-sixth Amendment) Act, 1990. | Retrospective | 48.6 | National Front (Janata Dal, Telugu Desam Party, Dravida Munnetra Kazhagam, Assam Gana Parishad, Indian Congress (Socialist)) |

# Appendix B: Political Responses to Declarations of Incompatibility in the United Kingdom

| No. | Case | Details of Declaration | Final/ Overturned | Mode of Response | |
|-----|------|------------------------|-------------------|------------------|--|
| 1. | R (Alconbury Developments) v. Secretary of State for the Environment, Transport and the Regions [Divisional Court,[20] House of Lords[21]] | The Divisional Court declared certain provisions of the Town and Country Planning Act, 1990, the Transport and Works Act, 1992, the Highways Act, 1980, and the Acquisition of Land Act, 1981 incompatible with Art. 6 of the European Convention for the Protection of Human Rights and Fundamental | Overturned | – | |

[20] [2001] HRLR 2.
[21] [2003] 2 AC 295.

| Prospective/ Retrospective | Response Time between Declaration and Enactment of Response (in Months) | Response Time between Declaration and Entry into Force of Response (in Months) | Party in Government at the Time of Enactment of Response |
|---|---|---|---|
| – | – | – | – |

| No. | Case | Details of Declaration | Final/ Overturned | Mode of Response | |
|---|---|---|---|---|---|
| | | Freedoms, 1950 (Convention). The declaration was overturned on appeal to the House of Lords. | | | |
| 2. | *R (H)* v. *London North and East Region Mental Health Review Tribunal* [Administrative Court,[22] Court of Appeal[23]] | The Court of Appeal declared sections 72(1) and 73(1) of the Mental Health Act, 1983 incompatible with Art. 5(1)(4) of the Convention. | Final | The incompatibility was removed by the Mental Health Act, 1983 (Remedial) Order, 2001. | |
| 3. | *Wilson* v. *First County Trust Ltd (No 2)* [Court of Appeal,[24] House of Lords[25]] | The Court of Appeal declared section 127(3) of the Consumer Credit Act, 1974 incompatible with Art. 6 and Art. 1 of Protocol 1 of the Convention. The declaration was set aside by the House of Lords. | Overturned | – | |

[22] 2000 WL 1720256.
[23] [2002] QB 1.
[24] [2002] QB 74.
[25] [2004] 1 AC 816.

| Prospective/ Retrospective | Response Time between Declaration and Enactment of Response (in Months) | Response Time between Declaration and Entry into Force of Response (in Months) | Party in Government at the Time of Enactment of Response |
|---|---|---|---|
| | | | |
| Prospective (but the order applied to applications and referrals pending before the Mental Health Tribunal). | 8 | – | Labour |
| – | – | – | – |

| No. | Case | Details of Declaration | Final/ Overturned | Mode of Response | |
|---|---|---|---|---|---|
| 4. | *McR's Application for Judicial Review* [High Court][26] | Section 62 of the Offences against the Person Act, 1861 (which at the time was applicable in Northern Ireland) was declared incompatible with Art. 8 of the Convention. | Final | The incompatible provision was repealed by the Sexual Offences Act, 2003 (SOA)—section 139 read with Schedule 6 (paragraph 4) and section 140 read with Schedule 7. | |
| 5. | *International Transport Roth GmbH v. SSHD* [High Court,[27] Court of Appeal[28]] | The High Court declared the penalty regime under Part II of the Immigration and Asylum Act, 1999 incompatible with Art. 6 of the Convention and Art. 1 of Protocol 1 to the Convention. The declaration was confirmed by the Court of Appeal. | Final | The penalty regime was amended by section 125 read with Schedule 8 of the Nationality, Immigration and Asylum Act, 2002. | |

| Prospective/ Retrospective | Response Time between Declaration and Enactment of Response (in Months) | Response Time between Declaration and Entry into Force of Response (in Months) | Party in Government at the Time of Enactment of Response |
|---|---|---|---|
| Prospective | 22.1 | 27.5 | Labour |
| Prospective | 8.5 | 9.5 | Labour |

| No. | Case | Details of Declaration | Final/ Overturned | Mode of Response | |
|-----|------|------------------------|-------------------|------------------|--|
| 6. | *Matthews* v. *Ministry of Defence* [High Court,[29] Court of Appeal,[30] House of Lords[31]] | The High Court declared section 10 of the Crown Proceedings Act, 1947 incompatible with Art. 6 of the Convention. The Court of Appeal overturned this declaration. The decision of the Court of Appeal was affirmed by the House of Lords. | Overturned | – | |
| 7. | *R (Anderson)* v. *SSHD* [Divisional Court,[32] Court of Appeal,[33] House of Lords[34]] | The House of Lords declared section 29 of the Crime (Sentences) Act, 1997 incompatible with Art. 6 of the Convention. | Final | The incompatible provision was repealed by the Criminal Justice Act, 2003.[35] | |

[29] [2002] CP Rep 26.
[30] [2002] 1 WLR 2621.
[31] [2003] 1 AC 1163.
[32] [2001] EWHC 181 (Admin).
[33] [2002] 2 WLR 1143.
[34] [2003] 1 AC 837.
[35] Section 303(b)(i).
[36] Criminal Justice Act, 2003, Schedule 22.

| Prospective/ Retrospective | Response Time between Declaration and Enactment of Response (in Months) | Response Time between Declaration and Entry into Force of Response (in Months) | Party in Government at the Time of Enactment of Response |
|---|---|---|---|
| – | – | – | – |
| Prospective (however, prisoners who were already serving a term fixed by the Secretary of State had the opportunity to have their minimum term re-set by the High Court.[36]) | 11.8 | 12.7 | Labour |

| No. | Case | Details of Declaration | Final/ Overturned | Mode of Response | |
|---|---|---|---|---|---|
| 8. | R (D) v. SSHD [Administrative Court][37] | Section 74 of the Mental Health Act, 1983 was declared incompatible with Art. 5(4) of the Convention by the Administrative Court. | Final | The incompatible provision was amended by section 295 of the Criminal Justice Act, 2003. | |
| 9. | Blood and Tarbuck v. Secretary of State for Health [Administrative Court (unreported)] | The Administrative Court declared section 28(6)(b) of the Human Fertilisation and Embryology Act, 1990 incompatible with Art. 8 and Art. 14 (read with Art. 8) of the Convention. | Final | The incompatibility was removed by the Human Fertilisation and Embryology (Deceased Fathers) Act, 2003. | |
| 10. | R (Uttley) v. SSHD [Administrative Court,[38] Court of Appeal,[39] House of Lords[40]] | The Court of Appeal declared sections 33(2), 37(4A), and 39 of the Criminal Justice Act, 1991 incompatible with Art. 7 of the Convention. The declaration was overturned by the House of Lords. | Overturned | – | |

[37] [2003] 1 WLR 1315.
[38] [2003] EWHC 950 (Admin).
[39] [2003] 1 WLR 2590.
[40] [2004] 1 WLR 2278.

| Prospective/ Retrospective | Response Time between Declaration and Enactment of Response (in Months) | Response Time between Declaration and Entry into Force of Response (in Months) | Party in Government at the Time of Enactment of Response |
|---|---|---|---|
| Prospective | 11 | 13 | Labour |
| Retrospective | 6.6 | 9.1 | Labour |
| – | – | – | – |

| No. | Case | Details of Declaration | Final/ Overturned | Mode of Response | |
|-----|------|------------------------|-------------------|------------------|---|
| 11. | *Bellinger* v. *Bellinger* [Family Division,[41] Court of Appeal,[42] House of Lords[43]] | The House of Lords declared section 11(c) of the Matrimonial Causes Act, 1973 incompatible with Arts 8 and 12 of the Convention. | Final | The incompatibility was remedied by the Gender Recognition Act, 2004. | |
| 12. | *R (M)* v. *Secretary of State for Health* [Administrative Court][44] | The Administrative Court declared sections 26 and 29 of the Mental Health Act, 1983 incompatible with the Convention. | Final | The incompatible provisions were amended by the Mental Health Act, 2007. | |
| 13. | *R (Wilkinson)* v. *Inland Revenue Commissioners* [Administrative Court,[45] Court of Appeal,[46] House of Lords[47]] | Section 262 of the Income and Corporation Taxes Act, 1988 was declared incompatible with Art. 14 read with Art. 1 of Protocol 1 of the Convention by | Final | The incompatible provision was abolished by section 34 of the Finance Act, 1999, before the case was heard at first instance. | |

[41] (2001) 58 BMLR 52.
[42] [2002] Fam 150.
[43] [2003] 2 AC 467.
[44] [2003] EWHC 1094 (Admin).
[45] [2002] EWHC 182 (Admin).
[46] [2003] 1 WLR 2683.
[47] [2005] 1 WLR 1718.

| Prospective/ Retrospective | Response Time between Declaration and Enactment of Response (in Months) | Response Time between Declaration and Entry into Force of Response (in Months) | Party in Government at the Time of Enactment of Response |
|---|---|---|---|
| Prospective | 14.7 | 23.8 | Labour |
| Prospective | 51.3 | 66.6 | Labour |
| Prospective | – | – | Labour |

| No. | Case | Details of Declaration | Final/ Overturned | Mode of Response | |
|---|---|---|---|---|---|
| | | The Administrative Court. Appeals against the declaration were dismissed by the Court of Appeal and the House of Lords. | | | |
| 14. | R (Hooper and Others) v. Secretary of State for Work and Pensions [Administrative Court,[48] Court of Appeal,[49] House of Lords[50]] | The Administrative Court declared sections 36 and 37 of the Social Security Contributions and Benefits Act, 1992 incompatible with Arts 8 and 14 of the Convention. The declaration was overturned by the Court of Appeal. The House of Lords agreed with the Administrative Court, but saw 'no point' in making declarations of incompatibility since the relevant sections had been repealed.[51] | Overturned by the Court of Appeal. The House of Lords did not reinstate the declaration. | The impugned provisions were, in any event, amended by the Welfare Reforms and Pension Act, 1999 before the case was heard at first instance. | |

[48] [2002] EWHC 191 (Admin).
[49] [2003] 1 WLR 2623.
[50] [2005] 1 WLR 1681.
[51] [2005] 1 WLR 1681, para 52.

| Prospective/ Retrospective | Response Time between Declaration and Enactment of Response (in Months) | Response Time between Declaration and Entry into Force of Response (in Months) | Party in Government at the Time of Enactment of Response |
|---|---|---|---|
|  |  |  |  |
| Prospective | – | – | Labour |

| No. | Case | Details of Declaration | Final/ Overturned | Mode of Response | |
|-----|------|------------------------|-------------------|------------------|---|
| 15. | *R (MH)* v. *Secretary of Health* [Administrative Court,[52] Court of Appeal,[53] House of Lords[54]] | The Court of Appeal declared sections 2 and 29(4) of the Mental Health Act, 1983 incompatible with Art. 5(4) of the Convention. The House of Lords overturned the declaration. | Overturned | – | |
| 16. | *A* v. *SSHD* [Special Immigration Appeals Commission (SIAC),[55] Court of Appeal,[56] House of Lords[57]] | The SIAC declared section 23 of Anti-Terrorism, Crime and Security Act, 2001 (ATCSA) incompatible with Arts 5 and 14 of the Convention. This decision was reversed by the Court of Appeal, but was later affirmed by the House of Lords. | Final | The incompatible provision was repealed by the Prevention of Terrorism Act, 2005. | |

[52] [2004] EWHC 56 (Admin).
[53] [2005] 1 WLR 1209.
[54] [2006] 1 AC 441.
[55] [2002] HRLR 45.
[56] [2004] QB 335.
[57] [2005] 2 AC 68.
[58] Prevention of Terrorism Act, 2005, section 16(4).

| Prospective/ Retrospective | Response Time between Declaration and Enactment of Response (in Months) | Response Time between Declaration and Entry into Force of Response (in Months) | Party in Government at the Time of Enactment of Response |
|---|---|---|---|
| – | – | – | – |
| Prospective (existing appeals against certification to the SIAC were not affected).[58] | 2.8 | 2.9 | Labour |

| No. | Case | Details of Declaration | Final/ Overturned | Mode of Response | |
|---|---|---|---|---|---|
| 17. | R (Sylviane Pierrette Morris) v. Westminster City Council and First Secretary of State (No 3) [Administrative Court,[59] Court of Appeal[60]] | The Administrative Court declared section 185(4) of the Housing Act, 1996 incompatible with Art. 14 of the Convention. The declaration was modified slightly and upheld by the Court of Appeal. | Final | The incompatible provision was amended by Schedule 15 of the Housing and Regeneration Act, 2008. | |
| 18. | R (Gabaj) v. First Secretary of State [Administrative Court (28 March 2006, unreported)] | The Administrative Court declared section 185(4) of the Housing Act, 1996 incompatible with Art. 14 of the Convention. | Final | The incompatible provision was amended by Schedule 15 of the Housing and Regeneration Act, 2008. | |
| 19. | R (Baiai) v. SSHD [Administrative Court,[61] Court of Appeal,[62] House of Lords[63]] | The Administrative Court declared section 19(3) of the Asylum and Immigration (Treatment of Claimants, etc.) | Final | The Asylum and Immigration (Treatment of Claimants, etc.) Act 2004 (Remedial) | |

[59] [2003] EWHC 2266 (Admin); [2004] EWHC 1199 (Admin); [2005] 1 WLR 865.
[60] [2006] 1 WLR 505.
[61] [2007] 1 WLR 693.
[62] [2008] QB 143.
[63] [2009] 1 AC 287.

| Prospective/ Retrospective | Response Time between Declaration and Enactment of Response (in Months) | Response Time between Declaration and Entry into Force of Response (in Months) | Party in Government at the Time of Enactment of Response |
|---|---|---|---|
| Prospective | 33.2 | 40.6 | Labour |
| Prospective | 27.8 | 35.1 | Labour |
| Prospective (but since the 'Certificate of Approval' scheme was eliminated, those who had | 32.8 | 33.3 | Conservative– Liberal Democrats Coalition |

| No. | Case | Details of Declaration | Final/ Overturned | Mode of Response | |
|-----|------|------------------------|-------------------|------------------|---|
| | | Act, 2004 incompatible with Arts 12 and 14 of the Convention. The House of Lords varied this declaration, applying it to section 19(1) and limiting it on the basis that it discriminated between civil and Anglican marriages. | | Order, 2011 addressed the incompatibility by removing the 'Certificate of Approval' scheme under the Act. | |
| 20. | *Re MB* [Administrative Court,[64] Court of Appeal,[65] House of Lords[66]] | The Administrative Court declared that the provisions of section 3 of the Prevention of Terrorism Act, 2005 relating to the Court's supervision of non-derogating control orders were incompatible with Art. 6 of the Convention. The | Overturned | – | |

[64] [2006] EWHC 1000 (Admin).
[65] [2007] QB 415.
[66] [2008] 1 AC 440.

| Prospective/ Retrospective | Response Time between Declaration and Enactment of Response (in Months) | Response Time between Declaration and Entry into Force of Response (in Months) | Party in Government at the Time of Enactment of Response |
|---|---|---|---|
| been denied this certificate in the past had the freedom to give notice of marriage). | | | |
| – | – | – | – |

| No. | Case | Details of Declaration | Final/ Overturned | Mode of Response | |
|---|---|---|---|---|---|
| | | declaration was overturned by the Court of Appeal. The House of Lords refused to issue a declaration of incompatibility. | | | |
| 21. | *R (Wright and Others)* v. *Secretary of State for Health* [Administrative Court,[67] Court of Appeal,[68] House of Lords[69]] | The Administrative Court declared certain provisions of the Care Standards Act, 2000 incompatible with Arts 6 and 8 of the Convention. This declaration was overturned by the Court of Appeal. On appeal, the House of Lords declared section 82(4) of the Care Standards Act, 2000 incompatible with Arts 6 and 8 of the Convention. | Final | The transition to a fresh statute, the Safeguarding Vulnerable Groups Act, 2006, which does not include a system of provisional listing, began even before the decision of the House of Lords. | |
| 22. | *R (Clift)* v. SSHD, *R (Hindawi)* | In respect of Hindawi and Headley, the | Final | The provisions in question had already | |

[67] [2006] EWHC 2886 (Admin).
[68] [2008] QB 422.
[69] [2009] 1 AC 739.

| Prospective/ Retrospective | Response Time between Declaration and Enactment of Response (in Months) | Response Time between Declaration and Entry into Force of Response (in Months) | Party in Government at the Time of Enactment of Response |
|---|---|---|---|
| | | | |
| Prospective | – | – | Labour |
| Retrospective | 16.8 | 19 | Labour |

| No. | Case | Details of Declaration | Final/ Overturned | Mode of Response | |
|-----|------|------------------------|-------------------|------------------|--|
| | v. *SSHD, R (Headley)* v. *SSHD* [Administrative Court,[70] Court of Appeal,[71] House of Lords[72]] | House of Lords declared sections 46(1) and 50(1) of the Criminal Justice Act, 1991 incompatible with Art. 14 (in conjunction with Art. 5) of the Convention. | | been repealed, but applied on a transitional basis to offences committed before 4 April 2005.[73] The response was statutory, in the form of section 27 of the Criminal Justice and Immigration Act, 2008, which removed the incompatibility in these transitional cases as well. | |
| 23. | *Smith* v. *Scott* [Registration Appeal Court][74] | The Court declared section 3 of the Representation of | Final | Although a draft bill,[75] proposing | |

[70] [2003] EWHC 1337 (Admin); [2004] EWHC 78 (Admin).

[71] [2004] 1 WLR 2223; [2005] 1 WLR 1102.

[72] [2007] 1 AC 484.

[73] Ministry of Justice, *Responding to Human Rights Judgments: Report to the Joint Committee on Human Rights on the Government's Response to Human Rights Judgments 2010–11* (Cm 8162, 2011), p. 42.

[74] [2007] CSIH 9.

[75] Voting Eligibility (Prisoners) Bill, 2012.

| Prospective/ Retrospective | Response Time between Declaration and Enactment of Response (in Months) | Response Time between Declaration and Entry into Force of Response (in Months) | Party in Government at the Time of Enactment of Response |
|---|---|---|---|
| – | – | – | – |

| No. | Case | Details of Declaration | Final/ Overturned | Mode of Response | |
|-----|------|------------------------|-------------------|------------------|---|
| | | People Act, 1983 incompatible with Art. 3 of Protocol 1 of the Convention. | | three options, was presented for parliamentary scrutiny, the law remains unamended. | |
| 24. | R (Nasseri) v. SSHD [Administrative Court,[76] Court of Appeal,[77] House of Lords[78]] | The Administrative Court declared paragraph 3 of Schedule 3 of the Asylum and Immigration (Treatment of Claimants, etc.) Act, 2004 incompatible with Art. 3 of the Convention. The declaration was overturned by the Court of Appeal. The House of Lords confirmed the overturning of the declaration. | Overturned | – | |
| 25. | R (Black) v. Secretary of State for Justice [Court | The Court of Appeal declared section 35(1) | Overturned | – | |

[76] [2008] 2 WLR 523.
[77] [2008] 3 WLR 1386.
[78] [2010] 1 AC 1.

| Prospective/ Retrospective | Response Time between Declaration and Enactment of Response (in Months) | Response Time between Declaration and Entry into Force of Response (in Months) | Party in Government at the Time of Enactment of Response |
|---|---|---|---|
| | | | |
| – | – | – | – |
| – | – | – | – |

| No. | Case | Details of Declaration | Final/ Overturned | Mode of Response | |
|-----|------|------------------------|-------------------|------------------|--|
| | of Appeal,[79] House of Lords[80]] | of the Criminal Justice Act, 1991 incompatible with Art. 5(4) of the Convention, since it left the decision on the parole of long-term determinate sentence prisoners to the Secretary of State. The declaration was overturned in appeal before the House of Lords. | | | |
| 26. | *R (F & Thompson) v. Secretary of State* [Divisional Court, Court of Appeal,[81] Supreme Court[82]] | The Divisional Court declared section 82 of the SOA incompatible with Art. 8 of the Convention. The declaration was confirmed by the Court of Appeal and the Supreme Court. | Final | A remedial order removing the incompatibility was made by the Secretary of State— the Sexual Offences Act 2003 (Remedial) Order, 2012. | |

[79] [2008] 3 WLR 845.
[80] [2009] UKHL 1.
[81] [2010] 1 WLR 76.
[82] [2011] 1 AC 331.

| Prospective/ Retrospective | Response Time between Declaration and Enactment of Response (in Months) | Response Time between Declaration and Entry into Force of Response (in Months) | Party in Government at the Time of Enactment of Response |
|---|---|---|---|
| | | | |
| Retrospective (existing offenders under indefinite notification requirements would be able to make an application for review). | 26.8 | 27.3 | Conservative– Liberal Democrats Coalition |

| No. | Case | Details of Declaration | Final/ Overturned | Mode of Response | |
|-----|------|------------------------|-------------------|------------------|--|
| 27. | R (Royal College of Nursing) v. SSHD [Administrative Court][83] | The Court declared paragraph 8 of Part 2 of Schedule 3 of the Safeguarding Vulnerable Groups Act, 2006 incompatible with Arts 6 and 8 of the Convention, as it provided for the automatic barring of persons under the statute without allowing them to make prior representations. | Final | The incompatibility removed by section 67(6) of the Protection of Freedoms Act, 2012. | |
| 28. | T v. Secretary of State for Justice [Administrative Court,[84] Court of Appeal,[85] Supreme Court[86]] | The Court of Appeal declared the disclosure provisions in relation to enhanced criminal record checks under the Police Act, 1997 incompatible with Art. 8 of the Convention. The | Final | The incompatibility was removed by executive order after the Court of Appeal judgment but before the Supreme Court judgment— Rehabilitation | |

[83] [2011] PTSR 1193.
[84] [2012] EWHC 147 (Admin).
[85] [2013] EWCA Civ 25.
[86] [2014] 3 WLR 96.

| Prospective/ Retrospective | Response Time between Declaration and Enactment of Response (in Months) | Response Time between Declaration and Entry into Force of Response (in Months) | Party in Government at the Time of Enactment of Response |
|---|---|---|---|
| Prospective | 17.7 | 22 | Conservative– Liberal Democrats Coalition |
| – | – | – | Conservative– Liberal Democrats Coalition |

| No. | Case | Details of Declaration | Final/ Overturned | Mode of Response | |
|-----|------|------------------------|-------------------|------------------|--|
|     |      |                        |                   |                  |  |
|     |      | Supreme Court confirmed the declaration of incompatibility. |  | of Offenders Act, 1974 (Exceptions) Order 1975 (Amendment) (England and Wales) Order, 2013. |  |

| Prospective/ Retrospective | Response Time between Declaration and Enactment of Response (in Months) | Response Time between Declaration and Entry into Force of Response (in Months) | Party in Government at the Time of Enactment of Response |
|---|---|---|---|
|  |  |  |  |

# Index

# About the Author

**Chintan Chandrachud** is an associate at the London office of Quinn Emanuel Urquhart & Sullivan LLP. He holds a PhD in Law from the University of Cambridge, master's degrees from Oxford and Yale, and a law degree from the Government Law College, Mumbai. His research has been published in prominent newspapers, journals, and books, including *The Hindu*, *Public Law*, and *The Oxford Handbook of the Indian Constitution*. He has undertaken several pro bono litigation projects and was chairperson of the Cambridge Pro Bono Project.